TROUBLE SONGS

Stuart Braithwaite

BLOOMFIELD₅

TROUBLE SONGS

MUSIC AND CONFLICT IN NORTHERN IRELAND

STUART BAILIE

Volume and text copyright © 2018 Stuart Bailie. All rights reserved.
No part of this book covered by the copyrights hereon may be
reproduced or copied in any manner whatsoever without written
permission, except in the case of brief quotations embodied in
articles or reviews where the source should be made clear.

Bloomfield Press is a collaboration between the author and Eastside Arts,
Belfast. This book has been produced with the support of the British
Council Northern Ireland and the Arts Council of Northern Ireland.

Lines quoted from 'The Ballad of Claudy' by James Simmons
are sourced from *Poems 1956-1986* and appear with express
permission from the author's Estate c/o the Gallery Press.

ISBN 978-1-5272-2047-8
Printed by Akcent Media

CONTENTS

Trouble Songs is the story of how music has connected with the conflict in Northern Ireland since 1968. At times, music has seemed slight and irrelevant against a death toll that has exceeded 3,700. What's the point of lyrics shouted hoarsely when the volume of bigotry and violence has been so deafening? What chance a protest song when the mainstream has been jammed with intolerance and bad faith?

This book has been written in the belief that music has not been a passive voice. It has called for subversion and disobedience. It has put out stories that have challenged the given histories. And in the place of the old, stuck ideas, music has imagined new fixes. *Trouble Songs* is inspired by lyrics that have given succour and a sense of collective worth. But this story also values the reckless impulse and the rare clarity of youth. The punk rockers, ravers and rogue strummers have all done their job.

The book covers remarkable songs written in prison, lyrics that took people on to the streets and anthems that persuaded grinning kids in some rock stadium far away to raise their arms and ignite their lighters. The Clash were thwarted, the Undertones were conflicted while Sting pondered. There were songs by Bono and Boney M and Bananarama. There was steel from Christy Moore and lamentation from the Cranberries. And there were, lest we forget, so many unbelievably bad pop records about the conflict that we can only hope they have been disarmed, forever.

It is also about the musicians in the tour van, returning from a gig, wise to the danger that the checkpoint ahead might be the prelude to a massacre. But they rolled, nevertheless. The later part of the story looks at the whiplash effect of trauma and internalised pain – a peculiar energy that has not dissipated and still works out in song.

It would be dishonest to ignore the fact that music has been used to celebrate killings and endorse sectarian acts. You can still hear these tunes at sports events and in certain social clubs. Northern Ireland life is nuanced and morality is often contested. The definition of an offensive song may be relative to the listener. The musical voice may not be always to our liking.

Many books have been written about the conflict. All of it is debatable. Essentially, there is a centuries-old argument between the Irish and the British about territory and identity. The six north-eastern counties of the island were established as Northern Ireland in 1921. Unionists would uphold this link to Great Britain. Nationalists and Republicans wish to be united with the other 26 counties of the Republic of Ireland. Status is often influenced by religious upbringing. Violence returned to the story around 1968 and the consequences were horrendous. There was an agreement of sorts in 1998 and the death rate has declined.

Trouble Songs has no inclination to tell the political story in full. Rather, there are moments when the music is inspired, agitated or brutalised by the times. That is our narrative. It gives us a different perspective on the era – hopefully a useful one. This book is for everyone who has joined in the chorus.

TAKE A LOOK WHERE YOU'RE LIVING

'Ladies and Gentlemen…' he announces, 'the National Anthem'.

Hey, it's the last minutes of a perfect event. Thousands of people instantly tighten up. There's a sense of pride, a great swell of belonging and shared values. Here it is, a tune that has carried the listeners for many years. They have played it to their children, glad to hear the words passing down the generations. Everybody gets it.

The guy on stage is called Jake. He plays a line on his guitar and allows the note to hang in the air. Then he plays a similar phrase that rises at the end like a question mark. He repeats the two lines with a bit more intent and finally, brings it all back to the root note. The conversation has been resolved. Seconds later, the band crashes down on it.

There is shouting and fever and beer spray. Teenagers on their mates' shoulders. Sharply dressed women with their hands in the air. Old fellas with barrel chests, squat legs and a default look of menace – now smiling freely. There's a lot of male pattern baldness out there but the heads are shaved and the self-possession is intact. A few of them have teased their remaining follicles into spikes or even a Mohawk strip. Now it is time to sing, with feeling.

'*Nothin' for us in Belfast!*' they complain, happily.

The anthem is called 'Alternative Ulster' and the band is Stiff Little Fingers. This is a sold-out show by the River Lagan in Belfast. A stage has been put up at the far end of Custom House Square and the outsiders are all here. It is 40 years since the band first heard the call, put away their blues and boogie records and made a loyal salute to the new wave. No more Deep Purple and Highway Star, time for SLF and songs about teenagers in Northern Ireland where sectarian conflict has been the rule and no fun is the collateral.

'Alternative Ulster' was released in 1978 and it endures as a document of the bad times and the youthful resistance. There really was nothing for them in Belfast back then. The city was bombed-out and anxious. One of the few venues in town was the Pound on Townhall Street and that was literally an old stabling yard. Sure, there was music in Bangor, along the south coast of Belfast Lough, but the trains stopped early. So, if you wanted to party with the strange ones at the Trident, then a 12-mile walk back home was part of the purchase. What a life, eh?

Even on the first verse 'Alternative Ulster' is an acute idea, a call for radical action. Then it builds up the pressure and the provocation. With the second verse it tells the listeners that they really should be self-aware. '*Take a look where you're living,*' is a mighty challenge. If these words were to hit you at the right moment they could be life-changing.

The two dominant tribes of Northern Ireland since the partition of the island in 1921 have been about group-think and party lines. You were either born into the Protestant/Unionist/Loyalist set or the Catholic/Nationalist/Republican tradition. Basically, you had an option to choose what part of either spectrum you belonged to – at the peaceful end or otherwise. You had your given emblems, flags, colours and history books. In 1978, most people lived in defined areas where they were schooled, married and buried. The housing stock was rotten, there were barricades, bollards and dead ends. Murder gangs were busy, paramilitary law was severe and the state response was heavy duty. Into this context comes a squalling song with a simple notion: is *this* what you want?

Jake Burns sang the lyrics in a hurry, like a guy in a phone box with no spare change. The air came out of his oesophagus with a retching sound. This was acceptable in the punk era, when vocalists like Johnny Rotten and Joe Strummer sounded alien, deranged, unwell. Jake had his own method and Stiff Little Fingers amplified the tumult. All this helped with 'Alternative Ulster'. In the bridge section of the song, Jake listed the obstacles in the way of a freshly liberated mind. There were controlling voices and old allegiances. Some people might deny that there was any other option. But yes, there was an escape route in self-realisation and action. It amounted to four words: '*alter your native land*'. Every person could make a choice and achieve change.

People have sometimes confronted Stiff Little Fingers with confessions. After hearing the music of SLF, they've said, they became open to new thoughts. They started to question their own traditions and received bigotry. They listened to lyrics like 'Wasted Life' and 'Suspect Device' and they made a decision to step away from paramilitary organisations. Thus, some killings were avoided. Given that each murder in Northern Ireland created a multiple in terms of tit-for-tat reactions, it's fair to suggest that scores of people in Northern Ireland owe their lives to a bunch of scratchy, shouty tunes.

Anti-anthems were always a speciality of punk. The Sex Pistols declared anarchy and listed armed factions, like the UDA and the IRA, on the UK streets. Johnny Rotten rolled his 'Rs' with contempt and on 'God Save the Queen' he aspirated his 'H' in the manner of an Irish Catholic. The Establishment, he claimed, had made the Monarch a moron, a potential H-bomb. He sang it for the Queen's Jubilee Celebrations in 1977 and he relished the outrage. At the same time, the Clash were banging on about 'White Riot' and changing the nursery rhyme 'London's Burning' into a fire-starter. They were looking for flashpoints and lines of attrition.

Before punk, the great anthem-shaker had been Jimi Hendrix, live at Woodstock in 1969. Without singing a word of the 'Star Spangled Banner' he gave judgement on America, at war in Vietnam and riven by street riots at home. With his Fender Stratocaster and six overloaded Marshall amps, he recreated the jungle casualties, carpet-bombing and urban shoot-outs. Jimi had served in the 101 Airborne Division – the Screaming Eagles – and he empathised with the lowly soldiers. During this festival performance of the nation's premier tune, he added a few seconds of 'Taps', the bugle call at military funerals, and then he buried it in fearsome noise.

The same impulse led Stiff Little Fingers to record a track called 'Johnny Was' on their debut album. It was based on the Bob Marley recording, credited to his wife Rita, a slow lament for a grieving mother whose son had been killed by a stray bullet during civic unrest in Kingston, Jamaica. In the chorus, she is fretting about whether her boy's soul will make it to Heaven. He was a good man, she keeps saying. In the Stiff Little Fingers version, the conflict has relocated to Northern Ireland and there's another woman who's left to mourn.

In their rendition of 'Johnny Was', some of the original reggae remained. But mostly it was about the snare drum, playing out a military pattern. This was a native sound, the accompaniment to so many marches about territory and identity and ancient battles. On record, it sounded remorseless, sucking all of the goodwill out of the air. It became a live standard and at Custom House Square they played it out as the encore. Jake followed the Jimi example with his guitar, creating an impression of discord and automatic fire. As ever, there was mention in the lyric of a shot ringing out in the Belfast night, and veterans in the audience winced at the memory of those crackling, after-hours exchanges.

Down in Dublin, the formative members of U2 heard 'Johnny Was' and it later imprinted on their *War* album – the snare drum, the shouting and the sense of injury. It encouraged Bono to start waving a white flag and it birthed 'Sunday Bloody Sunday', a trouble song (but 'not a rebel song') that many people in Derry detested. Then again, there were people at home who fiercely disliked Stiff Little Fingers. They felt that their music was contrived and melodramatic, making capital from the conflict. They took issue with Gordon Ogilvie, the journalist who co-wrote a deal of their lyrics. Some old-school Belfast punks sneered that they were merely rock opportunists while the political diehards shouted sell-out, insisting that the conflict should be a partisan story, not a liberal one. And then the Undertones also lobbed in plenty of insults, for a variety of reasons.

Stiff Little Fingers split up a few times but periodically reformed to find an ever-growing welcome from the international punk community. American acts like Green Day and the Dropkick Murphys gave them credit. Latin American youth found the reason in the songs and a parallel to their own hardships. Manu Chao said that *Inflammable Material* was one of the best albums ever. And so, SLF approached their 40th anniversary with world tours and new supporters who regarded them as the authentic deal. This integrity was tested in Paris on November 13 2015 when 89 people were killed by an ISIL attack at a gig in the Bataclan Theatre. The Belfast band had a Paris engagement on November 17 at Backstage by the Mill, by the Moulin Rouge. They determined to play their show and Jake made this clear in a Facebook post on November 16:

'When we were growing up in Belfast, I was always saddened by the fact that groups would never come and play there because of the political situation. I was deprived of another 'normal' part of life. With this in mind, and with the wonderful co-operation of our Parisian promoter, the SLF show at Backstage at [sic] the Mill WILL GO AHEAD AS ADVERTISED tomorrow night.'

They played the gig and then determined not to talk about it again. So, when the band readied to play Belfast on August 26 2017, their reputational value was firm. Old grudges had been buried and one of their support acts was the Outcasts, who had given SLF a rough time back in the day. This spikey détente took place by the formal setting of Custom House, part of a 19th Century build, now accessorised by water features and granite landscaping, part of a refit by the Laganside Corporation as the city embarked on a bid for modernity and post-conflict prestige. The city publicists rolled out their statistics about visitor spend, overnight stays and incoming cruise ships. They said less about the exponential youth suicide rates in North and West Belfast where the peace dividend has not made a material change. Northern Ireland is not healed. And trouble songs still matter. They serve as history lessons and they talk of unfinished business. They remember the dead and they animate old struggles. They are ciphers for the story since 1968, old editions of the tombstone blues.

There is no doubt that music was engaged in the story back then. Even the decision to have fun during those wretched years was a political act. And all this is manifest when Stiff Little Fingers appear for their home show before 5,000 locals and a gathering of supporters who have flown in to witness it. The night calls for a proper reckoning and their most durable anthem is deep in the ceremony. Time to re-capture the territory that Seamus Heaney once called the Republic of Conscience, what the punks have mapped out as Alternative Ulster. And tonight, there's one remaining line.

Jake has the prompt but everybody knows the song's final imperative.

'*Go get it now!*' they all shout.

WE ARE NOT AFRAID

On July 3 1968 they blocked the lower deck of the Craigavon Bridge in Derry and sang 'We Shall Overcome'. Most likely it was the first time the song had been used on the island for a disruptive purpose. Half a dozen people sat down on the disused railway lines, halting the official opening of this new route for cars across the River Foyle. Thus, they denied the new Unionist Mayor of Londonderry, Councillor William Beattie, his civic role.

The Derry Housing Action Committee was at work. Since February its members had made a persistent case: they saw a lack of housing stock and a sectarian bias in the allocation of homes. On June 22 they had blocked the Lecky Road with a caravan that was home for the Wilson family. It was a throw-down on a main route, an alert to poverty and excessive waiting lists. Here, they said, were citizens living without running water or sanitation, a child with tuberculosis, another had died in infancy and still no state provision. The Committee brought the caravan back out the following weekend, talking to the media, claiming that more than 1,500 local families were on housing lists. The DHAC members were also squatting empty homes, crashing meetings of the Londonderry Corporation and picketing landlords.

The DHAC favoured direct action. One of the organisation's movers, Eamonn McCann, had spent the previous three years in London, where he'd been party to the Vietnam Solidarity Campaign and the International Socialists. He'd returned home in March to meet with a sister, back on holiday from Canada. Then his old friend Dermie McClenaghan told him about John and Billie Wilson's wretched life in a caravan on Donaghy's Row and he decided to agitate in Derry instead.

By July, the Wilson family had been successfully rehoused at 417 Bishop Street and 11 of the DHAC protestors – including a Labour candidate, Janet Wilcock – had received summonses under the Road Traffic Act 1930. The hearing was set for the very same day of the protest on the Craigavon Bridge. This was an endorsement, rather than a deterrent. They occupied the bridge and carried their placards. One of these read 'HITLER-FRANCO-BEATTIE'. Eamonn recalls the effrontery:

'The opening ceremony was to take the amazing fucking form of Mayor Beattie walking from one edge of the bridge to the other, which is about 350 yards long, and ceremonially, that was it. He was a straightforward, Unionist party, Orange Order man. I am not going to miss a chance like that so we're in there, John Magee and Fionnbarra Ó Dochartaigh, Dermot McClenaghan and the rest of us.

'I think that 'We Shall Overcome' made its way quite spontaneously and I think the main reason for it is it is the easiest song in the world to learn. It is a very, very simple tune, very simple words and in fact it doesn't even matter if you sing the verses in the right order. It is a perfect song for that. Usually, in those situations it would be 'Kevin Barry' or more likely 'The Soldier's Song' or something like that.

'I remember immediately thinking, 'This is a bit *different*'. 'We Shall Overcome' – we shouldn't be singing that. That is the black people in America. But there was something romantic about that because it suggested that what we were involved in was much wider and more noble struggle, rather than just fighting about things about Northern Ireland.'

Fionnbarra Ó Dochartaigh, the DHAC Committee Secretary, had caused ructions at a Corporation meeting a few weeks before when he climbed out of the Public Gallery and took over the vacant Mayor's seat. He had declared himself First Citizen and issued various bold decrees before being removed. Now, one of his duties on the bridge on July 3 was to lead the singing. He would guide the activists through a song that was relatively fresh to Irish ears.

'We pretended to be spectators,' he says, 'coming along to welcome the Mayor. We had placards up our jumpers and under our coats. Just as he was supposed to cut the ribbon we jumped out in front of the cavalcade of cars.

'About six sat down – they volunteered to block the bridge, but we couldn't all do it. The rest of us were at the side, to cheer them on. At that stage the police arrived and people didn't know what to do. I just stepped forward, singing 'We Shall Overcome'. Very people knew the song at that time. Some of them would have known the chorus, but they didn't know all the verses.'

'We Shall Overcome' may not have been familiar to some of the Derry activists but it was the most resounding protest anthem in America. It had been sung on freedom rides and at sit-ins, in union halls, churches and rallies. It could be traced back to 1900 and a gospel song called 'I'll Overcome Some Day', published by Charles Albert Tindley. He was a Methodist Minister in Philadelphia, the son of a slave and many of his parish had also come north to rid themselves of the associations from that era.

It was a song about spiritual deliverance, about salvation for every soul that did not yield to temptation. Within ten years, striking miners were singing a version of it and by 1945 it had evolved into a union tune, 'We Will Overcome', performed at the end of a day on the picket line. Lucille Simmons sang it slow and heartfelt with the female tobacco workers in Charlestown, South Carolina. A union worker, Zilphia Horton, brought it to the Highlander Folk School in Tennessee, where emerging leaders in the movement were given support and training. The song was finessed there with the help of Guy Carawan and Pete Seeger, who published it in 1947 and who also helped with the lines about walking hand in hand, plus the title change to 'We Shall Overcome'. When you sang the word 'shall', your mouth opened wider and it sounded like you meant it, even more.

Seeger was a great ambassador for music with a message and he sent the song out into the world. The lyric was no longer about getting a reward in Heaven. This version called for justice on Earth. The call was for collective action and the reassurance that comes with it. Fear was part of the experience, but the people would prevail. The spirituality had not left the song – it still carried a deal of deep conviction. Now, the sentiments put faithful feet on the road; it was empowering and it proclaimed peace.

In 1960, the song was adopted by the Student Nonviolent Coordinating Committee. Three years later and Bob Dylan sang it at the Newport Folk Festival, on stage with Peter, Paul and Mary, with Joan Baez and Pete Seeger and the Freedom Singers from Albany, Georgia. They were joined by Theodore Bikel the actor, singer and festival co-founder. It was July 26 and the folk revival was alive and alert. They all crossed their right arm over their left, took the hands of their neighbours and presented an accord of black and white, north and south, various creeds and ethnicities.

Joan Baez took 'We Shall Overcome' to the March on Washington on August 28 and an audience of more than 200,000. It was the soundtrack to the Selma to Montgomery marches in 1965 led by Dr Martin Luther King Jr., asking for voting reform on behalf of the Civil Rights movement. He used the lyric often in his speeches, including his final public address on March 31 1968, four days before his assassination. Tens of thousands then sang it at his funeral.

Pete Seeger was in awe of this ongoing development: 'I don't think there was any political movement in history that had as much singing as the Civil Rights movement had.'

Now it was being transplanted to Northern Ireland. Not without a challenge, though. Fionnbarra Ó Dochartaigh led the singing on the bridge yet he had barely finished the first verse when officers from the Royal Ulster Constabulary (RUC) caused him to desist. The other protesters continued for a bit but they were also halted and taken away to Victoria RUC Station. Two individuals, Neil O'Donnell and Roddy O'Carlin refused to sign a bail bond and were sentenced to a month in Crumlin Road Prison, Belfast. There was a fine of £5 for Ó Dochartaigh. His work in conducting the peace anthem was filed as 'disorderly behaviour'.

Fionnbarra had been living in London in the mid-60s when he had learnt about the ongoing Civil Rights actions in America. He was selling *The Irish Democrat*, the newspaper of the Connolly Association, around the pubs. At the same time, Eamonn McCann was editing a Trotskyite paper,

The Militant, on behalf of the Irish Workers Group. He and songwriter Christy Moore used to sell it at Hyde Park on Sundays. Both publications were taking heed of Martin Luther King's example. *The Irish Democrat* also published the lyrics of radical songs, so the connection was underlined.

They sang the song again on the road from Coalisland to Dungannon on August 24. This was the first significant march from the Northern Ireland Civil Rights Association (NICRA), formed 18 months before. Again, an important theme was the fair allocation of housing. A related issue was 'one man, one vote', rather than a property qualification that favoured rate-payers and businesses. NICRA opposed the gerrymandering that went with the loaded, political arithmetic of Northern Ireland. Protestant rule west of the River Bann often depended on this creative accounting. NICRA wanted to see fairness in job opportunities, the disbandment of the quasi-military Special Constabulary (B-Specials) and the repeal of the Civil Authorities (Special Powers) Act (Northern Ireland) 1922. This broad, albeit left-leaning Civil Rights alliance included free-thinkers, Republicans, socialists, liberals and revolutionaries. Hence the value of a decent anthem. 'We Shall Overcome' was a wishful cover-all, a non-violent aspiration wherein they might find a common chorus.

Bernadette Devlin was on the evening march, a Queen's University student from Cookstown. Her background and her schooling were Republican. At the age of seven she had been able to sing 15 verses of 'The Croppy Boy', a song dating back to the 1798 Rebellion and the United Irishmen. At the age of 12 she had won £10 in a local talent contest, reciting the words of Pádraig Pearse, executed for his part in the 1916 Easter Rising. She had learnt this from a Michael MacLiammoir album of rebel speeches. 'Beware the risen people who will take what you would not give,' she had declaimed.

As the march began, it seemed like a carnival atmosphere, with the participants eating oranges, smoking cigarettes and dodging the drunks. Bernadette noted that people were singing 'Who Fears to Speak of '98' and 'Faith of Our Fathers' – the latter a Catholic hymn to those martyred under the reigns of Henry VIII and Elizabeth I, a refrain often sung at hurling matches. Soon after, she recalled that the hymn 'has been degraded by frequent playing at Nationalist gatherings and is one song I hate to hear at a political meeting, because it betrays the old mentality that equals Irish and Catholic. But we had a bash at 'Faith of Our Fathers' anyway: so much for being non-sectarian.'

That said, the 2,000 marchers were asked not to display political banners and stewards were on hand to deter stone throwers when the march was halted by a Loyalist counter-demonstration. Some of the speakers, such as Gerry Fitt, the Republican Labour MP for West Belfast, made angry speeches, but the non-violent ethos was largely maintained. The NICRA Chair was Betty Sinclair, a Communist and former mill worker, born to a Protestant family in the Ardoyne area of Belfast. She had joined the Revolutionary Workers' Group in 1931, a forerunner of the Communist Party of Ireland. She was part of the 1932 Outdoor Relief Strike in Belfast, a powerful moment for working-class unity when thousands came across the religious divide to seek better conditions. Back then, the non-sectarian anthem was 'Yes, We Have No Bananas'. They had sung it with feeling on the Falls and the Shankill Roads. Betty was keen to replicate this spirit in 1968, but others, like Bernadette Devlin, were more sceptical. Coalisland, Bernadette figured, was 90% Republican. Betty then determined to end the meeting at the police cordon and requested that they all sing the Civil Rights anthem. Bernadette related it thus:

'She raised her arms and started 'We Shall Overcome' and everybody else started 'A Nation Once Again'. By the time we'd got to the end of the first verse of our anthem, Betty and all her friends had scuttled into the lorry and driven off, leaving the population of Coalisland outside the town of Dungannon.'

Bernadette, Eamonn McCann and other marchers such as John Hume had come to appreciate that this era of contention would be televised. This source had shown them their counterparts in America and the students in the Sorbonne, Paris that Easter. They had watched the Tet Offensive in Vietnam plus the Prague Spring of '68, followed by the invasion of Czechoslovakia in August. McCann had sent a telegram of solidarity from the people of Derry, c/o the General Post Office, Prague. Bernadette had a similar view of the times: 'By such seeming osmosis did television help transmit the radical contagion from place to place.'

Music was also fit to carry the news. Eamonn would quote Phil Ochs and 'White Boots Marching in a Yellow Land' – a summer instalment from a US artist who regarded himself as a guitar-carrying journalist. The satirical sentiments of Country Joe McDonald and 'I Feel Like I'm Fixin' To Die' had been in the public domain since 1967, ready for the intense exposure of the Woodstock festival two years later. This also connected. Before this, McCann had independently sensed music's rousing power as a 13-year-old in the Bogside, just after 'Rock Around the Clock' had been shown at the City Cinema on James Street:

'They banned it in a number of cinemas in England as it was causing riots and ructions, so you had great expectations that there would be riots. You've got to face it, if they could do riots in Ipswich they could certainly do riots in Derry. We were not going to let ourselves down.

'I remember looking out the attic window from our house, 10 Rossville Street, and they stopped at the junction of Rossville Street and Eden Place right opposite our house. A huge circle of people clapping and singing the same song over and over again. And the brilliant dancing in the middle that was done by Frankie Roddy. He had a school of Irish dancing and he was a teacher and all-Ireland champion and we suddenly discovered he was a very good jiver. There was Teresa Shields – daughter of Paddy Shields, one of the legendary old IRA in Derry – and there they were, dancing. And naturally, the RUC came in to clear it up. So just the next night there were three times the crowd, naturally enough. Part of it was the craic, as much as wanting to riot. It was the first time I had experience of music actually producing a reaction. And this had nothing to do with the politics of the area or the politics of Derry. It was one of those moments when you could sense Derry opening up and the young people opening up.'

'We Shall Overcome' had a different dynamic and a different purpose in 1968, however:

'I think people were bored hearing it after a couple of days. It can get boring after a while. There wasn't much variation on 'We Shall Overcome'. There wasn't a middle eight, like. And 'We Shall Not Be Moved' was the same thing basically. Not bad at all, particularly if you were sitting down, which we frequently were. But at that time, the Rolling Stones were on the go, there was a lot of aggressive, upfront music and you could momentarily think that Mick Jagger was a revolutionary. Obviously, he was not. There was an awful lot of stuff at that time that you would have thought, "This is our stuff; they are part of the movement".'

When Frankie Mooney, the Derry tenor, sang the anthem at the Guildhall, Fionnbarra was nearby to prompt him on the verses. The latter was also duplicating the lyrics for public events and using the DHAC newsletter, *Reality*, to bed the song into the Derry psyche. He had no doubt about the song's value: 'It was important because when you're on a march it gave people a sense that we're all together in this, we have to see this through. You just couldn't walk along silently. It kept our spirits up. The songs had a part to play. You can't put it in material terms. You have to see it in emotional terms.'

The Folk Music Society at Queen's University Belfast was a source of quiet sedition. They had imported the creativity of the American protest movement and put these aside the Irish folk tradition. Bernadette was impressed. 'They sang black Civil Rights songs before anyone else in Queen's was interested in the race problem, and they were singing songs about unemployed in Belfast long before the Civil Rights movement took it up … there was more real politics in the Folk Music Society than in any of the parties.'

Anne Devlin, unrelated to Bernadette, had grown up in West Belfast, listening to the strident notions of Nina Simone and Bob Dylan. It was part of the family soundtrack. Her father, Paddy, had made a political journey from violent Republicanism to trade unionism and the Northern Ireland Labour Party (NILP). Her dad would actually disapprove if he heard a song like Dominic Behan's 'The Sea Around Us' in the Labour Party Club. Even that was too insular in its awareness for him. Socialism, in his view, aimed to transcend national borders.

'So, then Bob Dylan comes along with 'The Times They Are A-Changin'' and we get nothing else at home from Paddy. He sings his head off, he's even got the words, so protest songs are being laid down in around me. I join the Young Socialists and, of course, they all look like the CND guys and they all have long hair and long hairy jumpers. I find it via a fund-raising barbecue for the NILP and Jimmy Simmons [James Simmons, the poet and songwriter] comes along with his guitar and he is singing and his wife is singing blues and jazz.

'The Beatles are now in there. But it hasn't quite landed with me, because Paddy is trying to keep me away from anything too dangerous, so he is keeping me in the political songs – in fact, the most dangerous thing he could do, because he is laying down all this language. And suddenly a film comes out called *Yellow Submarine*. And I go with four Young Socialists on a Saturday afternoon and we hop into the Hippodrome and I sit down and I am gobsmacked. Everything opens up. It is the most wonderful, surrealist fantasy and they sing, 'Altogether Now' and it's really funny. But also – the Blue Meanies. It is absolutely perfect. It tells me who I am with, where I am, what I believe in. We're against the Blue Meanies.

'It made you feel that we are modern and this is going to be alright. And so never for a second were we afraid of anything because the music was so like: it's *us*. This is us, this is where we are going.'

Anne and her friends sang a version of the Beatles on a bus going to Derry on October 5, with a new chorus line: '*we all live in a fascist regime*'. It was the occasion of another Civil Rights march from the Waterside, across the Craigavon Bridge and into the centre of the walled city. A hundred students were traveling up by various means. Anne had made arrangements with her friend Patricia. They had made a Young Socialists banner with red letters and also a Starry Plough flag. They were singing and passing around an issue of the *Evergreen Review*. In terms of music for the march, there was discussion about rebel songs. 'Kevin Barry' was often sung on such an occasion. The words commemorated a teenage Irish Volunteer who was executed in 1920 after killing three British soldiers:

'At one meeting of the Young Socialists I met Tony Kennedy and he objected to 'Kevin Barry'. He said, "Oh, Kevin Barry was a terrible person. He shot soldiers in a bread queue." And I remember thinking, "I have never met anybody who criticised Kevin Barry".'

The protestors may have been armed with rousing choruses, but the people they were challenging had their own songbooks. The Apprentice Boys of Derry commemorated the 1688-89 siege of Derry with marches and ritual. Their ancestors had withstood the attack of the deposed King James II and his Catholic army. Part of the culture was defence and fortitude, involving a march in August to mark the relief of the siege. The Loyal Orange Institution also looked back to victories in the Williamite-Jacobite War. In 'The Sash' they honoured the campaigns of the Dutch-born King and sang of Derry, Aughrim, Enniskillen and the Boyne. In 'Derry's Walls', the faithful related to the start of the siege at Bishop's Gate and vowed to fight again if required. On 'The Ballad of Dolly's Brae' Loyalists remembered how they had enforced a County Down march on July 12 1849, despite opposition, resulting in at least 30 deaths. They sang 'The Crimson Banner' and vowed that their own flag would prevail.

Eamonn McCann had persuaded NICRA that the October 5 March was a reasonable notion. The Civil Rights people in Belfast were less sensitive to the city geography, less sure that he was taking an audacious step. McCann planned on flaunting an unwritten law that Catholics could not march within the city walls. Unsurprisingly, the march was banned but 400 people assembled at Duke Street, as per the original plan. They were prepared to cross the bridge and enter the city. However, the RUC contained the protestors in a cordon and then boxed them off behind. There was no great provocation from those present but batons were lifted and many civilians were beaten. Gerry Fitt was bleeding from a gash in his head that required three stitches. District Inspector Ross McGimpsey was swinging his blackthorn stick, knocking an 18-year-old to the ground and flailing at others. Two water cannons were hosing the civilians and a camera crew at a first-floor window.

RTÉ documentary footage of the RUC actions was shown internationally. Many supposed that the policing had been brutal. Bernadette Devlin felt that the authorities had given the Civil Rights movement a considerable bonus: 'they gave it life in one day'. Eamonn admitted that this was a gameplay of sorts: 'Our conscious, if unspoken strategy was to provoke the police into over-reaction and thus spark off mass reaction against the authorities.' Now there was a reckoning. 'Over and again, along Rossville Street on the morning after, we heard the exact same phrase: things will never be the same again.'

The students were mobilised, and a new group, People's Democracy (PD), was set up under a 'faceless' committee in Belfast. Almost immediately, they were confronted in the streets and in meeting halls by Unionist groups, often termed 'Paisleyites'. The PD plans relented for a short time while Prime Minister Terence O'Neill made his 'Ulster stands at the crossroads' speech on December 9. He presented a nightmare scenario – 'a separate, inward-looking, selfish and divided Ulster' – and there was assurance of some positive reform. But the radicals won out and the so-called 'Long March' was fixed for January 1969.

'I Shall Not Be Moved' was another song that had grown out of the American gospel experience and a verse from the book of Jeremiah about a tree by the river, nourishing the roots. 'I' was changed to 'We' as the song went secular. This was put to use as the march set off from Belfast, on January 1, destination over 70 miles away in Derry. Around 40 people at the start, but numbers grew along the way. Anne Devlin experienced this rolling effect:

'It builds as it reaches different towns. There are tailors standing in front of Royal Avenue, in front of their shops, coming out to watch us. I remember a whole hotel staff coming out, before Randalstown. We were so naïve. On the first night, in a hall sleeping in sleeping bags in Antrim, a policeman came into the room, the lights went on and he said, "We have been phoned and told there is a bomb in this hall". We said, "We're staying" – we turned out the lights and went to sleep. Whereas people like Betty Sinclair said, "This is very dangerous".'

Gospel anthems were not the exclusive ownership of the marchers. One of the high-profile opponents to Civil Rights was Ian Paisley, leader of the Free Presbyterian Church. A fundamentalist, a hulking presence, a vigorous critic of the Catholic Church ('baptised paganism', he called it) and of Protestant back-sliders and apostates. He had a church without a choir where women were expected to keep their heads covered, as understood by 1 Corinthians 11:2-16. Paisley scorned modernism, sang Charles Wesley hymns from the 18th Century and regarded Terence O'Neill and his allies as 'Iscariots of Ulster'.

This leader did not care for the work of Martin Luther King and, on his death, Paisley's *Protestant Telegraph* newspaper noted thus: 'He laid great emphasis upon the brotherhood of man rather than the Kinship of Christ. He chose liberal theology rather than fundamentalism. He chose ecumenism rather than separatism.'

Paisley's response to civic unrest was to Chair the Ulster Constitution Defence Committee and its subsidiary, the Ulster Protestant Volunteers. These groups harried the Civil Rights marches in Dungannon and Armagh. They contested the PD activities in Belfast and on their march to Derry. Much of this was directed by Major Ronald Bunting, who had seen active service in Korea and Malaya.

It was Bunting's mission to 'hinder and harass' the march to Derry. They blocked the way at Randalstown, Toome and Bellaghy. The Major asked for the aid of other Loyalists 'who wished to play a manly role' and to 'arm themselves with whatever protective measures they feel to be suitable'. They came with cudgels and home-made weaponry. As a soundtrack, they had mustered some traditional rope drums, huge and loud, doubled-sided in goatskin and neck-slung, beaten with Malacca canes. Bernadette Devlin was one of the marchers who sensed the import of the Lambeg drum: 'The unceasing pounding of the drums was beginning to get on everyone's nerves.' To diffuse the tension, a Protestant marcher called Wilfie Blackwood made a drama out of the tribal attraction of the rhythm. 'I'm in the wrong crowd,' he joshed at the police cordon. 'These Civil Rights people had me brainwashed, but the drums are calling me back.'

Bunting was ready at Burntollet Bridge, five miles from Derry. Around 300 associates had gathered on January 4 with nail-spiked clubs and piles of stones, fetched in from a nearby quarry. Off-duty members of the B-Specials were involved – some of them identified to each other by armbands. Civil Rights marchers were beaten into ditches. Anne Devlin was knocked unconscious and into the River Faughan. Thirteen people were hospitalised.

The marchers took the final stretch into Derry, past another attack in the Waterside area on the near bank of the Foyle. Now they were singing 'The Internationale', a 19th Century song of solidarity. '*Arise ye workers from your slumbers,*' they chanted, '*Arise ye prisoners of want*'. Fionnbarra takes some of the credit for this development:

'I went on the Burntollet march and I joined up with it at Antrim. I seemed to be the only one in that crowd that knew 'The Internationale'. I spent most of my time teaching it to people. So, by the time that we reached Derry, three days later, a lot of them knew it. When they got to the Guildhall, it wasn't 'We Shall Overcome' but 'The Internationale'. It was quite symbolic. It seemed to echo off Derry's walls.'

There were disturbances in the city that night involving the police. Some accounts say that the enforcers had sang a bastardised version of *The Monkees* TV theme as they smashed windows and doors. The Bogside residents put up barricades to resist them. Eamonn McCann took his lead from the Free Speech Movement in Berkeley, California and suggested a note of self-determination on the gable wall of St Columb's Street. It was first scrawled there by Liam Hillen on January 5 and later painted up more formally by John 'Caker' Casey, a house painter. YOU ARE NOW ENTERING FREE DERRY, it declared. Eamonn explains it thus:

"You are now entering a fragment of a United Ireland' – that is what it actually meant. We were very much against nationalism; we were very explicitly saying that the fucking border doesn't matter. That is what has held us back – let's sort this thing out here, as it were. We can sort the border if we get rid of sectarianism.'

Around 7pm on January 10 they plugged in a pirate radio transmitter that had been smuggled up from the Irish Republic by friends of People's Democracy. The transmissions were a feature of 1969, firstly from the Creggan and then from the top of Rossville Flats, an eight-storey feature of the Bogside. The equipment was installed by Jim Sharkey, an electrician from Rossville Street. Radio Free Derry went out on 240 Medium Wave and involved Eamonn McCann, Eamonn Melaugh, Tommy McDermott, Ross O'Kane and a few others. Their reach was the Creggan, the Bogside and the Brandywell – 888 acres and 25,000 people. They played folk tunes, pop music and they talked about resistance.

'It was, "don't weaken now", all that,' Eamonn recalls. '"Don't listen to so-and-so, they are middle-class wankers", and so on. "Stand by the people". There was no police and you could think about it as a liberation area. There was a lot of romance around at the time. This was a revolt against the way things were. We weren't just making it up.'

Over those first two days, the station played 'Please Surrender' by Elvis and sent it out as a request from the people of Lecky Road to the RUC ('Of course, the police force in Derry have a great number of smash hits in recent weeks'). There were skits about Paisley, they named and shamed slum landlords and cued up 'I Am the Walrus'. Radio guests gave eye-witness stories about Burntollet and the supposed collusion between the police and Bunting's militia.

'I seen the police talking to these people before the ambush,' said one voice. 'Definitely, they were hand in hand.'

The playlist had space for the Spinners and local artist Majella Brady. Their station theme tune was a recent release called 'The Derry Civil Rights' song on a Monaghan indie label, Shamrock. The band was the Moonlighters, a reference to the secretive Kerry insurgents during the land crisis of the late 19th Century. The tune was on loan from 'Down by the Sally Gardens' and the lyric (apparently written by Tony O'Doherty, a DHAC campaigner and songwriter from Lone Moore Road) was a fairly restrained account of the October 5 March. It was the first recorded trouble song of the looming conflict.

> 'The police were there in hundreds and on mercy they did frown
> As they freely used their batons that day in Derry town.'

Radio Free Derry name-checked the vigilantes and sent out peaceable messages to their Protestant neighbours in the Fountain area. 'Why do you stone us when some of you don't have the vote, when your houses are in a disgusting condition?'

And then some more Elvis, getting urgent with 'It's Now or Never'. The DJ added some banter at the end of the tune, 'which may or may not have any relevance to the Civil Rights campaign, but it was the only song on the gramophone at the time'.

So, music was a feature in the dramatic churn of events. Anne Devlin recognised this:

'It sort of carries you. You are out of the shallows and there you are in the new thing and you can't go back. That's the point, you don't go back.

And I find that really extraordinary. 'We Shall Overcome' did travel. And it travelled bravely. I sang it in Poland one night with my friend Jimmy Simmons. We walked along the street and we started singing 'We Shall Overcome' and Jimmy turned to me and said, "But *will* we?"

'There was a terrible confrontation that took place when we came back from Derry, and the Republicans who objected to it turn up at the PD meeting for the first time and go in and criticise that march. They are furious and these are the people we lost out to, in a way. This is what I feel. We weren't just dealing with the Loyalists, if you like – the effect of the Burntollet collusion that was going on between the B-Specials and various other groups. We were actually dealing with *them* as well.

'And the enemies were on both sides and quite formidable. You can't win with those odds, it seems to me. Those were the odds you were against. Police and Protestant attackers on one side and then the Republicans on the other. They were what I call the military mind-set, those are hierarchical, patriarchal, military mind-sets. The PD calls a meeting in St Mary's Hall and I walk away. I actually walk away from it.

'It [the People's Democracy March to Derry] didn't start the Troubles single-handedly. I think they lost control. It was a failure but it wasn't the intention to actually create this level of mayhem. We were simply doing what is part of being human, which was carrying our civilisation forward.'

There was much for Eamonn McCann and his colleagues to consider also:

'October 1968 was almost like a mass endorsement of what this tiny gang of left-wing people had been preaching in Derry and trying to put into practice. We were saying, "It's a Housing Action Committee, we are going to concentrate on that, no green stuff". We just told people to fuck off who were coming along, talking about tricolours – "Fuck off". At the Burntollet march, the tricolours went off the march. Consensus, you know – "Take that down, it's not happening". So, October 5 represented what we thought at the time was an explosion of activist radicalism that could sweep over sectarianism.

'You got a glimpse of north and south rising up together, about economic and class issues – that's the answer. I still believe this. I still fervently believe that is the only thing that is going to make Ireland united. They can fuck off with their armed struggle and their "We'll negotiate with the European Union, that's what will do it". October 5 was a really buzzy experience. To think the future is going to look like something as we envisage it. Also, the sense of mass participation, that we were making the future ourselves. I was coming back from London, from a Trotskyist position which held that workers have to create socialism themselves. Only in rising up themselves could people slough off what Marx called the muck of ages – all the ideological things, nationalism and chauvinism and all the other things that weigh down on people.

'And I thought I was seeing it happen. That is a very heavy thing to happen to you when you are in your 20s and you are totally committed to what you are doing. So, in that sense, it was an epiphany for me. It was an epiphany that didn't last very long, you know, because within 18 months 'We Shall Overcome' was gone, it was 'The Soldier's Song', 'Kevin Barry' and so on. And for a couple of years – sort of wasted years when I look back on it now – I was arguing against that in the Bogside. When I look back on it, I was never going to win the argument. People just thought I was an eccentric.'

Nevertheless, Eamonn had carried out his wish to ramp up the political situation in Derry and beyond.

'Whether it was by wise means or not, history will judge.'

BETWEEN THE VIADUCTS OF YOUR DREAM

Van Morrison was in New York during September and October 1968.
He was working on an album called *Astral Weeks* – his first for the label
Warner Bros. He was singing about wonderment, joy and slivers of dread.
The songs had connections to Boston, New York and California. But mostly
he was singing about Belfast.

The sessions took place at Century Sound, 135 West 52nd Street. Some
jazz players had been hired to accompany the work. These veterans were
used to the various demands of Miles Davis, Charles Mingus and the
Modern Jazz Quartet, but Van's songs often circled around two or three
chords and he didn't seem to be prescriptive about the gig. Neither were
there charts or scores. So they took their steers from the swirling voice, the
rapture and hurt.

Two of the three sessions took place in the evening, and that added to
the trance-like method. Van could sing a word like 'Ballerina' and take all of
the word parts to bits, raving and stretching at the meaning. Just 18 months
earlier he had recorded 'Brown Eyed Girl' in New York, a jaunty pop tune
with a calypso beat that was perfectly tuned for a million transistor radios.
But this new music did not put much value on structure, chorus or the rules
of the Medium Wave. He was elsewhere, away from the known.

On 'Beside You' he ached for his lover across the Atlantic, and tried to
reach her by breathing intently, aiming to rise out of the physical world.

Mention of the Sunday Six Bells located the song in the village life of Bloomfield, near the belfry of St Donard's, Church of Ireland. This part of East Belfast was covenanted land, where the sale of alcohol was forbidden while churches, mission halls and street preachers managed to thrive. Van's patch was the cheap slob land by the marshy hollow of the Beechy River. In his imagination he reached for the rich heights of Cyprus Avenue, rising from the Beersbridge Road to the North Road, a seeming boulevard lined with 85 trees: Corsican pine, lime, beech, sycamore, maple and more.

Van later described Bloomfield as his 'Blakean micro-cosmos'. It was a place of innocence and child-like visions. He could be utterly shaken up there by the intensity of his feelings. The red brick mansions on the hill had biblical echoes – the home on high that was promised in the gospel of John 14:2. It was only minutes away from the terraced houses that served the shipyard, the ropeworks, the mills and the engineering works, but the difference was vast.

The poet William Blake had concerned himself with the harmful side of the industrial age, the slide from innocence into experience and decay. That was reflected in *Astral Weeks* also. The girl in 'Slim Slow Slider' is taken by heroin, set to die prematurely. The subject of 'Ballerina' endures a lonely time in the tower block. Most fascinating of all is 'Madame George', who flits along Cyprus Avenue in high heels, flaunting convention, headed for an eventful night with a soldier boy and a bottle of wine.

The roof of St Donard's Church had been damaged during the Belfast Blitz of April 1941. Ravenscroft Avenue nearby had been flattened as the German bombers had targeted the industrial heart of the city, killing over 900 people across Belfast and damaging 55,000 homes. By 1968, most of the hardships had passed and the baby boomers had grown into a reasonable economy. Van, born in 1945, would pay his respects to the parents' generation in the song 'War Children', but he was also testing the boundaries, pushing at the door.

Astral Weeks conveys a mood of Belfast in this time of flux. The figure of Madame George is doused in perfume and walking the broad avenue that houses the captains and doctors, the Reverend, the lawyers and their beautiful, distant daughters. Madame George is headed to a party and time spent in the corner, '*playing dominoes in drag*'. Quite the statement. In Britain, the Sexual Offences Act 1967 had provided a partial decriminalisation of homosexuality. But this did not apply to Northern Ireland. So, Madame George is behaving boldly in a place where the old values were not inclined to give way without a battle.

There's a pivotal moment in this song when the party is interrupted by a rap on the window. In a moment, the woozy joy is replaced by paranoia as they suspect a police bust. Madame George throws some possessions out of the window and soon after makes plans to quit the city. A few dear companions go to the train station to say their farewells yet others have already gone cold and walked away. There's a moment of compassion when a friend hands over a glove. This leads to an outburst of love and sadness and a hundred goodbyes. The future may be less giddy, but a change has begun, as Eamonn McCann has noted:

'The release of *Astral Weeks* was as revolutionary an event of relevance to Northern Ireland as anything that happened at the time. Just in the way that all young revolutions do, it opened up minds and hearts to possibilities they had never dared dream of.'

The characters in the songs may have been unusual, but Van's vocals were not so far removed from the singers in those mission halls around him. The Baptists, the Congregationalists, the Presbyterians, the Brethren, the Elim and sundry other proclaimers and splitters who wanted a direct, personal discourse with God. They would recount their testimonies and act them out with all the dramatic thrills, fever, babble and charismatic effects. The Pentecostals took their lead from the verses in the Acts of the Apostles when the Holy Spirit lights up the disciples, causing them to speak in tongues and to behave intemperately. 'These men are not drunk,' Saint Peter explains. Rather, it is a fulfilment of the prophet Joel – when the anointed ones will prophesy, see visions and dream dreams. This, Peter says, is a sign of the last days, a time for urgency and commitment. 'And everyone who calls on the name of the Lord will be saved.'

So, it is perhaps not so strange that in the sensory rush of 'Astral Weeks', the song, Van finds himself in the avenue of trees – a kind of birth canal – and declares his own spiritual connection. This has been suggested by

John 3:7 and he barely changes the words when he sings it:

> *'In silence easy,*
> *To be born again.'*

Eamonn McCann hears a significant trait in all this. 'Van Morrison couldn't be a Catholic. His background didn't burden him with duty, but gave him freedom to define himself other than by reference to the place and people he came from. Being himself, he could be anybody and anything at all. *Astral Weeks* revealed that the north could nurture, unbeknownst, beautiful visions of things we haven't dreamt on enough, even now.'

Derry might have been looking to Berkley for a model of disobedience and revolution but youth culture in Belfast was taking some of its style and expressions from San Francisco. The alternative Californian lifestyle had been nurtured in 1966 around Haight Street, a low-rent convergence of heavy hippies, psychedelic rangers, swap shops, audacious artists, seekers and pranksters. The scene had an underground paper sprayed with jasmine scent called *The Oracle* and a mission to feed the drop-outs in the Panhandle with Digger bean soup. They held out at Golden Gate Park, resisted linear thinking and thought they might manage outside the financial system.

The scene was damaged by over-exposure, drug busts and commercialism; therefore, they staged 'The Death of Hippie' in October 1967. By then, the freak flag had been raised across Western popular culture. Belfast publication *City Week* had uncovered its own subversives on the grass in front of the City Hall. This was the cover of their issue dated August 3 1967. There was an image of some flower children in a circle near Wellington Place. A security guard with a peaked cap and gleaming boots provides the generational contrast. 'City Hall Love-In', says the banner headline. The sub-head is less dramatic: 'But Belfast Not Ready For Hippy Cult'.

On this Tuesday interlude on the lawn, a girl called Janet allowed the paper to take a photo of her smelling a summer bloom. But she withheld her surname, seemingly disdainful of the square-minded reporter. Brian McGoohan wore a lime green shirt, a red floppy hat with a tall crown and a handlebar moustache. 'Drugs are not necessary,' he stressed. 'Peace and happiness are what we want. We have no enemies.'

A bit of alarmism and youth-baiting was the norm for such a publication, but there was also truth in the story. The city's counter-culture was in decent shape, as Terri Hooley remembers:

'There were 80 clubs in or around Belfast, where you could go to hear music. The town was buzzing. We were talking about freedom of thought, action and expression. On a Sunday night, you used to get 1,000 people at the City Hall, so they had to open up Donegall Square Methodist Church and let all the people in. The Rev Hedley Plunkett opened it up so that the kids could have tea and coffee They called it Heaven.'

Terri was a poet, a DJ, a contrarian, folk-devil and chancer. His father was a trade union man and a Labour Party candidate. He had found his own political focus after the Cuban Missile Crisis of 1962. He signed up for the ideals of the Campaign for Nuclear Disarmament (CND) and tried to stage a coup with his local branch when he supposed that they were overly fond of pints in the Duke of York. He brought down his mates from the Maritime Jazz Club to sway the vote, but the CND guys had batted him away on issues of governance and so he formed the Northern Ireland Youth Campaign for Peace and Nuclear Disarmament.

'We were very active,' he notes. The NIYCPND marched along the coast of Belfast Lough to Bangor and also shut down traffic at Wellington Place in town. For this, Terri and his accomplice Paul Murphy were arrested under new civil disobedience legislation. Murphy had been playing 'We Shall Not Be Moved' on his guitar when they took them away. Hooley attended the court hearing but confusion followed:

'This policeman came in looking for change for the phone. He said, "What are you doing here?" I said, "I'm here because I believe in the fight for the abolishment of nuclear weapons and the preservation of humanity and an end to the war of aggression on the men, women and children of Vietnam – dropping their Lazy Dog missiles and their Napalm bombs."

'He said, "You're in the wrong court, son. This is the Maintenance Court." So, I went down to the other court and apparently everybody thought that I hadn't turned up as a protest. I got fined £20.'

Terri had lost his left eye during a childhood accident with a bow and arrow and he would remove the glass replacement for dramatic effect, placing it in pints of beer or in the trusting hands of potential partners. He took over a High Street premises from the World Socialist Party and encouraged misbehaviour. He harangued Bob Dylan in 1966 for paying his taxes to the war-mongering US government and Bob told him to "fuck off". In time, there were publications such as *Id* and *Ego* – poetry, prose and random thought, inspired by London's *International Times* and *Oz*. Terri's style and his focus was unconventional but it found a sympathetic chime with the era.

'My revolution was never about killing my brothers and sisters because of an accident of birth or religion. I was never really interested in Northern Ireland politics. I was interested in what was happening in Vietnam, Cambodia, Chile and Latin America. I was inspired by the riots in Paris and I really did think we could change the world. I was very much interested in the Civil Rights movement in America and singers like Nina Simone. There was all sorts of stuff, like 'Marat/Sade', recorded by Judy Collins about the French Revolution and lyrics like: '*Down with all of the ruling class, throw all the generals out on their ass*'.'

There was consternation during the Lord Mayor's show on May 18 1968. A Vietcong flag was raised that morning in Donegal Square by the Communist Youth League. American sailors from the USS Keppler took part in the parade but, on a pre-agreed signal, local protesters lay down on the road. The sailors marched on.

'The American Navy just walked over everybody,' says Terri. 'The ship was down at the docks and we would be running around the ship. We'd be writing things on wall, sticking leaflets in the bogs. Anti-Vietnam leaflets and stuff like that.'

The examples of old revolutions in France and America were sometimes remembered, as was the Society of United Irishmen that had responded to those 18th Century notions of fraternity, enlightenment and religious tolerance. Many of the agents for change in Belfast during that century had been Presbyterian. The dissenter tradition had resisted slavery and the Anglo-Irish ascendency. They went into battle in 1798 while singing 'La Marseillaise' under the banner of *Erin go Bragh*.

Ruth Carr was at school in the late 60s, preparing for Queen's University, a future poet and a co-conspirator with Terri Hooley. She remembers those historical footfalls:

'It was a bit like the United Irishmen time. All these ideas flooding in from elsewhere that make you think, "Oh, the world doesn't have to be the way it seems to be here". In 1969, because of everything that happened, there was a curfew – you were banned from meeting more than three people in the street. I was just a kid running around with flowers on my face. We were all laughing, saying we were gonna get arrested because there were more than three of us.

'A lot of people were waking up to a kind of idealism that was floating around. As if we could be something. I was very influenced by ideas. There was peace and love and notions that you could live in a different way. There was the death of the family, living in communes, being free. I would have gone around with people that called themselves Heads, who were probably into dope more than anything.

'To the majority of people I met at school, this would have been anathema. I remember in school, different people would do the assembly. I arranged to have the 'I have a dream' speech on. And people started booing it. The teachers weren't doing anything about it.'

Hence the attraction of a counter-culture in Belfast.

'There was Terri's Tribe, as it was called then. He would have always wanted to be a sort of leader. A sort of *anti-leader*, maybe. It was around culture as much as it was around music. All sorts that things were just like, "rebellion – we'll do things the way we want to do them because we don't want to grow up like our parents".'

Fr Tony Marcellus was a Passionist Priest at Holy Cross in the Ardoyne area of Belfast. He was active on the ground during the restless summer of 1969, trying to quell potential riots as the marching season continued. He was part of the Citizen's Action Committee but this was also a stressful issue as opportunists had tried to hijack the social cause. On occasion, the newspapers called him 'the hoodlum priest', after the old film about a Jesuit street-worker in St Louis. The Passionist Order had been preparing to mark its centenary in the city, but had been advised by the police to be wary of any high-profile event close to sectarian fracture lines. Instead, Fr Marcellus put his name to 'Pop for Peace'.

The event was scheduled for August 4. It was partly inspired by the Rolling Stones and their free concert at Hyde Park, July 5. At least 250,000 had attended the London happening as Mick Jagger said a farewell to the recently departed Brian Jones, releasing thousands of cabbage white butterflies, many of which expired in the heat. The Belfast version was less ambitious, but still aimed for 10,000 people. Venues such as the City Hall and the King's Hall were not available, so the setting was assigned to Minnowburn, a National Trust property near Shaw's Bridge in South Belfast.

'We want to show that most young people are not interested in hatred,' Fr Marcellus reckoned. Various names were mentioned in the July newspaper reports, including Tyrannosaurus Rex, John Peel, Jimmy Savile and Joe Dolan, the showband powerhouse from Mullingar. But, chiefly, they wanted John Lennon and Yoko Ono, who had recently recorded a song during a bed-in session on the 19th floor of the Queen Elizabeth Hotel in Montreal. Featuring Hare Krishna chanters and celebrity stompers, 'Give Peace a Chance' was released in July and rapidly became a standard for street demos and sit-ins.

'In my secret heart I wanted to write something that would take over 'We Shall Overcome',' Lennon told *Rolling Stone*. 'That's the one they always sang. I thought, why doesn't somebody write something for the people now? That's what my job and is. Our job is to write for the people *now*.'

The Pop for Peace Committee included Paddy Devlin, the Northern Ireland Labour Party MP, plus local media figures Sam Smyth, Donal Corvin and Colin McClelland. They tried to get a line to John Lennon and expressed their public wish that he would see the importance of a Belfast appearance. Unfortunately, he had crashed his car on a family tour of Scotland on July 1, requiring stitches. And at the actual time of the concert, he was recording the *Abbey Road* album in London. Colin McClelland, who had been flagging up Pop for Peace in the pages of *City Week*, recalls the ask:

'Lennon sent two telegrams to us. One of our group had contacts with Apple or the management. He kept getting in touch – "is John coming over, has John got something to say?" What we got was: "all we are saying, is give peace a chance – love John and Yoko". I think those telegrams were auctioned off on the day. However, what we didn't know was that John was going through cold turkey at the time.

'The intention for the gig was that the kids were all together. It was naive but well-intentioned. It was a show of strength – that the kids were all opposed to this. And it bucketed out of the heavens. I remember meeting Paddy Devlin the day before and saying, "Are we gonna call this off?" He said, "Under no circumstances do we call this off". And, right enough, when I drove to it on the day, the kids were thick on the ground up the Malone Road, even in the pelting rain. Probably about a thousand. It wasn't a huge turn-out, but considering the day that was in it, it was huge. All the bands played, everybody had a good time.'

Marmalade did show up as promised – Glaswegian pop familiars who had topped the charts in January with their version of 'Ob-La-Di, Ob-La-Da'. Irish acts also persevered in the rain, including the Dreams, Boutique and Joe Dolan, now a chart feature and a *Top of the Pops* face with 'Make Me an Island'. Ordinarily, this would have amounted to a positive news story and a riposte to the bad narrative elsewhere. Colin remembers the actuality:

'TV cameras were there from everywhere because Northern Ireland had become a flashpoint. But rioting broke out in Unity Flats as the concert was taking place. So, all the newsmen rushed off – we didn't know where – and in the news that night it was all Unity Flats and then a postscript at the end – "and also a crowd gathered at Minnowburn, blah blah blah…"

'You couldn't think of what to do next. Reality hit us on the face. This is not the story. The rioting was the story. They didn't even put us on TV. There was one photograph in the paper two days later. We had a quick education in reality that day.'

One week later, a section of Derry was encircled with barricades and declared itself an independent entity. The Battle of the Bogside had sparked off on August 12 after the annual Apprentice Boys' march around the walls of the city. The British Army arrived two days after, relieving the RUC, but did not intrude past the 30 barriers that sealed off the Bogside, Brandywell and parts of the Creggan. Inside, it was marshalled by 400 associates of the

Derry Citizens Defence Association, organising deliveries of bread and milk and keeping internal discipline. Radio Free Derry was operational again, a source of information and motivational words.

'Tommy McDermott was a hippie,' Eamonn remembers, 'one of the few genuine hippies from the Bogside, and he was always preaching peace, as hippies do. And he got two hours on his own. He locked the door and didn't come out and played the Incredible String Band for two hours and he would say, "Hey, keep cool, don't be fighting with the cats in the Fountain".'

It was McCann and Mary Holland, writer for *The Observer*, who planned the Free Derry Fleadh Cheoil, a festival over the weekend of August 30-31. The banner read DERRY MERRY DERRY FREE and the entertainment included donkey rides and candy apples. Traditional music and dancing was central to this 'Liberation Fleadh'. Special guests included the Dubliners, who performed on Westland Street by the Bogside Inn. They also played a long session at Dermie McClenaghan's house on Wellington Street, sustained on whiskey and endless nicotine fixes of Gallagher's 'Blue'.

Tommy Makem was folk royalty, an Armagh man from a music family who had connected with the Clancy Brothers in New York and witnessed the rise of Bob Dylan and the Bleeker Street scene. He played on a makeshift stage in the Bogside on the Sunday evening and was taken by the sense of occasion and purpose. 'To me it was like being asked to sing for people behind the Berlin Wall,' he said later. 'They were standing up for themselves and thanks be to God, somebody has the courage to stand up and say, no, we're not taking any more.'

Tommy's repertoire included 'Four Green Fields', a song that he'd written in Ireland 1967 after driving across the border. He had noticed that an old woman with her livestock seemed immune to this notion of divided territory. Makem's lyric drew on an older tradition of the grieving woman, lost and bereft, a symbol of Ireland unfree. The poet W.B. Yeats had visualised this figure as Kathleen Ni Houlihan. In previous centuries, the *aisling* poets had pictured a grieving, female ghost, and wrote up their nationalism in such loose code. So, Tommy Makem had plugged into a depth of understanding. The three rescued fields were the provinces of Munster, Leinster and Connacht. Part of the Ulster province had been recovered, but the six counties of Northern Ireland were still awry. Tommy put this ballad out to an audience in the Bogside that was more than sympathetic.

'When I sang that song, it was like a huge electrical storm. It seemed like the whole city was electrified and lit up. *Seared* by it. That evening I got the impression that this was more than a song. It was touching a lot of people in their soul, in their heart:

> *'My fourth green field will bloom again, said she.'*

And she was right.'

Riots and killings had intensified during August in Belfast. After the weekend of Pop for Peace, the *Irish News* announced the rioting as 'the first major clashes between Protestants and Catholics since 1935'. Following on from this, scores of families were displaced and burnt out of their homes in the north and west of the city. The Army had been summoned but still there were disturbances across September and October as factions on both sides gathered their weaponry. Colin McClelland remembers how Belfast had become entrenched by the end of 1969.

'There were about a dozen of us in the Abercorn Bar in Cornmarket on a Saturday afternoon, drinking and shouting or whatever. We walked out and the streets were empty and all the shops were shuttered. We asked a passer-by what was going on. He said, "Oh, everyone's been sent home". He pointed towards Royal Avenue. You could see smoke rising. He said, "the rioting is moving into the city centre". And everyone had been told to shut up the shops and send their staff home.

'So, we're standing there with this group of maybe eight or nine. There was no public transport. Someone said, "How do we get home, who has a car?" Two or three people put their hands up. Now these were people that we had been associating with and drinking and partying with for the past two or three years. They were good friends, people who we knew and trusted. We'd slept over in their houses and gone to parties with them. And for the first time ever, people said, "Where do you live again?" And we immediately polarised into the ones going to Protestant areas and the ones going to Catholic areas. And you took a lift with the person going up your route, as it were. And I remember that vividly. It was the first time we stopped and said, "What religion are you?" Because we thought we had beaten that.

'I think it was alarming to both sides of the paramilitary leaders that for the previous two years in Belfast, Catholics and Protestants had been mixing. Kids were mixing. They were getting married. And that had never happened before. I think the old guard on both sides saw the beginning of the Troubles as a welcome ghettoisation of the younger generation. No one will understand 1967 to 1969 unless you put it in the context of what had come before and what had come after. We had dull, grey, industrial Belfast through the 1950s and early 1960s, and then suddenly this explosion. People with flowers in their hair – we *did* have that. Clubs were opening, bands were being formed at a ferocious rate, and then suddenly, *whooof* – it's all closed off. The curtain comes down and nothing's happens again until… I don't know if anything ever *did* happen again.'

Weldon 'Juke Boy' Bonner was a bluesman from Bellville, Texas. He had been born into a sharecropper family, the youngest of nine children, orphaned at the age of six. He had worked in the fields during the cotton season before moving to Houston as a teenager, keenly learning from the jukebox. His musical career had been sporadic and halted for a time in 1963 when half of his ulcerated stomach was cut out. But in November 1969 he was set to perform at Belfast's War Memorial Building.

He had come to Europe for six weeks at the invitation of the National Blues Federation in the UK. His trip across the Irish Sea on November 14 was part of that overall plan – prompted by record shop owner Dougie Knight and the Belfast Blues Society. Terri Hooley was Secretary of the Society. They had put a lot of effort into poster design and promotion and arranged to sell food at the venue to cover some of the costs. Interest in the blues was holding up and there was audience enough during this period for a series of valued guests: Champion Jack Dupree, Memphis Slim, and Mississippi Fred McDowell. But it was going to be a challenge for the Juke Boy gig, as Terri remembers: 'That Friday night, because of rioting, all the bars in Belfast city centre closed at teatime. The only place you could get a drink was at our concert on Waring Street.'

They brought the singer in through diversions and around roadblocks. And the night was reasonably well attended. Everyone there had made a personal effort to be present. They were keen to make Juke Boy feel welcome and one of Terri's friends, Pauline Harrison, got up on stage and kissed the man on the cheek. Juke Boy responded in kind, singing with a sweet, fragile edge, detailing his troublesome life. His songs also reflected on the modern world and the anxieties of a black artist in America. One of his emerging tunes was called 'Going Back to the Country' and the punchline was a sore comment on the situation at home: '*if I move back in the sticks, at least I ain't got to worry about being killed by no sniper's fire*'.

The concert organisers in Belfast cut their losses and gave most of the food away. The night might have been meaningful, but it wasn't a profitable one. Still, they heard that Juke Boy wasn't making a great success of it either, so they passed around the hat for extra cash and let him know just how much he mattered before his trip back to London.

One of the singer's last engagements during his transatlantic visit was a recording session in Regent 'A' Studios on Tottenham Court Road. This was also a National Blues Federation production with Chris Trimming plus Ron Watts, who also booked acts for the 100 Club on Oxford Street. And while Juke Boy was self-reliant with voice, guitar and harmonica, they had a backing band on standby for a few tracks and a keyboard player, John Lewis, later known as Jona Lewie. 'Juke Boy Bonner was slightly on the shy side,' Jona says. 'And slightly on the gentle side. He wouldn't force the issue. But what could be worse than London in November – and he's coming from the sunny side of America.'

It was severely cold, and the singer had lost many of his clothes in a mishap with the hotel laundry. But he sat there without any socks and he settled on new songs that detailed his eventful visit. One song related a conversation back home with his friend Lightnin' Hopkins, who assured him that the upcoming trip was going to be a swell experience. But the songs also revealed the downside of life overseas, the lonely times at Bexhill-on-Sea and the prohibitive cost of phoning his lover back in Houston. The mood was blue and regretful.

He also fetched up a song called 'Belfast Blues'. It was a one-man rendition, a recollection of his evening at the War Memorial Building in a city with a worsening international reputation. The memory was only a few days old, but already he had a theme and a riff. He gave it a unique feel.

'You normally associate the blues with 12 bars,' Jona says. 'That's the sequence. But Juke Boy Bonner might do eleven and a half or twelve and a half. He was more country blues than city blues. He was less formal. It was very personal and the lyrics were very spontaneous. Obviously, Bonner had thought about what he was going to sing about, but the framework of the music was so loose. The way he rhymed '*surprise*' and '*smiling Irish eyes*'. It was a great song, really.'

Juke Boy Bonner had this extraordinary gift in him, the ability to take a contrary view from the newspaper headlines. Belfast, he declared in his song, was a surprising place. The men were friendly and the women were sweet and kind. It was a highlight of his six-week journey, so he picked at his Fender Mustang and he told his listeners that the city had floored him, that a woman had even come up and kissed him on the cheek. He made it sound joyous.

It was a while before the record was released and longer again before Terri Hooley got to hear 'Belfast Blues'. By then, the concerts had become less frequent and the city centre was a place of random violence. The song was an emotional keepsake.

'The 60s for me was like a great big party which I thought would never end – but by November 1969 l knew it was over. It was the night we stopped partying. A lot of the people who had gone to places like the Jazz Club and the Maritime went back to their own ghettoes and people lost contact with each other. And we were going into a horrific part of history in Northern Ireland. That was the night when the kissing had to stop.'

BEHIND THE WIRE

Dana won the Eurovision Song Contest in Amsterdam on March 21 1970. She wore a white *báinín* dress embellished with Celtic whorls. It was designed by Maura O'Driscoll and the rhinestones had been sewn on by nuns from the west of Ireland. She was 18 and it was her first trip abroad.

'All Kinds of Everything' had been written by two newspaper compositors from Dublin and arranged by Phil Coulter, another Derry figure on the rise. Dana was the last performer of the evening and she sang the lyrics with the artless lilt of youth. She took 72 votes, well ahead of Mary Hopkin and the British entry, 'Knock, Knock Who's There?'. The latter was an invitation to love from a successful Welsh voice but Dana was on the side of snowdrops and daffodils, butterflies and bees.

Dana was a native of Londonderry or Derry, depending on the given political allegiances. She was really called Rosemary Brown but her schoolmates from Thornhill College had come up with the stage name – Irish for bold and also an allusion to a mythical goddess from Gaelic lore. It was her second run at Eurovision and, happily, she won the prize for Ireland.

That was her prerogative. She had been born in Islington, north London, but the family had returned to Derry when she was five. She had lived in the Creggan and the Bogside and in 1970 her home was in the high flats at Rossville Street. Under Articles Two and Three of the 1937 Constitution of Ireland, all 32 counties of the island were designated territory – even the six counties of Northern Ireland under actual UK rule. So, Dana could claim allegiance to her preferred nation for this cultural event and was lauded for her Irish victory. Her father Robert had put down a £10 bet at 10/1 odds, so he was especially delighted.

The national airline carrier, Aer Lingus, staged "operation Dana" to bring her home in a Boeing 727. She sang on the steps of the plane at Dublin airport and talked to reporters before flying to RAF Ballykelly in the North, welcomed by the Nazareth House Céilí Band and John Hume MP. It was the first time an Aer Lingus plane had landed in Northern Ireland. There were 5,000 people and a couple of Bishops at the Guildhall reception in town and many more waiting around her home. The Army helped to remove obstacles at the Butcher Gate for this part of the victory trail. She sang to the crowd from the fifth floor of the flats, her former vantage point, where she had followed the Battle of the Bogside, seven months before. 'It was like watching a war movie,' she remembered. There was a minor riot on the evening of Dana's return, and several days later the *Derry Journal* reported that soldiers had taunted the locals, claiming that Dana was in fact a British subject. Meanwhile, the song lyrics were translated into a worsening political landscape by an unknown author.

> *'UVF, IRA, British forces too,*
> *All kinds of violence, reminds me of you.'*

There was a market for recordings about political opinion and national identity. Two enterprises handled the bulk of the demand: Outlet and Emerald. Neither of them showed an especially partisan hand. They pressed up records from male voice choirs, rebel balladeers, pipers, céilí outfits and Protestant marching bands. By the early 70s, there was an established network that took in record shops and independent retailers but also saw value in street traders and market stalls in Glasgow, Blackpool, Crossmaglen, wherever.

Outlet was fronted by Billy McBurney, whose parents Patrick and Bridget had founded the Premier Records shop in Smithfield Market, Belfast in 1926, There had been profitable sidelines in gramophone needles and sheet music. They sustained the business over many difficult eras and claimed with some pride that it was the oldest record store in Ireland. Nineteen-sixty-six had been a fervent time for recordings, 50 years on from the Easter Rising and the proclamation of the Irish Republic. Patriotic songs had been selling well and Billy found the words and the occasion to exact the best result.

Dublin had rid itself of many symbols from the British Empire but there was still a statue of Lord Nelson on the main drag of O'Connell Street, on top of a granite column, 121 feet high. A splinter group of militants deposed the statue with explosives in the early hours of March 8 1966. Billy wrote a lyric to commemorate the event, called 'Up Went Nelson'. It was matched to the melody of the American Civil War anthem, 'The Battle Hymn of the Republic'. A band of Belfast schoolteachers from St Thomas's Secondary Intermediate on the Whiterock Road recorded it as the Go Lucky Four. Stomping and gleeful, it topped the Irish charts for eight weeks. Others followed – Tommy Makem wrote 'Lord Nelson' and the Dubliners had their say with 'Nelson's Farewell', but Belfast had trumped the major names.

From the mid-60s, the McBurney labels Homespun and Outlet produced local pressings for the football supporters' market (Linfield and Glentoran) and for anyone partial to Lambeg drums or 'The Bold Orange Heroes of Comber'. By 1968, Billy had taken over a recording studio in St Mary's Hall in Bank Street and was working on sessions with his trusted engineer Cel Fay. They caught important moments with their rudimentary gear, involving the champion whistle player Tom McHale and the fiddler Seán McGuire. Versatile studio musicians were expected to fit with the style and the sentiment. The records became more audacious, such as Chuck McGuigan and the Bogsiders, who presented a 1969 release, 'The Battle of the Bogside', using the melody of the prime loyalist anthem 'The Sash'.

'Sessions musicians are an ecumenical breed,' Cel Fay explained. 'They provide the background music no matter whether the origins are orange or green. There's no religious barrier in a recording studio.'

So, when the studio proved too small to accommodate an Orange band, they took them to a hall on the Falls Road. Conversely, a pipe band from

Andersonstown needed a drum major for a Bank Street session and Outlet sourced them a true defender from the Shankill Road. A 1970 release, *Songs of Irish Civil Rights*, was credited to Owen McDonagh and the Bogside Men. It remembered Burntollet and the Long March, the Battle of the Bogside and also included the famous American freedom calls. Events were accelerating and it already felt like a historical document. On many of the new lyrics, the Civil Rights narrative had turned into an issue of nationality: the tone had gone green.

Outlet expenses were tightly handled. Session fees and artwork could be managed for less than £500. A popular record could deliver £10,000 a year for five years or more. Billy's catalogue grew over the first six years to 126 vinyl albums and as many on cassette and 8-track, plus 100 singles. He was also distributing other Irish labels such as Claddagh, Hawk, Gael-Linn, Glenside and Shamrock. Annual turnover was in excess of £500,000. 'Partly as a result of the Troubles and the emphasis on home entertainment,' he told *Music Week*, 'a greater market than many of the major labels imagine exists now throughout Northern Ireland.'

By Billy's reckoning, he suffered 14 separate incidents of bomb damage on the Smithfield business in 1971. He was from Durham Street towards the north of the city, an Official Sinn Féin man. His son Martin would later suggest that his politics went back to non-sectarian, 18th Century ideals. 'His philosophy was sort of in the Wolfe Tone tradition, you know, Protestants, dissenters and everyone – there was no issue in that, they were all Irish men at the back of it all.' However, McBurney was in the crossfire of opposing forces, as the photographer and author Bobbie Hanvey remembered: 'He was shot by the Loyalists, he was blown up by the Provos and he was put into Long Kesh by the British. His nickname was Lucky.'

Operation Demetrius was enacted by the British Army on August 9-10 1971 in consultation with the Unionist government of Northern Ireland. This was internment without trial and 342 people were lifted, many in dawn raids. The Army had targeted supposed Republican militants, although Civil Rights figures were also on the list of suspects and several of these names evaded arrest. The accuracy of Army intelligence was later questioned. No Loyalists were interned until 1973. Some Protestants taunted their neighbours with a chant adapted from 'Chirpy Chirpy Cheep Cheep', the 1971 hit single by Middle of The Road: *'where's your daddy gone?'*

Many of the internees were moved to HMS Maidstone in Belfast Harbour and later to HM Prison Magilligan and into Nissen Huts at Long Kesh Detention Centre, a former military airport on the outskirts of Lisburn. This is where Billy McBurney spent a period of time and whence Outlet Records was directed during his confinement. Bobbie Hanvey explains: 'His accountants and all were going into the prison and getting his books right and he was telling them what people to record.'

'The Men Behind the Wire' was released on December 14 1971. The author was Paddy McGuigan, a plumber from Springview Street in West Belfast, and the track was recorded in the Outlet studios with his band Barley Corn (later Barleycorn). It was issued by the Andersonstown Civil Resistance Committee on the CRC label as a fund-raiser for the families of internees. Billy McBurney managed the logistics. It was pressed in England due to sensitivities at home and, on its release, RTÉ and the BBC declined to play it.

The song described the dawn raids and the arrival of the Army in their *'armoured cars and tanks and guns'*. It is debatable whether tanks were actually involved in the operation, but the line became branded into the Republican imagination. The RUC was now sidelined in rebel lyrics and the British soldier was the object of hardening hatred. There was an allusion in the words to Oliver Cromwell and his brutal Irish wars of the 17th Century. The song urged the families to be steadfast and supportive. It was a song of community and it proposed that, ultimately, Ireland would be 'a nation once again'. This had been promised in the same-titled Young Ireland anthem of 1844 by Thomas Osbourne Davis. So, 'The Men Behind the Wire' was an immediate protest song with crashing consonants, but also a history lesson for the Republican movement. It topped the Irish charts in January 1972 and returned there again in February, after Bloody Sunday – five weeks as the nation's best-seller and a feature of the charts throughout the year. Conflict was number one in the hit parade.

Back then, Máirtín Ó Muilleoir, aged 13 from Andersonstown, was impressed:

'We listened to it and it was, "Wow, what a song". When he started singing about Cromwell and armoured cars and tanks and guns, we were living that, but the history was totally alien to me. I had no idea there was any kind of constitutional conflict. I was only a child. You talk about the power of a song to change a nation – those songs did change people's views and introduce you to stuff. In hindsight you say, "Oh, he's saying that because they would all understand". We'd never heard of that stuff. Those were terrible years. British soldiers were killed every second day in the streets I lived in. Civilians were killed. Nobody suffered like the civilians suffered.'

Paddy McGuigan was interned for three months afterwards. His allies felt it was punishment for writing the song. Whatever, the ballad was irrepressible and was covered with thigh-slapping gusto by the Wolfe Tones and others. There was even a Loyalist variation with the imagery flipped and the colours a different hue.

Also in Belfast, the Men of No Property took their name from a Wolfe Tone quote and some of their political ideas from revolutionary Marxism. Brian Moore, Dave Scott and Joe Mulheron had been encouraged by folk mainstays Ewan MacColl and Peggy Seeger. Bernadette Devlin wrote their sleeve notes. Their 1971 debut album, *This Is Free Belfast! Rebel Songs of the Six Counties*, included 'The Bogside Man', a startling re-write of the old sea shanty, 'Hog Eye Man':

> *'Steady on your aim with the petrol bomb,*
> *Don't throw it son, 'til the peelers come,*
> *I am the Bogside man.'*

'It was a protest group,' says Joe Mulheron. 'We weren't your average rebel band in that sense. Our songs came out of the Civil Rights and People's Democracy and that sort of stuff. We were singing mainly in the shebeens back in '69 and '70. The different ghettoes opened up their own sort of social clubs, for want of a better word. We tended to play up and down the Falls Road, in the Ardoyne and the New Lodge Road. We were constantly on Radio Free Belfast.

'We toured England a couple of times – the Troops Out movement hosted us. In '69, Ewan MacColl and Peggy Seeger brought us over to their club in London. We rammed the place. MacColl was a dry boy. He said, "Mulheron's introductions lasted longer than some of the songs". I said, "That's 'cos youse know fuck all over here – we have to explain ourselves".'

The American folksinger Barbara Dane financed their records and released them on her Paredon Records imprint, which she managed with Irwin Silber. Their label specialised in international revolutionary music. 'She was very left wing, to say the least,' says Joe. The first album mixed the raw news of 'Cry Murder!' and 'Ballymurphy' with the innuendo of 'Rubber Bullets'.

'The line-up tended to change as people moved about. Dave Scott wrote 'Rubber Bullets'. Dave was from the Protestant tradition, but his father was a shop steward in Shorts [Short Brothers aerospace] and was involved in left-wing politics. You might have thought differently by listening to the likes of 'The Bogside Man' but we tried to keep the sectarian thing out of the mix. What we also found was that we'd be singing these deep, political songs and half the time the working-class people in the ghettoes would be clapping away and not really listening to the words. I ended up consciously having to write some of the songs where there was a twist or a funny bit at the end. Just to get the people's attention.'

While Joe and his colleagues were adding wit to their repertoire, other writers were coming up with stirring, sentimental songs like 'The Broad, Black Brimmer'. Attributed to Art McMillan, this song evoked the paramilitary uniform of the original IRA, bequeathed from the late father to the son – the brimmer being the headgear worn during the 1919-21 Irish War of Independence. Later, Joe would respond with a piece of satire, writing a Palestine Liberation Organisation anthem in an Irish rebel style – 'The Wee White Turban'.

'It was a tongue-in-cheek, a take-off. It's very difficult to explain. We were pissed off with 'The Broad, Black Brimmer' because every drunk in every pub in Belfast was singing it, whether they could sing or not. So, I wrote that song as a spoof. But I tried to put a bit of politics into it – I didn't want people to think I was sending up the PLO. I was really sending up the Republicans. You're gonna have to take your oil, as they say in Derry. Take a bit of criticism.'

The Provisional IRA had emerged in late 1969, taking a more offensive position than their predecessors, who became known as the Official IRA. On March 10 1971, the Provisionals killed off-duty soldiers for the first time. Brothers John and Joseph McCaig were from Ayr and Dougald McCaughey was from Glasgow. They were 17, 18 and 23, serving in the Royal Highland Fusiliers. They had been unarmed and had left a bar in Belfast's city centre, thinking they were headed to a house party. Apparently, they had been encouraged into a car by females connected to the IRA operation. Their bodies were discovered off the Ligoniel Road at the outskirts of North Belfast, two of them shot in the back of the head, the third in the chest.

There were protests and walk-outs across Northern Ireland, involving workers from the shipyard. Thousands gathered at the cenotaph by the City Hall in Belfast. A song, 'Three Scottish Soldiers', was written to the melody of 'Silent Night'. When Sylvia Pavis from Dee Street later sang it, she was slow and sorrowful like Patsy Cline or Tammy Wynette.

Other songs started to appear in Loyalist papers. 'A Wee Spot in Europe' portrayed the six counties as being resolute in the face of difficulty. They had endured the Belfast Blitz in 1941. Their grandfathers had fought in the Great War, and many had died. The song admits a feeling of vulnerability but there are also allies close to hand:

'Say you're side-by-side with Scotland,
They won't let us down.'

That year, Coca Cola rolled out a lavish commercial that saw all the nations of the world united by their product. The advertisement, filmed on an Italian hilltop, massed up scores of grinning youths in ethnic costume, singing of harmony and turtle doves. They wanted to buy the world a Coke. The Loyalists of Belfast were unimpressed. Their version of the lyric was cranked out in backstreet printers, presently a feature of work places and school satchels:

'I'd like to buy The Pope a rope
And hang him from a tree
With Bernadette and Gerry Fitt
To keep him company.'

There were multiple verses. In each stanza, various enemies of Ulster were dispatched in graphic style.

The 50th anniversary of Northern Ireland was officially marked by an exposition, Ulster '71, ranging across 37 acres in Botanic Gardens in Belfast. There were amusements, jousting tournaments and a festival pavilion with performances by acts such as Derek Bell and the Canticle. It was opened in May 1971 with an investment of £800,000. Visitors were invited to walk through a darkened 'Tunnel of Hate', painted with State-approved graffiti ('SLUMS', 'VIOLENCE', 'REMEMBER THE PENSIONERS') into a wonderland of contemporary culture. This included a vibrating venue, Disco '71. One of the DJs was Michael 'Hendi Henderson.

The age of the discothèque had begun in Belfast in the mid-60s with figures such as Dennis 'Dino' Martin, a red-headed resident at The Plaza, part of the Mecca organisation. Other early adopters were Stevie 'Wonderful' Wilson and George Carroll. The Marquee Club at the Astor Ballroom in 1969 had been the peak DJ experience for Hendi: busy nights in the city centre, alternating with visiting name acts, records, go-go dancers and local players. Hendi had also been a compere at the Pop for Peace Concert:

'I was forever optimistic about it. And I did feel that music brought both sides together. It didn't matter where you were. It was good to get away from it and be entertained. We strung together equipment. We were into quad and electrostatic speakers, a wee Phillips slide amp and what they called E-boxes. When we went to Queens, we met some electronic engineers who made us some great stuff. Then we had ultraviolet lights and a slide show – we had a branch-off from the Marquee work that was called Fanny Flickers Light Show. The Freshmen hired us to go round and do these shows all over Ireland. That was another aspect of it.

'I was doing wee daft clubs – shebeens up the Shankill, drinking clubs. And also on the other side of the market. Because we'd done the Snack Bar at Queen's for so many years, we had so many people on both sides and we'd be asked up to the Falls Bowling Club or somewhere. There was a well-known guy on the Shankill called Billy McCarroll; he used to phone me up. We always kept it quiet – I'm sure some suspect people were running it. You didn't want to be allied to them. Then we did Ulster '71. We got the franchise for the disco. We had the dome for the disco for most of the summer. The Grand Met Hotel had the franchise for the catering and we managed to get it off them and we ran it every day and night. And we encountered the notorious Tartan Gangs.'

The Tartan Gangs were working class and Loyalist. They were loosely modelled on the Young Team street gangs of Glasgow. A box of tartan scarves had been stolen from a gift shop during a trip to a Glasgow Rangers game in the late 60s and so the Shankill Tartan had their identity. As noted by the author Gareth Mulvenna, they wore Wrangler jackets and boots and Ulster Covenant badges. They adopted lyrics by T. Rex ('*we are the children of the Shankill Tartan*') and Jeff Beck ('*hi ho, Shankill Tartan*'). Over in East Belfast, 'Get It On' by T. Rex was an anthem for the Woodstock Tartan.

Rod Stewart started to wear tartan and that was noted with approval. The Belfast gangs had their individual clan patterns, commissioned from local stores such as The Spinning Wheel and The Paragon: a yard long, four inches wide. The gangs were aware of the band Slade, their early skinhead image and superyob tendencies. The Ulster Bootboys from Ballygomartin read the Richard Allen *Skinhead* books, printed by the New English Library. At some level, the droog culture from *A Clockwork Orange* was also an influence. The Tartan Gangs would be summoned to the barricades of Protestant Belfast at moments of resistance and then filtered into paramilitary organisations. At the time of Ulster '71, they were already a potential bother. Hendi remembers his encounter:

'We had a brilliant team of bouncers, we never had any trouble worth talking about. They kept the troublemakers away. The only thing that happened was the Woodstock Tartan and the Village Tartan both wanted to run the place. We didn't want any of them to run it. It was our gig, you know. So, we brought the two leaders of the gangs together and said, "Look, why don't you both work together on that, and then you can both come?

Otherwise, nobody gets in." So, they came to an agreement and it was great. They just enjoyed themselves.'

While the Tartan Gangs made use of popular songs, they were also the subject of new music. John McKeague, a sometime associate of Ian Paisley, was printing up regular issues of *Loyalist News* and also an annual collection, *Loyalist Songs*. A lyric, 'Woodstock Tartans', was written to the tune of 'South Down Militia' and it featured in the 1972 edition. But this was not the most remarkable feature of *Loyalist Songs*. In May 1971, McKeague was prosecuted under Northern Ireland's Incitement to Hatred Act for his lyrical content.

The musical *Paint Your Wagon* had a cinema release in late 1969, the story of California miners during the Gold Rush. Lee Marvin was a prospector, Ben Runsome, and he drawled the song 'Wand'rin' Star' on the soundtrack. This topped the UK charts in February 1970 and it provided the basis of an entry in *Loyalist Songs*. Now it was titled 'I Was Born Under a Union Jack' and it ended with a malevolent couplet:

> *'If guns are made for shooting, then skulls are made to crack.*
> *You've never seen a better Taig than with a bullet in his back.'*

Taig was an abusive term for an Irish Catholic. John McKeague and two others avoided prosecution on appeal. In 1972, he continued to publish inflammatory words but put much of his energy into the foundation of the Red Hand Commando, a paramilitary organisation that absorbed many of the Tartan Gang members.

Every entertainer needed to be aware of political sensitivities and the expected ceremony at the end of the night. Cinemas in Northern Ireland concluded with 'God Save the Queen' and there was often a rush to exit the cinema before this obligation to stand to attention. Likewise, at the end of a concert, although in Nationalist or Republican areas they expected to finish with the Irish national anthem *'Amhrán na bhFiann'*, aka 'The Soldier's Song'. Hendi, like others, had to be prepared for each eventuality:

'I used to carry both national anthems with me. I remember we did a disco down by Donaghadee where the majority of people would have been

Protestant. And I'd forgotten the anthems. I did a very casual sign off, and the boy said, "What about the National Anthem?" I said, "Oh, I haven't got it with me". He said to me, *sing it*. And I was waiting for him to say to me, "Sing the second verse". You had to be aware of that.'

Ulster '71 was jokingly called Explo' '71. However, the irony had worn thin during the introduction of internment, when visitor numbers crashed and violent unrest was the year's legacy. Ten civilians, including a priest, were killed by the 2nd Battalion of the Parachute Regiment in just over 36 hours. An eleventh man died of a heart attack. The event became known as the Ballymurphy Massacre.

Operation Demetrius was also followed by mass displacements in mixed-religion areas such as the Ardoyne. It was reported that 240 houses in Farringdon Gardens, Cranbrook Gardens and Velsheda Park had been set on fire as Protestants left the area. The houses were deliberately burnt to prevent new tenants moving in. Flatbed trucks and lorries were commandeered from Loyalist areas and brought to those streets to aid this evacuation. The fall-out of such actions was that other residents had to flee for their own safety. Thus, the O'Shaughnessey household packed and left at speed when their home on Cranbrook Gardens caught fire:

'There were tensions simmering for about three days,' Anthony O'Shaughnessey recalled. 'People did not know what was going to happen. I thought it was a dream and, in the morning, everything would be okay.'

London's *Evening Standard* used a photograph of this disturbance. The image shows 13-year-old Anthony with a grip bag in his left hand and a cardboard suitcase under his right arm. He looks at the camera in a distracted manner. His mother Kathleen is in the background and his brother Kevin is at his right elbow, in a duffel coat. On the other side, his brother Gerard is carrying a plastic bag with some personal effects, being led onto the pavement by a man in a Wrangler jacket and jeans. The children are understandably distressed. Behind the boys, a man is clambering on to the back of a coal lorry. Anthony would later remember the immensity of the moment.

'That day was probably the biggest evacuation since World War II, where so many people retreated into their own communities. The Protestants were evacuated from Ardoyne. Later that night a Loyalist mob from outside the area started burning the houses two streets behind us. Our house caught fire from the houses behind us and burnt to the ground.'

A cropped version of the image was later used as the album cover of the 1980 debut from Dexys Midnight Runners. Anthony had not been aware of the cover until a friend spotted a copy in Smithfield Market. There were several meetings with Kevin Rowland from the band afterwards and bemused quotes from Anthony when vintage marketing posters featuring his image began reaching high prices on the collectors' market. The unwitting cover star also told reporters that he had come to terms with the trauma, that he had no desire to return to his old neighbourhood: 'I don't think I would like to live in a shared community as I couldn't trust it.'

Many people were buying James Young records. It was said that he outsold the Beatles in Northern Ireland with a quarter of a million sales. He was an actor, a ham, an impressionist. He played the roles of Orange Lil, Derek the camp window cleaner, the blethering trade unionist and the snooty lady from Cherryvalley. He had found his audience on Radio Ulster and also at the Group Theatre on Bedford Street. His shtick was derived from Music Hall and he put the mockers up the bigots. When he moved on to a Saturday evening television show, he signed off with a wishful catch-phrase in a Belfast street vernacular: *'would yez stap fightin'.'*

His 1970 album on the Emerald label was *Behind the Barricades*. The title track is about rash love between a girl from the Shankill Road and an English soldier called Cyril. She is the daughter of a B-Special and the liaison has caused ructions at home. But the female is determined. *'The Troubles brought me romance, and it may be my last chance,'* she bleats with some urgency, to the tune of 'Muirshin Durkin'. She imagines giving birth to Cyril's child and she says that she will hang the baby's nappies on the peace line.

On an earlier James Young track, 'The Year 2001', a worker suffers a fatal accident and reports back from Hell. In this nightmarish world, the Irish flag is flying above City Hall and the border has been abolished. They are speaking Gaelic at the shipyard, there are *'Fenians in all the high places'* while Protestants are queuing for soup. In this live recording, the audience laughs in disbelief as James turns the world on its head: '*The Pope was living in Stormont and Paisley was cleaning' the jacks.*' He signs off with the admonition that if we chose to love one another, then this vision of Hell may just be averted.

George Jones was a jobbing musician who played on James Young records and watched him create his precarious edge. 'You could hear intakes of breath, but they turned around and laughed. I think it's the inbuilt dark humour that we have in Northern Ireland. I remember saying to James – who was a great soothsayer – I said, "James, we're in really big, troubled times". He said, "Do you know what, George, the day that Ulster stops laughing is the day we really will have problems".

Emerald Records had been founded by Mervyn Solomon around 1964 and had flourished with George Docherty as the in-house producer and *consigliere.* They had made capital out of 'Up Went Nelson' and also with Bridie Gallagher and Big Tom. In 1971 they had George Jones back in the studio with his band The Club Sound (later Clubsound) and a track called 'Belfast, Belfast'. The song's lyricist was a Welshman, Tommy Thomas who had married a girl from Omagh and put down roots in Northern Ireland. Previously, he had served with the band of the Royal Lancers. He later joined the Coldstream Guards, a military musician at the funeral of Winston Churchill in 1965. In his civilian life, he played jazz drums, worked with the BBC Light Orchestra and supplemented his income on the cabaret scene.

'Belfast, Belfast' is the story of conflict in the city, told from the perspective of an Indian immigrant. He has taken up residence in Gilnahirk, in the east of the town. He makes a resourceful living as a door-to-door salesman, where he meets local figures such as Ian Paisley plus random females in Sandy Row, the Grosvenor Road and the Falls. He sets up a stall on the Shankill with a particular pitch: '*lucky knickers in red, white and blue*'. The narrator takes endless abuse, but his optimism is undented, even when Mrs McVickers wants to know if his underwear is bulletproof. In the Tommy Thomas lyric, the immigrant is also delighted with unemployment benefit, known locally as 'the bureau' or 'the burroo', hence the chorus:

'Belfast, Belfast I love you,
If you're out of work, you can get de borroo.'

The song is delivered in an assumed Asian accent, akin to Peter Sellers in the 1960 hit, 'Goodness Gracious Me' (coincidentally, Sellers visited Unity Flats in Belfast with Swami Vishnudevananda in 1971). In terms of its musical form, 'Belfast, Belfast' is a calypso, a West Indian form that was popularised by Harry Belafonte in America and by the Trinidadian musicians who had settled in Britain during the Windrush era. Part of the calypso method was improvisation and innuendo and so it was used by UK comedians such as Lance Percival, Bernard Cribbins and Benny Hill. And so, Clubsound went to work on it. George Jones:

"Belfast, Belfast' is based in a calypso thing. It's a close as we could get to Indian music at the time. We tried to create a wee sitar thing at the start of it. In those days there wasn't as big an Asian community as there would be now. So, having a guy walking around Belfast with a turban on was an odd thing to see. So, Tommy came out with this idea. How would a wee Asian guy who had come to settle here – how would he view the different roads or how would he understand it? Where to go and not to go? And this no-go scenario? Espccially if he was selling his wares, which just happened to be lucky knickers.

'We did question ourselves when we were writing the stuff. And we obviously had a trial basis and tried them out, but there was always this laughter about it. Although we still do it, nobody has ever questioned the racist thing in it. You know, you talk about crossing the line and where do we go with this stuff.

'I was talking to George Docherty about that first album, *Clubsound Capers*. He said that, by today's terms, it would have gone nearly quadruple platinum. It has sold around the world, because it took a sort of a message of light – hope to people who had left for Australia and ex-pats, living away – that there was still a bit of laughter in Northern Ireland.'

Decades later, another layer of meaning became apparent in the Dexys sleeve of *Searching for the Young Soul Rebels*. The two adult males in the picture were identified. The figure in the denim jacket was a regular on the

Shankill Road. The other man, leading Anthony O'Shaughnessey on to the pavement is Robert 'Basher' Bates, who was imprisoned for his involvement with a gang, later known as the Shankill Butchers. This team, led by Lenny Murphy, killed upwards of 19 people, chiefly Catholics. For the most part, the victims were pedestrians taken at random from the streets around North Belfast. The gang operated with butchers' knives taken from a meat warehouse. Even by Belfast standards, their work was appalling.

THEY SHOT THE PEOPLE DOWN

John Lennon and Yoko Ono were active in London on August 11 1971.
They walked the length of Oxford Street to a rally at Marble Arch, a green
space with a tradition for free speech, used by George Orwell, Karl Marx
and the Chartists. They sang 'Power to the People' and hundreds of fellow
travellers joined in.

They were marching in support of the underground magazine *Oz*, which
was fighting a drawn-out obscenity trial. Issue 28 had been written by
young people and billed as 'Schoolkids' Oz'. A satirical image of Rupert the
Bear had led to the arrest of the publishers, who became known as the Oz
Three. Lennon had written a couple of songs, 'God Save Us' and 'Do the
Oz', which were aired in the summer. Comedians, academics and popular
figures were also supportive while the defence lawyer John Mortimer QC
made a case for 'the boundaries of our freedom to think and draw and write
what we please'.

The Marble Arch rally was only two days after the introduction of
internment in Northern Ireland and so this also became a pressing story
for John Lennon. As he walked through the West End, he held a copy
of another publication to his chest, plain to see. This was *Red Mole*, the
work of the International Marxist Group. The Editor was Tariq Ali, who
had fronted the Vietnam Solidarity Campaign march in 1968, gathering
upwards of 80,000 in Trafalgar Square before leading 8,000 people to the

US Embassy at Grosvenor Square, an event that had caused Mick Jagger to write 'Street Fighting Man'.

The early August issue of *Red Mole* showed a montage of soldiers with gasmasks and rifles. The headline read, 'FOR THE IRA: AGAINST BRITISH IMPERIALISM'. Lennon, in his double denim and poor-boy cap, made sure that the image of himself holding the cover was in full view of the press photographers. He also posed with the issue for a newspaper shoot at his home that week. These were sentiments that he did not want the world to miss.

The *Red Mole* cover story had been written by Bob Purdie, a Marxist from Edinburgh. It ran over the centre pages, rightly guessing that internment was about to happen and reflecting some of the delirium of the time. It praised the Provisional and Official IRA and 'the remarkable military success in recent months', citing the bombing of Springfield Road barracks, a weapons raid and an explosion that had disabled a *Daily Mirror* pressing plant on the outskirts of Belfast. The story discussed a strategy of Chairman Mao whereby 'the guerrilla must move amongst the people as a fish swims in the sea'. According to Bob Purdie, this was now evident across the Irish Sea: 'both IRAs today are larger, better armed and have a wider support amongst the Nationalist population in the North than at any time in their history'. The *Red Mole* feature concluded that 'the struggle … is moving towards its bloody climax'.

Previously, John Lennon had shown mixed feelings about conflict. The recording sessions for the Beatles track 'Revolution' (May-June 1968) had resulted in three different narratives. The single version of 'Revolution' was a snub to violence and the Maoist diehards. The inference was clear: John was a lover, not an aggressor. He had recently returned from an ashram at Rishikesh, India and the notion that everything would be '*alright*' was touched by his experiences of Transcendental Meditation. However, the slow version of the song, which appeared on the double album *The Beatles*, found him wavering between '*count me out*' and '*in*'. He was trying out both options and he later stressed that this recording had been the original one. Meantime, 'Revolution 9' was cut-ups, random noise and avant-garde fever as Yoko brought her art theory and sedition into the Beatles' camp.

Lennon unpacked his contradictions in an interview with *Red Mole* in January 1971. Yoko and himself met with Tariq Ali and Robin Blackburn at his country pile, Tittenhurst Park, near Ascot. He was pleased that people were adopting Beatles' lyrics for their own purposes. 'Yellow Submarine' had become an anthem for striking workers, revised as '*we all live on bread and margarine*'. It was a conversation that led him to write 'Power to the People' later that evening. 'You can't take power without a struggle,' he had supposed. Yoko had been more hopeful of a different, youthful order. During the interview, John had doubled back on himself at one stage: 'I don't know what the answer is'.

In a September 21 interview with *Sounds*, John was more forthcoming about the situation in Northern Ireland. The first half of the quote was used many times afterwards to suggest his clear support for an armed struggle. But he was more ambivalent, as the second part of the answer reveals:

'I understand why they're doing it, and if it's a choice between the IRA or the British army, I'm with the IRA. But if it's a choice between violence and non-violence, I'm with non-violence. So, it's a very delicate line ... our backing of the Irish people is done, really, through the Irish Civil Rights, which is not the IRA. Although I condemn violence, if two people are fighting, I'm probably gonna be on one side or the other, even though I'm against violence.'

Back in Belfast, Terri Hooley was aiming to muster his own underground energies. Through the sales of his poetry magazine *Id*, he planned to use the proceeds to create a 'Bust Fund' with information sheets for those arrested for drugs misdemeanours, similar to the Release organisation in London. 'The police say they have 1,700 names in their drug users' files,' he figured. 'I hope they have a few interesting things in my file as some of the stories I have been told about this Terri Hooley bloke are quite unbelievable.'

A second publication, *Ego*, was launched in July 1970, this time a newspaper with a cover price of 6d. '*Ego* belongs to you, the progressive-minded youth of today,' he wrote. He printed up 1,200 copies and he claimed that he sold 800 on the streets within a few days. He made a formal declaration about his new community – The Tribe – and launched a campaign in the October 1 issue of *City Week*. They were planning to raise £1,000 to found the Belfast Arts Lab (BAL), possibly incorporating an independent press, poster workshop and a head shop. There was also going to be a record release, a split single featuring his friend John B plus Ed Emmett, the folk blues guitarist. To illustrate the potential of his plans, Terri offered some poetry:

'BAL is a phone call.
BAL is in the mind.
BAL is not LAL.
BAL is BAL is BAL.
BAL is you being you...'

In the same *City Week* feature, Terri took the journalist to a derelict building on the Oldpark Road. This northside wreck was a potential site for BAL, he enthused. The locals were less approving and a restless mob gathered outside. The police arrived in a Land Rover, confiscated the photographer's film and demanded identification from Hooley. This tense scenario resulted in a rethink. 'I might have to try somewhere else,' he mused. Only later did Terri reveal that he had been under the influence of LSD during his Oldpark visit.

Free radio was another of his ambitions. 'If we start talking about love, peace and happiness on the air,' he imagined, 'the powers that be would more than likely jam the frequency.' So, in the early months of 1971, himself and Tommy Little from The Tribe were broadcasting from an abandoned house on the Rocky Road, high up in the Castlereagh Hills. During one pirate session, an army patrol arrived at the door. Tommy had been playing 'Alone Again Or' by Love and was rigid with anxiety, but the squaddies were only looking for directions. Radio Harmony persisted.

The pair of them went to London to search out radio equipment and fetched up at a party on the Portobello Road. John Lennon was there, but masses of dope had been consumed and recollections were hazy afterwards. However, they did visit a lock-up garage, possibly in the Highbury area. Terri was confounded. 'Lennon was completely off his rocker. One of his friends took us to the garage and showed us these boxes of rifles and wanted to know how we could get them back to Northern Ireland. I said, "We're the boys, but we're not *those* boys…"'

Next day there was a meeting with some of the *Oz* people and a party in a well-heeled part of the city. Lennon was there again and words were spoken, as Hooley remembers. 'The discussion turned to Northern Ireland and Lennon started spouting what I can only describe as green, Nationalist, graveyard shit. We began to argue, it got nasty and I ended up swinging for him.' In another account, Terri recalled the final confrontation being outside. 'We had a big row in a graveyard and John beat me up in the end. He could fight better than me.'

Radical chic had become a concern in Derry, as Eamonn McCann explains: 'There was a constant stream of revolutionary tourists in the Bogside. There were German and French students, Baader-Meinhof, Rudi Dutschke and so on. They came over and at one time there was about a hundred of them and they were billeted in the dressing rooms of the GAA park and they loved it. A lot of us did come to resent them because they had no connection with what was going on. So, people said, "Why don't we fuck them out?" It was a short-lived honeymoon with them and we were probably too unfriendly to them at the time, looking back on it.

'And, of course, you had the Americans coming – the Ancient Order of Hibernians – who we absolutely shunned. So, there were different sorts of people who represented different strains, really. Politics were marbled through the situation in not such a simple way as people imagine.'

John Lennon had been supporting anti-apartheid activists as well as workers in the Upper Clyde shipyards and sundry erratic causes. His tone became more strident when he moved to New York in August 1971 and connected with figures such as Jerry Rubin and Abbie Hoffman. The pair had famously disrupted the Democratic Party's National Convention in 1968 and so now the John and Yoko orbit was busy with Yippies, Black Panthers, White Panthers, feminist themes and issue politics.

They headlined the John Sinclair Freedom Rally in Ann Arbor, highlighting a severe sentence for the MC5 band manager for a minor drug infringement. In December 1971 they played a benefit at the Harlem Apollo for the families of prisoners who had been killed in the Attica Prison uprising in New York State. There was talk of a 1972 tour, billed as the John and Yoko Political Plastic Ono Band Fun Show, and they were aiming to shadow Richard Nixon on his way to the Republican National Convention that Summer. There was a new song in their live repertoire called 'The Luck of the Irish', a fresh commentary on the land of Lennon's paternal grandparents.

They wrote the song with a film in mind. John and Yoko had met with John Reilly, a documentary maker from the Global Village Collective, also engaged with the National Association for Irish Freedom. They felt that Joko Productions might make a film about Northern Ireland, and so this track was a musical overture. It was loaded with sentiment and shamrockery – images of the old country seemingly gleaned from parlour songs like 'Galway Bay' and 'The Boys of the County Armagh'. It was Yoko's role to perform these parts, while John worked in a political commentary, how the land had been '*raped by the British Brigands*', how youth and the IRA were seemingly scapegoated while the English were perpetuating '*genocide*'.

These New York activities were duly noted on the other side of the Atlantic, and thus Lennon joined a debate in the letters pages of the music weekly *Disc* in January 1972. Raymond Stewart from Northern Ireland had taken exception to John's new lyric and the author retaliated. 'I hope the readers noticed Raymond Stewart's last name – it is in fact Scottish, right? If you want to be British, Mr Stewart, I suggest you move to Britain. Otherwise leave Ireland to the Irish.'

Bloody Sunday changed the tone entirely. Soldiers from the 1st Battalion of the Parachute Regiment shot 13 people in Derry on January 30 1972. The death toll reached 14 when another casualty died of bullet wounds four months later. The deaths came after a disrupted Northern Ireland Civil Rights Association march against internment. The military had insisted that the deceased were carrying firearms or throwing bombs, but this was discounted after several enquiries. The killings had taken place in daylight, in view of the world's media. Reactions were swift and emotional. In Parliament, Bernadette Devlin, an Independent Socialist MP, attacked the Home Secretary Reginald Maudling on the Commons floor after he had presented the British establishment line. 'I'm just sorry I didn't get him by the throat,' she told reporters afterwards.

There was a general strike in Ireland on February 2 when 12 of the funerals took place and the British Embassy in Dublin was burnt down while a large crowd applauded. The British Ambassador to Ireland, Sir John Peck, related the impact in his memoirs:

'Bloody Sunday had unleashed a wave of fury and exasperation the like of which I had never encountered in my life, in Egypt or Cyprus or anywhere else. Hatred of the British was intense. Someone had summed it up: 'we are all IRA now'.'

Tommy Skelly, a performer from Inchicore, Dublin, wrote 'Go on Home, British Soldiers', hours after hearing the news. It was later recorded by the Wolfe Tones and it became a staple of the rebel songbook: '*Go on home British soldiers, go on home / Have you got no fuckin' homes of your own?*' Conversely, in Loyalist areas, they sang a triumphalist variation on the children's counting song 'This Old Man', with a tally of the Derry casualties.

Paul McCartney recorded his reaction two days after Bloody Sunday. 'Give Ireland Back to the Irish' was co-written with his wife Linda and sought to endear the UK listeners to their reasoning. The song was written in a light, reggae-boogie style, the chorus was plaintive and the verses tried to flip the story, locating the conflict to an English town, marshalled by Irish military. '*Would you give in, or go berserk?*' he asked.

This was the first release credited to the McCartney project Wings; it was recorded at Abbey Road on February 1 and was out before the end of the month. The Chairman of EMI, Sir Joseph Lockwood, had called McCartney and asked him to rethink. But the artist was adamant. 'He thought it was too inflammatory. I told him that I felt strongly about it and they had to release it.' Unsurprisingly, it did not feature on radio playlists and an EMI marketing campaign tried to turn this into an asset, publicising the channels that were withholding goodwill. 'BANNED EVERYWHERE,' the adverts said. The BBC explained that 'the lyrics adopted a definite viewpoint on the Northern Ireland situation and are therefore clearly politically controversial'.

'My family comes from Ireland,' McCartney reflected afterwards. 'Half of Liverpool comes from Ireland. That was the shocking thing. We were fighting us. And we'd killed them, very visibly, on the news.'

The track topped the Irish charts, alternating with 'The Men Behind the Wire'. It was the best seller in Spain. 'Basque separatists loved it,' McCartney said. The UK and American buyers were less keen. Meantime, the Wings guitarist Henry McCullough felt bemused after his first session with the band. He had been raised in Portstewart, County Londonderry, a showband veteran and the only Irishman who had played Woodstock, during his tenure with Joe Cocker and the Grease Band. He would later dismiss the song: 'That was his little cotton wool protest'. Unfortunately, his brother Samuel suffered a broken nose after singing the lyric in a London pub.

The Lennons joined with Jerry Rubin in a February 5 rally outside the offices of BOAC, the national UK airline, on 5th Avenue. They sang 'The Luck of the Irish' and made a power salute to a gathering of 5,000. 'We were there to show our sympathy to the 13 people who were mercilessly shot down by the British imperialists.' He amplified the rhetoric in a letter to the *International Times*: 'we also ask for the American Irish to wake up to their responsibilities in the same way Jewish people respond to the problems of Israel'.

Most remarkable of all was the new song 'Sunday Bloody Sunday', a howling exchange that John and Yoko had recorded during the March sessions for the new album, *Some Time In New York City*. There was little in the way of a tune and local combo Elephant's Memory did not show any particular flourish. It was invective, seemingly without a filter. He rejected any claim that the British army had been acting in self-defence – '*not a soldier boy was bleeding*'. He questioned the mathematics of Partition and surmised that Unionists did not have a majority on an island-wide percentage. The internees, he stated, were being held in concentration camps. But he saved most of his venom for the '*Anglo pigs and Scotties*' in Northern Ireland. He called for a flaming reckoning and a mass repatriation of the non-Irish. Get back, his message said.

'Most other people express themselves by shouting or playing football at the weekend,' he told the *NME*'s Roy Carr. 'But me, here I am in New York and I hear about the 13 people shot dead in Ireland, and I react immediately.

And being what I am, I react in four-to-the-bar with a guitar break in the middle. I don't say, 'My God, what's happening? We should do something'. I go: *It was Sunday Bloody Sunday and they shot the people down…*'

The cover of *Some Time In New York City* was a mock-up of the *New York Times* and some early issues featured a postcard of the Statue of Liberty giving a Black Power salute. The critics were dubious. *Melody Maker* talked of 'the full fist of revolt' but also 'mindless overkill'. *Rolling Stone* went for 'embarrassingly puerile'. The *Irish Times* reviewer was Stewart Parker, the playwright and poet from Belfast. He was appalled by 'Sunday Bloody Sunday' and bothered by Lennon's assumed New York accent – rather than singing '*burn*' he chose '*boin*'. For Parker, the lines sounded as if they were loaned out: 'it seems likely that they were gleaned from some boozy New Yorker wearing a green bowler in the St Paddy's Day Parade'. But even if Lennon was singing in the character of an American-Irish figure, Parker wrote, 'that hardly reduces the ugliness of the song's crude sectarianism, nor its arrogance coming from an uninvolved pop star'.

John had talked of a New York benefit for the Civil Rights movement in Northern Ireland, and for concerts in Dublin and Belfast. He was also meeting the militants. In an interview with Johnny Rogan, the IRA figure Gerry O'Hare remembers John Lennon talking of several gigs. 'I got the impression that he was keen to do one for the Protestant community as well.' But his plans were already being curtailed in the spring of 1972 by the American Immigration and Naturalization Service, who had denied his request to extend his six-month visa. There was a deportation order and a three-year legal process. He did not take part in the disruption of the Republican Convention in Miami. When he did play at Madison Square Garden on August 30, the beneficiaries were children in care homes, not Irish causes. 'Sunday Bloody Sunday' and 'The Luck of the Irish' did not feature on either of the two shows.

The FBI, under J. Edgar Hoover, had also been looking into the Lennon affairs, supported by MI5 in the UK. They noted his drug use and suspected that he had donated to groups such as the Workers' Revolutionary Party. There was a story that he had assigned the royalties of 'Luck of the Irish' to NORAID (Irish Northern Aid Committee) and made a significant contribution to this group. A former MI5 operative, David Shayler, later claimed that Lennon had funded the IRA. Yoko dismissed this, claiming that the intended recipients had been 'children, orphans and women in need'.

Later, when he was later asked about his radical stance in a 1980 *Newsweek* interview John was self-critical. 'That radicalism was phony, really, because it was out of guilt. I'd always felt guilty that I made money, so I had to give it away or lose it. I don't mean I was a hypocrite. When I believe, I believe right down to the roots. But being a chameleon, I became whoever I was with.'

Only a few other mainstream acts mentioned Northern Ireland in 1972. McGuinness Flint had reached number 2 in the UK charts with the single 'When I'm Dead and Gone' two years before. Tom McGuinness was a former bassist with Manfred Mann. His father had been in the original IRA, 'so I was raised to be very aware of the Irish Republican tradition. I knew that Northern Ireland was an English colony.' He told the author Peter Doggett that when internment was introduced, he had been in Ireland. 'It was a huge blow. Everybody in the Irish Republic was really shocked.'

They released 'Let the People Go' in February 1972. There were congas and acoustic guitars and a song title that echoed the Bible via the gospel songbook of Paul Robeson. Like Paul and Linda McCartney's work, the song stressed the nearness of the conflict and the lack of outrage in England. It was a fundraiser for families of internees and there was radio play in Ireland, but the UK did not respond with a chart placing.

Derry songwriter Phil Coulter played it differently. He had co-written Eurovision favourites for Sandi Shaw ('Puppet on a String') and Cliff Richard ('Congratulations'). Along with co-writer Bill Martin, he had delivered England's World Cup anthem 'Back Home' in 1970. The decade would also favour him with hits by the Bay City Rollers and Elvis Presley. But he also worked with the Dubliners, mainstays of the Irish ballad tradition, fronted by Luke Kelly and his socially aware presence.

It was Luke who had encouraged Phil to add his voice to the Irish conflict. A 1971 effort, 'Free the People', was recorded by the Dubliners and popular in Ireland, but the writer had not been satisfied with the sloganeering. The next statement took many months to craft. Coulter wrote from the perspective of his home city in 'The Town I Loved So Well', a lament for

Derry that watched in dismay as stacks of barbed wire encroached on the skyline. The army was keeping guard by the gasyard wall and the landmarks with their happy associations had been degraded. Now there was CS gas in the air, rather than music. The song was written for the compassionate fibres of Luke's voice, and he sang well about the matriarchal nature of the town – the men on the dole, keeping house while the women earned a livelihood in the shirt factories.

It was a nuanced song that lasted for six minutes, far from the anti-internment slogans of 'Free the People'. Phil's background was Nationalist, but his father had been a member of the Royal Ulster Constabulary, so the song was not entrenched. The final verse talked of civic fortitude and a possible way out of the conflict. Like many significant songs, it adapted itself to changing circumstances.

'When the song came out first,' Coulter remembered, 'people on the extremes of Unionism would have dismissed it as a rebel song, and that was before they even listened to it. I was very aware it could have become a rabble-rousing song, which then was the last thing we needed, but no, it's been accepted for what it is, a love song to a city.'

After *Astral Weeks*, Van Morrison began to document his life as a settler in America. He sang about bucolic times in old, old Woodstock, about Tupelo honey and moonshine whiskey. He moved with his family to the west coast and further stories of redwood trees and the Pacific joys around Marin County. But the new life was interrupted by thoughts of Belfast. He was in Reno, preparing for a gig at the University of Nevada, when he read about a mass in St Dominic's Church, San Francisco. The theme was peace in Northern Ireland. This report inspired the title track of his 1972 album *St Dominic's Preview*.

The song starts in the backstreets of Belfast as the window cleaner gets busy with his chamois leather, musing about Edith Piaf, about Paris and her life theme, 'Je ne regrette rien'. The scenes flicker from San Francisco to New York and back to Van's hometown. Things are overloaded and tense there. Yet unthinking life continues in America – beyond the discarded waste of supermarkets and into the vacant rituals of a record company promotional launch.

The singer realises that there is a new release to promote and, sure enough, a music journalist is ready to sidle up for a quote. But the artist is painfully distracted. He's been thinking about a clash of culture back over the ocean – about colours, symbols and historic bitterness. There's a flickering remembrance of the Flags and Emblems (Display) Act that had been introduced in Northern Ireland in 1954. After this, the Union Flag was legally beyond reproach, but the Irish tricolour was not. During the Queen's coronation in 1953, loyal flags had been removed in parts of Belfast and replaced with the green, white and gold. Consequently, this legislature was a safeguard for the Union, and it would be tested in 1964 when a tricolour was placed in a window on Divis Street and Ian Paisley threatened to bring a mob down to remove it. The riots that followed caused Gerry Adams from the Falls Road to become more radicalised. Flags in Belfast had a deadly dimension.

St Dominic's Preview has a spectral, lost feeling – the same mood that Jimi Hendrix explored on his requiem, 'The Wind Cries Mary'. Things are broken, the good times have expired. Van takes us away from the ostentatious wealth of the music business, the hip and the high flyers. Instead, there's a parade of orange boxes, tramping feet and strained faces. He's writing like Bob Dylan or Baudelaire. There may be a vigil in the Californian church and votive candles may be lit but, away from this, something is happening:

'Freedom marching, out in the street.'

CHAPTER SIX

THE POUND'S SO OLD

It opened in 1880 as the Central Railway Hotel. Charlie McManus was originally in charge. Later, it was renamed the Law Courts Hotel but the locals all called it Roddy's. It was a three-storey building on the corner of Oxford Street and Townhall Street with elegant mouldings around the windows and a deal of Victorian assurance.

Larry was the first of the Roddy family to set up in the building before his son John took over. They served drinks to commuters and passing trade plus cattle traders and locals from St George's Market, Allam's Yard and Colgan's Yard. There were characters like Silver McKee, a cattle drover, a cow walloper, a street fighter.

'He was notorious,' says Chris, the third generation of the Townhall Street Roddys. 'He was Patrick Joseph Aloysius McKee. First time I met him he was bending old pennies between his thumb and his forefingers. It was a kind of party piece. He brought a horse into the public bar for a Guinness. For him and the horse. He poured a half pint into an old Harp ashtray. The horse was slurping up its drink when the Health Inspector arrived. He was so blind he walked straight past the horse and wanted to see the Gents, to give it a bill of health. The horse was smuggled out the back door.'

There were six bars at the premises. A lounge bar and a public bar on the ground floor, another upstairs called Miss Mac's Lounge and three in the Pound, the old stabling yard at the back. That was where John Roddy cut a deal with promoter Arnie Knowles to put on folk music gigs in 1967, starting with the fiddle player and Outlet recording artist Seán McGuire. Chris remembers the good times. 'It was quite a trendy, upmarket place when it originally opened: antiques, grandfather clocks, muskets on the walls. Then it became the Pound, alright.'

So rather than disguise the fact that this was a former animal pound, the venue conversion worked this into the aesthetic. The cast iron columns remained, brickwork and roof timbers were exposed and seating was arranged around the old livestock pens. Several months later, the Pound started to put on current music, beginning with rhythm and blues act the Group.

'In 1969,' Chris says, 'a consortium offered my father an awful lot of money for the premises. Crazy money. He went down to Dublin to tell his mum he was going to sell it. It was about three times actually what it was worth. But the weekend he went to Dublin was when all hell broke loose here. And then there was the 10 o'clock curfew on all the pubs. So, a late-night venue wasn't gonna happen. It was closed for a couple of years after that.'

In the early 70s, Irish acts like Thin Lizzy, Horslips and Fruupp were sounding bold and self-aware. All of them had a direct connection to the North. Sometimes they embellished their music with the accents of traditional music and themes from Celtic mythology. Horslips populated their songs with bristling warriors and cattle raids from the centuries-old narrative, *Táin Bó Cúailnge*. All of these acts insisted that they would keep touring in Northern Ireland. This was not simply bravado, as Barry Devlin from Horslips confirms:

'We were scared witless a lot of the time. There was a gig at the same ballroom that the Miami Showband were playing when they were killed. We played it earlier that summer, three months before [in 1975]. About three miles down the road there was a car parked in a laneway. It came out after us and tried to overtake us. Eventually, it kept banging into the back of us and it had a thing on the roof that was a flasher. But it wasn't a police flasher. In those days, the road forked at Loughbrickland, and you went through Loughbrickland. We were going about 100 miles an hour trying to keep ahead of these guys. I dunno, maybe they were just being friendly, but subsequently when the Miami thing happened I thought, "Maybe it wasn't just a hiding we were going to get…." Who knows?'

The payback was feverish audiences and a deal of loyalty that lasted well beyond the normal churn of popular music. A song like 'Dearg Doom' by Horslips blasted out for the duration of the conflict in student flats and house parties, localised fun and internalised thrills. The city's fondness for the band was evidenced on a live album, *The Belfast Gigs*, recorded at the Whitla Hall across two shows in 1980.

'Even though I was the only northerner, we had a real connection to Belfast. The band loved the place and I think that Belfast kind of liked us back. We wanted to do a live album and the place we figured out would be the most fun to do it was in the Whitla Hall in Belfast. We also finished our career as a band in the Ulster Hall [prior to a series of reunion shows in recent years]. Everybody in the band remembers that Charles took his fiddle and flung it out into the crowd and of course you make more of these moments than maybe they are, but I still see it in slow motion arcing out and obviously a Gaelic footballer, possibly from Down, climbing crane-like into the sky and hauling it down, and that was the end of it. That was where we finished.'

Also, there was Rory Gallagher. He had been born in Donegal and raised in Cork, but Belfast was an important deal for Rory. He had paid his dues at the Maritime Hotel, Sammy Houston's, Romano's Ballroom and the Whitla Hall. The city's blues scene understood and encouraged him and that's where he sourced many of his outstanding band members. Rory played every year in the city during the 70s. He was the match of Eric Clapton, a nearly Rolling Stone while Jimi Hendrix purportedly offered him the crown of guitarist *sans pareil*. He played roaring blues with occasional, delicate touches. His manner was humble and this served the feeling that the G Man was on a level with his listeners. 'I've a sort of home feeling for the place,' he said of Belfast. Rory's arrivals at the Ulster Hall were often timed for Christmas or early January and the sense of occasion was immense.

He was there on New Year's Day, 1972. Ten bombs had been detonated the night before, a statement of intent from the IRA. Outside, Terri Hooley's friends from The Tribe had been leafleting with their newsletter, *Take One*, and a new cause, the Music to Belfast Campaign. They were proud of Rory but unimpressed by the timidity of the music industry. After all, Led Zeppelin had played this same venue on March 5 1971, allowing a world preview to 'Stairway to Heaven' and other tracks from their fourth album. But such nights had become rare.

'Belfast has now become a graveyard for music,' The Tribe declared in *Take One*. 'We must create enough noise in order that the hypocrites in England (the capitalist agents who think nothing other than pulling in a lot of bread) become aware that they are most needed in this torn city. We want action now, for too long the groups in England haven't given music where it can give the most help. Lennon tells us to give peace a chance, but has he visited us? All we want John, baby, is the truth. Perhaps he is furthering the peace movements somewhere in Hyde Park.'

Rory's concert promoter was Jim Aiken, a former schoolteacher who had worked in easier times with Roy Orbison, Bill Haley and the showbands. He had arranged the Led Zeppelin gig in 1971. After they had played their strange new song about a bustle in the hedgerow, he took drummer John Bonham to see some riots on Leeson Street, off the Falls Road. Jim's old friend Roy Orbison had been so concerned at the violence that he had offered to rehouse the Aiken family in America.

Rory Gallagher was the *Melody Maker* 'Best Guitarist' that year and its writer Roy Hollingworth was in Belfast for this auspicious show on January 1 1972. After the gig, he spoke to the guitarist and promoter. He put a question to Rory. Was it worth it?

'Yes, oh yes, I think it was. Once it got over the feeling that they were thanking me for coming. Once they'd got over that, they were into just the music. Then it was darned marvellous. They're wonderful kids you know.'

The writer asked Jim if there was too much importance given over the music.

'No, it does do something which nothing else can do. If we can still hold a concert, then it can only be doing good.'

Ralph McTell made his first visit in 1969, during the Belfast Festival, playing seven nights in the Great Hall. 'I loved my visit and was invited back several times by the festival and loved all those occasions too. It was the time of the first Civil Rights marches and I was both shocked and horrified when the facts of the riots and the general situation regarding minorities emerged.

'I continued to visit all through those troubled times and did my best to persuade others to visit. Being a soloist, I was the only one I had to convince. A band, however, only needed one detractor and they were scuppered, even if they had wanted to play. I was held in higher regard than warranted and the people who came to the shows were not required to show which political leaning they had. I assumed it was a chance for both communities to have a night out and was happy and relaxed about the whole situation. Perhaps my fondest memory is on one visit during a particularly nasty part of the Troubles I walked on stage and got a standing ovation for several minutes. I was deeply moved and have always held the NI people in warm and high regard.'

Elsewhere, in the more upmarket, popular venues, the dancefloors were getting smaller, seats and tables were added and the waiter was ready to take your drinks order. Bass player George Jones remembers the transition. 'Since the late 50s through to the 60s, the primary hobby of nearly every village town in Ireland had been dancing. But then the ballrooms started to add a wee bar. So, people said, "We'd like to go out and watch a live show and we can have a drink". That's when the bars became cabaret clubs. Each one had to have a resident band. That was the statutory thing. And they all had good musicians. Although people weren't going to dances, they felt the cabaret scene was a little bit safer.'

It was changing when Dermot O'Donnell, owner of the Queen's Court in Bangor, put a seated audience in the middle of the dancing area. People started going there early for some live music. They sat down in a licensed space and bought a few drinks before heading off to the dances at Caproni's and Milano's. Encouraged by this, Dermott and his business associate Trevor Kane took over the use of the Abercorn on Castle Lane, Belfast, and turned the upstairs space into a sit-down venue with a capacity of 250. They hired

George and his mates as the resident players in 1970 and Dermot decided to call them Clubsound.

At one point there were around 13 cabaret clubs, running Monday to Saturday. Every venue had a band at the core of the entertainment, plus a compere. Roy Walker worked the Talk of the Town at Bridge End. Trevor Kelly was at the Abercorn with his Elvis routines. The chart hits of the day were reprised and then Tony Morelli might come forward with a Mario Lanza tune. There were visiting acts from America or England, like Vocal Perfection from Liverpool, who became famous on *Opportunity Knocks,* rebranded as the Real Thing.

In 1970, Granada TV introduced a popular series called *The Comedians.* It was filmed in Manchester and it captured the rough humour of the working men's clubs. It made stars of the performers and many of these were featured at the Abercorn. Frank Carson and Jimmy Cricket were homecoming favourites but there was also a welcome for emerging acts like Cannon and Ball, Little and Large.

Saturday afternoons were busy with women who had finished the shopping and wanted a laugh and a tune. Evenings were less popular given the disruptions and fatalities. McGurk's Bar at North Queen Street had been one of the early targets when 15 civilians were killed by a UVF bomb on December 4 1971. Loyalists and Republicans had become more intent on killing for their particular causes. Car bombs were set to become a feature in 1972 as the Provisional IRA built up its capacity and logistics. It developed a strategy that was later outlined by Brendan Hughes, former OC of the Belfast Brigade: to damage the economy and to draw soldiers into the city, away from the areas that they regarded as their own communities.

Clubsound were rehearsing on a Sunday in February 1972 when they received a visit from three uniformed fire service officials. One of them carried a clipboard and he talked the band through a new requirement. Should there be a bomb warning, the resident band would play a special piece of music that would alert the staff to imminent danger, allowing them to follow their pre-arranged plan for an ordered evacuation. So, they asked Clubsound to nominate a fire tune. Eddie McCrudden sounded disgruntled. He normally took care of the sheet music and this seemed like an extra ask. He picked something at random. "Three Blind Mice', put that down. That will do rightly.'

The visiting act on March 4 1972 was Max Beesley, a jazz drummer who had branched into comedy. The Saturday afternoon crowd had taken their places. A feature of the Abercorn décor upstairs was a large rug that had become caked with dust and many layers of spilt drink. This was not so unusual, but security checks were something new that Belfast was coming to terms with. The Abercorn had several staff for this role, including Terry Milligan, a former Olympic boxer who had reached the quarter finals in Helsinki in 1952. The club was aware of potential danger, George says.

'The terrorists designated that Belfast had to be shut down. They started to bomb the cabaret clubs. They literally wanted to take the heart out of the city. The Abercorn was the prime place. But the only way into the Abercorn was up a single set of stairs. And there were the statutory security checks, as laid down. Every handbag had to be checked before you came in. And I remember on a Saturday afternoon, Terry Milligan was one of the bouncers. He was a nice guy, lovely temperament with him. There were queues coming up the stairs.

'He stopped this fella and girl, saying, "I have to look in your bag". And the guy pulled the bag away and says, "No, you're not looking at it". Terry was convinced that it was those two people that went straight out, into the restaurant underneath.'

Other witnesses say that the two suspects were female but George believes it was a mixed couple that left the device under a table on the ground floor. Indisputably, a bomb went off in the restaurant area at 4.30pm. Two young women, Janet Bereen and Ann Owens were killed immediately. There were 130 injuries, many of them severe. Fourteen limbs were amputated as the Victoria Hospital put their disaster plan into operation for the first time. One of the people they treated was Rosaleen McNern, who was engaged to be married. She lost her legs, her right arm and an eye. Her sister Jennifer lost both legs. The device had been left in a handbag and the shock of the explosion brought down the Abercorn ceiling, as George recalls:

'We're in the middle of Max Beesley's act and there's this huge thud.

The whole building shook. And I remember going into slow motion... the windows coming across, bits of glass, waiters flying through the air. And suddenly it stopped dead. It was the reality that it had been a bomb in the building. We thought the place was on fire, but it wasn't – it was the dust of four or five years coming off the old carpet. It had been Guinness-laden. It was like leather and it blew the dust up.

'So, everybody started screaming. All the fire exits had been blown out, of course. We had a guy in the band, Harry Hickland, who was one of the top musicians in the Ardoyne Silver Band and he's been brought up primarily to read music. He was always specific about how everything was. And in the middle of this chaos, Eddie McCrudden shouted out, "Quick, play the fire tune!" Everybody's screaming and Harry turned around and said, "What key?" Eddie says, "Any effing key!" Right to the end, Harry was a musician in the midst of this.'

Gloria Hunniford was a semi-professional cabaret singer and recording artist but in 1972 she was also a reporter for *Good Morning Ulster* at BBC Northern Ireland. Given the shocking nature of the news, she received a commission from the *Today* programme in London to report on the Abercorn bombing:

'The emergency services had just removed the dead and injured when I got there, but all around me were their possessions, leather handbags with their contents spilling out over the road; teddy bears with charred faces – people's everyday lives broken and tossed aside by the force of the blast. I really felt the futility of the conflict that day – women and children who had become victims, simply because they happened to be out shopping on a Saturday afternoon.'

The fatalities might have been much worse, George supposes:

'That bomb, they reckoned, was about four or five pounds, quite small in size. But it was strategically placed underneath. If Dermott O'Donnell hadn't had that carpet, which was like leather, and if that bomb had been about half a pound or even one pound more – those 250 people would have come down through that floor. The carpet literally held the floor together.

'You're always saying, "Ah, I'm a musician, I'm not into all that". Suddenly, reality was there. I walked out to where the phone booth had been – there was a call box phone in the upstairs foyer – to try to phone my wife. Because in those days they used to break into the television broadcasts saying, "We have to interrupt this programme…" and if they had said it was the Abercorn, my wife would have known I was playing there. I was balancing on two open beams, looking at the bodies, downstairs, in the restaurant.'

Dermott O'Donnell had wanted to open the Abercorn on the following Monday. Trader resilience became a recognised trait in Northern Ireland and glaziers were ever-busy. George talked it over with his colleague. 'I says, "Dermott, reality here. People were killed." He says, "I'll not let them beat me". He waited for a week, got the place refurbished and kept going until the tumbleweed was literally rolling down the streets of Belfast. We were playing to about 20 people. Some nights only half a dozen braved to come out into Belfast.'

The Abercorn bombing was not an exceptional act. The Provisional IRA set off more than 20 bombs in Belfast on July 21 1972. During an 80-minute operation it targeted bridges, stations, depots, road and rail networks plus residential areas. Nine people died and 130 people were injured. This was remembered as Bloody Friday and the Oxford Street Bus Station was the scene of the worst fatalities, with six dead. Corpses were wrapped in tarpaulin on the road and newsreels showed body parts being lifted on shovels. Moments after the explosion, Silver McKee, the regular drinker at the Pound, walked into the bus station on a rescue mission. He lifted up a roof beam that had come down and trapped people underneath. His coat was on fire but he managed to get them free.

Many casualties were taken across the road to Roddy's Bar, which became a makeshift field hospital. 'We used it as a first aid station,' Chris says. 'It broke my dad, crippled him. The front bar was used like a morgue.'

Reginald Maudling, British Home Secretary, had talked about 'an acceptable level of violence' in December 1971. This was a premature call. 1972 was the worst year of the conflict. There were 500 deaths, 2,000 explosions and 10,000 shooting incidents. In July alone, there were 100 deaths. 'The 70s were horrific,' Terri Hooley says. 'You were afraid to go out. There were times when I said goodnight to people and never saw them again. I lost a lot of friends. The country was having a nervous breakdown and everyone was living in fear.'

Three car bombs killed nine people in the village of Claudy on July 31. The poet and songwriter James Simmons wrote 'The Ballad of Claudy' in response. He sang it in a folksy, solemn style. In the first four verses, he depicted the rural setting in County Derry by the Sperrin Mountains and the Faughan River. Then he detailed the workaday activities of the nine individuals around Main Street before the explosion. He named each person and their actions: fixing shop, cleaning and sweeping, serving petrol, delivering milk, searching for the cat. And then he related the mutilation.

> *'For an old lady's legs are blown off, and the head*
> *Of a man's hanging open, and still he's not dead*
> *He is shrieking for mercy while his son stands and stares*
> *And stares, and then suddenly – quick – disappears.'*

The IRA bombers had not sent a warning in time. It later transpired that some of the phone connections had been damaged in a previous explosion and the payphones were useless. Hence, the closing lines of the Simmons lyric:

> *'Meanwhile to Dungiven the killers have gone*
> *And they're finding it hard to get through on the phone.'*

Saturday afternoons at the Pound became a refuge for the 60s players, many of them veterans from the Maritime Hotel on College Square North and those nights that had nurtured the blues boom of Them, the Mad Lads, the Just Five, Rory Gallagher and others. Artists like Jim Armstrong and Kenny McDowell had become internationally known and they brought it back to Belfast with Spike and later in splinter acts such as Light and Bronco. The musicianship was well regarded by an assembly of denim, cheesecloth, heads, tokers and the biker fraternity.

'The Chosen Few were the motorbike gang and they were a heavy metal vibe,' says Chris. 'They were the peacekeepers. You didn't fuck with the Few, y'know. The rest was mainly hippiedom, really.'

Some of the bar's weekend customers were on their way back from Purdysburn, a psychiatric hospital in Newtownbreda on the outskirts of South Belfast. 'The bus from Purdysburn used to drop all the outpatients off on Oxford Street on a Friday afternoon. But they all got off a stop early and came round to the bar. We were actually glad to see them. It was a wee bit of sanity.'

The drinkers in Townhall Street were a tolerant crew, but many of them grew weary of the alarms and random stresses:

'When there were bomb scares in the vicinity, people became blasé about it. They didn't want to leave their pint. And they would say, "Look, if you let us sit at the counter, we'll leave a couple of pound out until the bomb scare is over". They didn't want to have to take their pints outside.'

In Belfast, George Jones had reached the limits of his endurance:

'I lived in a place called Pottinger Street, which was halfway up the Woodstock Road. And I remember a knock on my door. They all knew who I was in the area – that I was a musician in a band. Three or four of the guys, they said, "You're on vigilante duty tonight". And I said, "What are you doing?" He said, "We're standing on the corner to make sure nobody's coming up into our area to bomb". They said, "We know you're a musician and all, but you have to come out with all the rest of us". I finished up standing beside a brazier, wondering what I was doing there.

'And there were cars coming up in the area and they were stopping and the drivers were terrified. This was blossoming out of sheer fear. One time at Short Strand, at the bottom of the Woodstock Road, they starting bringing up guns and shooting up the long entries. Now that terrorised the people and made the Loyalists in our area even more fervent.

'At the front of the road which backed onto our house was a Jet petrol station. This is how bad it got: they found that Jet petrol originated in the south of Ireland. So, to protect their area – as they called it – they cut down all of the lamp standards, to make sure all the light switches wouldn't be switched on. And they were falling down on the road. This was a really bad night where the fever was getting high. They cut the petrol pipes and the petrol was flowing down the Woodstock Road. And it got worse and worse. I got my wife and my young son – he was only about seven or eight months old – up to Castlereagh with my sister. And I stayed in the house to try to protect it, if I could.

'It just all came back, the bombing came back. I didn't want my wife involved in something like I'd been through, in the Abercorn. That was the decision to uproot and leave Northern Ireland, give it up. It was the first time I'd ever given up on my country. I didn't really want to do it, but I had to look to my family. I had no idea what I was leaving behind and what was gonna go on.'

CHAPTER SEVEN

A MILLION MILES

Their fans took an old Al Jolson song and they made it their own. They said they'd walk a million miles for one of their smiles… *Miami.* They adored the band with their fresh repertoire, their smiles and their moves. In particular, they lit on the singer Fran O'Toole, the boy from Bray whose vocals revealed a love for soul music and whose face was kind and gracious. He looked like the American star David Cassidy. The other band members were half-joking when they said that they were jealous.

Onstage, it was all about the lightness but it was also a serious business. There were set codes of behaviour, about talking to their audience after a gig, about how to answer fan mail, about good behaviour in public. They had their own hairdresser. Their manager, Tom Doherty from Topline Promotions, even sent the Miami Showband's brass players to dance classes, encouraging them to move it like the Four Tops and to swing and dip their instruments, just so.

At their prime, they travelled in a bespoke coach with a big palm tree on the side panel and a built-in wardrobe inside where they hung up their Louis Copeland suits. There was a reel-to-reel recorder that ran off a 12-volt battery and they used this to rehearse during the endless hauls across Ireland. Five or six nights a week and maybe another Dublin show at the TV Club in Dublin on a Monday, playing to their off-duty peers and to rockers like Phil Lynott.

There were over 600 showbands in Ireland in the 60s, playing up to four hours a night, packing the brass and a line-up that was still based on the Dixieland model. It had started around 1954 when the Clipper Carlton from Strabane had dispensed with the sheet music and their seats, adding comedy skits and energy. A year later and Dave Glover was calling his combo a showband but it was the pure verve of Brendan Bowyer and the Royal from Waterford that defined the age. He crooned and he jumped. He threw shapes and he did the hucklebuck.

The Dixies had made it out of Cork and so it was imperative that Dublin had its own stars. The Miami rehearsed in the Palm Beach Hotel in Portmarnock and in the late 60s they were at the top of their game. Dickie Rock sang the ballads and Sinatra show tunes. Impassioned females would shout, "Spit on me, Dickie", happy to get the slightest recognition. Fran would play keyboards and favour the husky tones of Smokey Robinson and Wilson Pickett. Des Lee from Belfast sang pops and horn player Brian McCoy from Tyrone handled some of the country material. Three songs fast, three songs slow and then the same again. Two thousand people in the dancehalls many nights, simple rites of courtship and never the harm in it.

'We entertained everybody,' says Des Lee, the saxophone player from Andersonstown. 'Didn't matter what colour, what creed, where we were playing, whether it was north or south at that terrible time in Northern Ireland. We looked upon it as giving two hours of fun to people to get away from it.'

When they successfully toured America in early 1968 they heard the potential of a pop tune by a New Jersey act called the 1910 Fruitgum Company. It had enormous showband crossover – the stomping rhythm, the big chorus and the audience participation. They made a transatlantic phone call to the Radio Éireann DJ Larry Gogan, presenter of *The 17 Club* on a Sunday evening. Larry told the band that 'Simon Says' had not been released at home. Des recalls: 'We got off the plane on the Monday, we were in the recording studio the next day and the following day that was ready to go, a number one for the band.'

Gerry Anderson, the late broadcaster and showband veteran, was in awe of the Miami. 'They were almost ruthless in pursuing their objective to be the biggest band in Ireland. And they made it.'

Dickie left in 1973 and Fran moved to the centre of things as the band renewed its act, getting closer to contemporary pop, even glam. The lapels on the suit jackets got wider, the shoes were taller and the gull wing collars were ready for take-off. The bass player Stephen Travers joined in the early summer of 1975 and Fran relaxed him into the job with practical jokes and silly games on the road. By then, they were wearing casual clothes and had removed the 'Showband' tag. Fran was preparing for a major project, a solo album launch at a Las Vegas music convention in the autumn. The lead song 'Love Is' was co-written by Des. It grew sweetly and steadily into a gospel anthem and the singer was in commanding form. A hit, surely.

Des sighs.

'Unfortunately, his life was taken short.'

What has become known as the Miami Showband Massacre happened around 2am on July 31 1975. Three musicians were shot at point blank range on the way home from a gig. Fran was hit by 22 bullets, many of them in the head. Guitarist Tony Geraghty was shot five times in the back and twice in the back of the skull. The pattern of the bullet holes suggested that he had put his arms up for protection. There was also a bullet in his scrotum, fired from a revolver at close range. Brian McCoy was shot four times. They had asked their killers for mercy, but none was given.

Two of the band members survived: Des was blown into a ditch and Stephen survived a dum-dum bullet that fragmented in his body and seared through his internal organs. These jobbing musicians with no involvement in the conflict had become targets. The paramilitaries had literally shot the piano player.

Des and Stephen recount the details of this incident with unending patience. They remember the early morning drive from a booking at the Castle Ballroom in Banbridge. It didn't seem like a major deal when they were stopped by for a roadside check around Buskhill. There were around eight men wearing uniforms of the Ulster Defence Regiment – legitimate soldiers, mostly part-time, sourced from Northern Ireland. It did seem strange that an English army officer with a public-school accent moved from the left into the middle of the gathering and took command but, to Brian, this had been reassuring. 'It's OK Stephen,' he said, 'this is British Army.'

Yet, the UDR soldiers were also members of the mid-Ulster UVF connected to the brutal Glenanne Gang. The latter's territory was the murder triangle that extended from north Armagh to the border and west into Tyrone. They had decided to put a bomb in the Miami's van. At least ten pounds of commercial gelignite on a short fuse. The musicians would be killed in transit back to Dublin. The point of all this has never been made clear. Possibly it was intended to further destabilise Northern Ireland, to make border controls more rigid. Perhaps they wanted to make even the humble players look like they were transporting bombs, seemingly part of the armed struggle. Human trust would have been further damaged.

Whatever, the mission failed. The bomb went off prematurely. Two of the paramilitaries were killed trying to hide the explosives under the driver's seat of the VW van. One of these was later identified by a UVF tattoo on an arm fragment. In the original plan, the musicians would have died and there would have been no witnesses to the checkpoint and the bomb planting. A new plan was required. It was quickly decided by the uniformed gang that the Miami Showband should be dispatched with Sterling sub-machine guns, Luger and Star pistols.

'I remember as a child watching all the GI and Vietnam war movies,' says Des. 'You lie down, pretend you're dead, hold your breath and that's exactly what I did. That's what probably saved my life. The ditch was on fire from the explosion and as the fire was coming very close to my body I realised that if I stayed here I'm gonna burn alive. So, I had to run up the ditch not knowing was going on. Was I gonna get mowed down? Are they still around?

'The first thing I did was call out the lads' names – Fran, Brian and Tony. No response. Then there was Stephen Travers. I got a moan off Stephen and I explained to him that I was going to Newry police station to get help. A lorry came around with a big trailer and I asked him would he take me to the police station and he refused. I said, "I'll get in the trailer in the back" and he refused to even let me on the trailer. Then a young couple came along and they took me into the police station but as I was going in, my hand was on the door handle of the car, in case. I was ready to jump out but, thank God, they did take me to Newry.'

Stephen remained on the murder scene for a further 45 minutes while the police carried out searches and worked out that the area was safe. Thereafter, he was taken to Daisy Hill Hospital for intensive treatment. The bullet had entered his right hip, collapsed his left lung and exited just under his left arm. One of the killers had almost put another bullet in him but had refrained. A parting comment from an accomplice was, 'Come on, those bastards are dead. I got them with dum-dums.'

Earlier, Des and Stephen had both stepped out of line at the roadside check, to make sure their instruments were safe and to reassure the military that nothing in the van was suspect. This was the saving of them. They changed places in the line when they returned, thus escaping the worst. And while they have been involved in other musical projects and different businesses since 1975, they also concede that they must keep telling their story. It's an essential work of testimony, Des affirms.

'I can't understand that people who were there to protect you actually planned your murder to the finest detail. I found that absolutely appalling.'

There is a monument to the band outside the National Ballroom on Parnell Square, Dublin. Friends of the band gathered there on August 1 2015 to mark the 40th anniversary. There's now a Fran O'Toole Bridge in Bray over the River Dargle and a plaque outside the singer's old home nearby. Des insists that there should be proper recognition in the North.

'Where the actual massacre occurred, we've got nothing in Northern Ireland. This was one of the worst tragedies, and it should never be forgotten.'

Stephen has responded with a book, *The Miami Showband Massacre*. At the end of his account he spends five hours in conversation with 'The Craftsman', second-in-command of the UVF's Brigade Staff. It's an abrasive meeting as Stephen brushes aside the UVF narrative that the bomb would have detonated much later when the band had reached home and left the van. But he sees value in the meeting. 'My contention is that you must speak to terrorists. Unless you do, you don't understand people. It's not excusing it, but it's understanding it.' The book has been optioned by a film producer and a Netflix documentary has been scheduled. Meantime Stephen visits conferences and gatherings at The Hague, in Amsterdam, Omagh and Spain. He doesn't flinch from graphic content and feels that this is defensible.

'Unless we are graphic, unless we are convincing and unless these people face up to the fact that violence will get them absolutely nowhere, then it's counterproductive for every single one of us. If we stay silent then people will say that they didn't know. So that's as much as we can do.'

There is ongoing litigation against the PSNI and the Ministry of Defence. In the course of all this, Stephen was diagnosed with Enduring Personality Change, a syndrome that was first noted with survivors of concentration camps. He gave evidence at the Barron Tribunal in 1997. Both Stephen and Des are affronted that their testimony to British Army involvement in the massacre has not been reflected fully in the Historical Enquiries Team (HET) findings.

'The HET looked into the whole Miami tragedy,' Des days, 'and they came out with a document. We all got a very, very thick document. Each one got an individual one. For example, Stephen Travers' case was totally different from my case. And they come with the whole thing that it was collusion. We are currently going through the High Court in Belfast with our lawyers.'

Des believes that the British voice at the checkpoint was Captain Robert Nairac, later believed to have been executed by the IRA in County Armagh in 1977. This was also the view of former MP Ken Livingstone, who named Nairac in Parliament in 1987 as being party to the massacre.

'There's a lot of dispute about that. I am still convinced he was there. But the HET report – we asked them to look into that – they said that they've got no evidence whatsoever that that was the case. But, on the night I remember telling the police that there was a man who stood out for me he had a very, very posh English accent. And Nairac was actually educated in a Catholic college in the UK. He had a posh English accent. Later on, I remember Nairac being on television and that voice – I recognised that voice. But as I saw, the HET report didn't come out with any evidence for that.'

Stephen is not so sure.

'I've never said that it was or it wasn't Nairac. The man that I saw appeared to have fair hair. I would never speculate like that. People have come forward – ex-British Army people – to the researchers from the film. They have given them information that has been followed up but… if it's not something that you can bring into court, I certainly wouldn't put my name to it. I'm absolutely certain without a shadow of a doubt that there was a British Army officer there.

'The documentation disclosed in public records shows that there were concerns about an infiltration of the UDR by the paramilitaries and that was years before the attack on the Miami, and nothing was ever done about it. There are members of the UDR who raised concerns about infiltration while they were serving members. I've spoken to a lot of ex-members of the UDR and to RUC officers. In every case that I've spoken to them there was this sense of this thing should never have happened and that they didn't want to be tarred with that brush.'

For some time after the massacre, Stephen had articulated a message of reconciliation and had affected a relatively normal demeanour. It was the 30th anniversary of the massacre that prompted a change. For the first time he began to regard himself as a victim, with the attendant trauma.

'The study on trauma tells us that most of the effect of trauma is that there aren't any words to express it. I have a background in journalism, I used to own the *Irish World* newspaper and for a while I was the Editor as well. I've written articles and been the co-writer of a book and now I'm a co-writer of the screenplay of the film. You would imagine that somebody that practiced could articulate how you feel – whether it's a sense of depression or whatever – but there's a study now on trauma that tells us that it's like a child, that there are no words to express how you actually feel and that's just a result of psychological damage.'

On August 15 1975, a DJ, Norman Kerr, was killed after a night's work at the Carrick Bar in Armagh. He had finished loading his equipment when three masked IRA men arrived and shot him. The organisation claimed that Kerr had been familiar with Captain Nairac. According to Kerr's mother, her son was an associate of Harris Boyle, a UVF member who had died during the planting of the bomb in the Miami van.

The showband killings were widely reported and visiting musicians cancelled their shows. Queen's University social secretary Gary Mills told *NME* that he had lost Be-Bop Deluxe, Osibisa, Sailor and the Sutherland Brothers. For the respected promoter Jim Aiken, it became a major challenge to retain international names. Charlie Pride, the country artist, was in the ascendant and in 1975 Aiken had secured four dates from a 40-date UK package. However, this was now in question. Charlie's band was unwilling to play the dates and the anxieties were shared by his wife and the executives at RCA Records. Jim determined to make an arduous trip to Ohio to meet the singer backstage and to deliver the persuasion in person. The late Jim Aiken explained it thus in 2005:

'Suddenly we became a place *not* to go to. I wouldn't say it was anti-northern. It was… we can do without the north. Every atrocity affects you in some way and some in a particular way. And this was a particular way because it was a business that I was in and we foolishly thought that we were immune and entertainers were immune because entertainers weren't attacked in the world, or anything like that. We thought that bringing normality through music was the story. We told the people – come here, everything's not right, but there's music that people want to hear and that's it.

'I had no other job, so I immediately wanted to start again. And in 1976 I tried to encourage people to come and tried to tell people that there was an audience who would appreciate them, that there was an infrastructure that would put on concerts. The only thing we didn't have was restaurants and bars.'

Eventually, a date at the Ritz Cinema in 1976 was confirmed and Aiken was in business again.

Charlie Pride: 'I couldn't have refused Jim Aiken. He had to take four internal flights there and back, including one in a puddle jumper and then drove miles to the Ohio concert hall to see me.'

The showband industry was in decline at this stage. Discos were providing cheap competition and now the northern market had become perilous. The bands were advised to cover up the logos on the side of their vans. It was the same for rock acts, although Rory Gallagher and a few bold exceptions would still play to appreciative audiences in the north. It was always a risk though, as Barry Devlin from Horslips remembers:

'It was a time of your life when you saw headlights behind you at three in the morning and you just never knew who they were. It was kind of creepy. You just didn't know what stuff meant. Up until then, there had been a belief that you didn't shoot the piano player and bands travelled happily – and occasionally a bit nervously – on the basis that it wasn't personal, that the entertainer will always be alright. But that gave the lie to that. It was the end of an age of innocence.'

Stephen and Des have an undimmed love for the Miami Showband and their legacy. Des points out that another fan, Louis Walsh, even took his own acts to the Miami's tailors: 'When I look today and see what Louis has done with Westlife and Boyzone in the white suits – it's just like the Miami.'

Amidst the blackness, the talk of collusion and cover up, there is a proud realisation of the importance of music during the worst times. Stephen is emphatic:

'People often say that music was harmless fun. It wasn't. It must have terrified the terrorists. When people came to see us, sectarianism was left outside the door of the dancehall. They came in, they were brought together and they enjoyed the same thing. They looked at each other and thought, "There's not much difference here", and nature was doing its course. That's the power of music and I think that every musician that ever stood on a stage, north of the border during those decades, every one of them was a hero.'

I WANNA RIOT

The Clash were supporting the Sex Pistols at the 100 Club on London's Oxford Street on 31 August 1976. In mid-performance, a string snapped on Keith Levine's guitar. There was no other instrument and so the punk energy was stalled until a new string could be fitted. Instead of silence and inaction, singer Joe Strummer decided to improvise with a transistor radio that he'd just bought from the market on Portobello Road. He lifted this 50p bargain from the top of a piano nearby, switched it on and held it close to his microphone.

This random act delivered a news programme into the basement bar. It was a panel discussion about the IRA bombing campaign in London. The content was severe but it made peculiar sense. And so, Dave Goodman, the soundman at the gig, made some adjustments to the mixing desk. He added a dub echo effect onto Joe's microphone input and thus the broadcast became an instant art bulletin, swirling and repeating this message of dread in the capital city.

'Bombs... bombs... bombs... Piccadilly...'

The scene was still finding a voice and an identity but this seemed appropriate. Many of the early punk songs were about decay, menace and deceit. They declared a war on illusion and happy endings. Civic society was a mess and the idea of national unity was being mocked in Sex Pistols lyrics like 'Anarchy in the UK'. Johnny Rotten was a north London boy with family from Tuam in Galway and he seemed to delight in the notion that England's dreaming was in terminal decline. He too had decided to make art out of the newsreader's script:

'Is this the UDA, is this the IRA,
I thought it was the UK.
Or just another country,
Another social tenancy…'

There had been serious rioting in west London the night before the 100 Club gig involving 1,500 police and 60 arrests. Joe and Paul Simonon from the Clash had been at Notting Hill and watched as the West Indian carnival tipped into confrontation and brick throwing. They saw a connection to their own art. Photos from the riots would feature on their first album sleeve. Before that, there was a debut single, orchestrated by sirens, breaking glass and a hurtling fire engine. At first, listeners were concerned that 'White Riot' was a right-wing anthem. This was at a time when the National Front could muster 10,000 people on the streets of Lewisham. But the lyric was actually a call for every citizen to engage actively and directly, as song writer Joe Strummer explained:

'This was a case of people saying, look, I've had enough, and that's what gave rise to 'White Riot'. We participated in the riot but I was aware all the time that this was a black people's riot – they had more of an axe to grind and they had more guts to do something physical about it. After the riot I sat down and wrote the lyric. In its clumsy way it's trying to say to white people, if we're going to do anything we're going to have to become anarchists or activists. We can't just sit around and be pummelled by society or plastered over.'

The Clash took their name from an issue of the *Evening Standard*. There seemed to be conflagrations on every page. The band began to spray such headlines onto their clothing: 'Hate and War' subverted the hippy ideal; 'Sten Guns in Knightbridge' referred to a six-day siege at a spaghetti restaurant in 1975; 'Creative Violence' was a promise and a threat. This informed their songs about call girls, traffic seizures and dead-end employment. On 'Career Opportunities', Mick Jones remembered his time as a clerical assistant in the Department of Health and Social Security on Praed Street in the summer of 1974. In June and July, IRA bombs had been planted at the House of Commons and the Tower of London. Part of Mick's job was to intercept devices in the post. The IRA had been addressing targets in Whitehall, Birmingham and Manchester.

'The Social Security made me open the letters during the letter bomb time,' said Mick, 'because I looked subversive. Most of the letters the Social Security receive are from the people who live next door saying their neighbours don't need the money. The whole thing works on spite. One day an Irish guy they had treated like shit and kept waiting for three hours picked up a wooden bench and put it through the window in Praed Street. And they degrade the black youth even more. No one can tell me there ain't any prejudice.'

Many punks found a valid message in reggae music. Jamaican artists were singing about shootings, corruption and disorder. The island had achieved independence in 1963 but in 1976, the Premier Michael Manley had declared a State of Emergency, leading to 500 arrests. The resourceful music producer Joe Gibbs borrowed the line for a new recording. Additionally, the artist Prince Far I made use of the phrase 'Under Heavy Manners'. Another maverick, Lee Perry, produced 'Police and Thieves' with Junior Murvin singing about the guns and ammunition that were scaring the nation. The commentary was steady and ongoing.

Within reggae, the Rastafarian sect had created an outsider ethos. They read their Bibles and connected to the story of exile in Babylon and eventual deliverance. There was a lamenting strain with some of the artists who tuned into the 'sufferah' role, singing of injustice and hardship. Others saw a significance in numerology and the looming date of 1977. They felt that these were end times. Hence, the Culture album, *Two Sevens Clash*, with its millenarian rapture. Reggae was rich in attitude, emotion and expectation, assets that were lacking in music elsewhere.

So, in September 1976, when the Clash talked to *Sniffing Glue* fanzine about that night in the 100 Club with the broken guitar string, the transistor radio and the discussion about the IRA bombing campaign, they were already working on the mythology, a fracture line from Kingston to London, Belfast and beyond. Joe told the story of the gig and Mick Jones delivered the punchline:

'A state of emergency…'

On 20 October 1977, the Clash took the 8.30am flight from London to Aldergrove Airport, County Antrim. The Ulster Hall in Belfast was the first date of their 'Out of Control' tour. By now, the band had been toughened by events. They had taken part in the Anarchy Tour with the Sex Pistols and others in December 1976. The tabloid media had affected outrage and only seven of the 21 scheduled shows had actually taken place. In the following May they headlined their own 'White Riot' series of gigs, another turbulent passage. At the Rainbow Theatre in London, fans ripped out 200 seats. There was no tour support in the band's recording contract. They accrued a loss of £28,000.

The self-titled album sold well, but the Clash bristled about their relationship with CBS Records. They had signed voluntarily, yet there were many dramas between themselves and the corporate. The label had put out a single, 'Remote Control', without their consent. They answered with a 23 September release, 'Complete Control', with a lyric about the cost of ownership, press infamy, the challenge of revolution and the duty of a band to its audience.

This was the keynote of the new tour. It was about empowerment, about keeping the movement straight. Outwardly, the Clash seemed stern. 'The situation is far too serious for enjoyment,' Joe had remarked to *Sniffing Glue*. Meantime, Mick was troubled by the stage backdrop for the new dates, a reportage photograph of youths from Northern Ireland in mid-riot. It was perhaps questionable to use this in Belfast.

'I feel we might be rubbing their faces in it,' said Mick. 'It's great in Bournemouth because everyone is fucking asleep. But in Belfast you don't need to be reminded.'

Northern Ireland had much to be concerned about. The death toll was currently at 2,062. Recent fatalities included fireman Wesley Orr, killed by an IRA bomb at the Ulster Brewery on 16 November. A Royal Marine, Gareth Wheddon, had died, aged 19, after being injured by a booby trap in Crossmaglen on 9 November. William Smyth was shot in the back of the head on 25 October by the UDA as he returned home from a Catholic Ex-Servicemen's Club in North Belfast.

While the Clash visit would make the cover of the *Belfast Telegraph*, the lead story next day was a police warning to business owners about the threat of incendiary devices. Civic premises had been targeted from the start of the decade and since Bloody Friday in 1972, the prime instrument had been the car bomb. Consequently, the city centre was surrounded in 1974 by 17 steel gates, 10-12 feet high. Two years later and the plan was advanced to create a single security zone out of the four security quarters. This was 'the ring of steel'.

The photographer Pennie Smith said that working with the Clash was like a commando raid staged by the Bash Street Kids. There was drama and posturing, comedy and bathos. Now here they were, headed for a reckoning with the most perilous location in the UK. In the aftermath of the Miami Showband Massacre, few touring acts had bothered with Belfast. So, this gig was a test for the band and also an important measure of the movement. The subculture had emerged from New York and London, a fusion of decadent poets, garage bands, seditionary French thinkers, deviant apparel, camp codes, student riots and Babylon burning. Here then was a test: punk's proof of concept in the city of the dead.

'They'll think we're here to entertain the troops,' Joe mused. As the plane descended, a stewardess delivered a message from the Ministry of Agriculture. It was a request for anyone who was travelling with food or livestock to make a declaration.

'That includes me,' said Mick. 'I'm a chicken.'

The Clash travelled with new drummer Nick 'Topper' Headon, with manager Bernie Rhodes, Caroline Coon from *Sounds* and Ian Birch from *Melody Maker*. CBS had brought along a photographer, Adrian Boot, who had already worked with the band, taking their first record company session by the concrete buttresses of the Westway flyover.

Adrian had lived for a time in Jamaica, teaching physics in Port Antonio,

Jamaica. He became friends with the singer Junior Murvin there and later the MC Mikey Dread Campbell. He was an amateur photographer and came to document Rastafarian culture in a book, *Babylon On a Thin Wire*. So, when he was taking shots of the Clash in Notting Hill Gate and he saw posters and graffiti about Jamaican music, he found a creative backdrop and also a shared interest with the musicians.

'It provided a contact with the band,' he says. 'It enabled me to have a conversation about something that was interesting. Otherwise, it would have been difficult. I wasn't a natural born punk. I was quite scruffy but more inclined to be a hippy. I hadn't much of a clue what punk was. I had missed out on quite a lot of this by being in Jamaica. Punk was already a force by the time I'd got back.'

Besides her role as the punk diarist in *Sounds*, Caroline Coon had co-founded the Release organisation in 1967. This was a legal support service for drug-related arrests. She had a particular concern with police stop-and-search powers.

'As a youth in the 60s, I was engaged in politics in my art and also in direct political action on the street. We confronted an ever-more militaristic police force whose tactics, we believed, were honed on the streets of Belfast. The police in the UK first got shields after the riot in Ladbroke Grove that was the foundation of the 'White Riot' song. But the police then got tooled up with the same manufacturer who was making tools for Northern Ireland. Before that, they didn't have shields.

'As naive as we were about the politics of Northern Ireland we were very close. It affected us. We were being warned that if we go into Oxford Street on this Sunday, you could be bombed. And many people were. Not as many as people as in Northern Ireland, obviously, but it was very real for us. Real for the Clash to their own eyes.'

Five years before, Caroline's younger brother had been involved in environmental politics and had despaired at the progress of a private member's pipeline bill. He considered blowing the pipeline up and travelled to Belfast on March 3 1972 to 'see some people'. He had been close to the Abercorn Restaurant the following day, when the IRA bomb exploded. 'His political orientation was changed forever.'

Therefore, she was cautious about the band's interest in extreme action groups:

'Making political change, via democratic political and peaceful means is a long, painstaking slog. Which is why, as a youth, violent political action was potentially seductive. I witnessed the Clash being youthfully seduced by the politics of Baader-Meinhof, the Red Army Faction and the Italian Red Brigades. Only later, as they realised the danger of moral shortcuts that can lead people to the wrong place, did they regret some such youthful endorsements. Joe Strummer and the Clash chose to do their politics with and through the artistry of their music.'

The Ulster Hall gig was promoted by the Northern Ireland Polytechnic Students' Union (NIPSU), based at Jordanstown on the north shore of Belfast Lough. They transported the band from the airport to the Europa Hotel on Great Victoria Street, famously the most bombed stopover in the Western world, and explained that the soundcheck was going to be delayed. As a courtesy, the NIPSU minibus was at their service and so was the driver, Peter Aiken, Vice President of Clubs and Societies.

At this stage, the band was unaware of a logistical problem. The promoters, headed by Austin Smith from the Polytechnic, did not have a letter of liability cover from an insurance company. This had been expected from Medical Professional Insurance Limited and all had seemed fine three weeks ahead of the event. But the cover was not confirmed on the day of the gig. It had actually been withdrawn. Austin had offered a premium of up to £500, but this was turned down. Given that the Ulster Hall was the property of Belfast City Council, there would be no gig without a cover note.

'As the gig approached,' Peter says, 'there was a problem with insurance. Because the music was quite revolutionary, given the context of Belfast and the unrest and the troubles, the insurance company felt that there could be elements that could possibly hijack this, and then there could be endless problems. It was as a result of that, and I remember the discussions internally, without letting the Clash management know anything about this, [that we thought] "What are we going to do? What can we do?" This was a few days before. "Let's see what we can do in trying to organise alternative insurance for it."'

This delay allowed the band more time in the city and the photo session was the next priority, as Adrian recalls:

'I wasn't expecting to take photographs of the Clash in the street, I was expecting simply to cover the event, to do backstage shots and some live photography. That's what I was commissioned to do. That's what it was meant to be. Just a photo session, of the kind that I had done many similar photos sessions before in the street with bands. Except the street here, of course, was Belfast in 1977.

'I saw an opportunity. "Can I do a photo session?" They agreed. There was a bit of reservation about where we went. The record company guy suggested that we just wander around the Europa and find a few rooms or a white wall to shoot against. But I thought, "Well look, this is an amazing city..." Amazing in the sense that it was almost like a war zone. A perfect backdrop for pictures of the Clash. Luckily, the band wanted to go out, so that overrode anything that the record company said.'

As it was a winter day, the light was poor. Adrian was using a Leica M4 camera, small, quiet and unobtrusive, favoured by documentary photographers such as the Magnum Agency. His film of choice was Kodak Tri-X and given the conditions he decided to push the sensitivity of the film to 800 ASA. This gave him longer shutter speeds and the ability to work without flash but the payback was grainy, black and white imagery. No matter, this was sympathetic to the nature of rock and roll.

Peter Aiken took them on a tour of North and West Belfast. They stopped near the Crumlin Road Gaol, their backs to the Carlisle Memorial Church. They encountered an army patrol and Adrian got a series of memorable shots:

'For me, visually, they were really good. The Clash certainly didn't look ordinary. And they didn't have to pose – they just wandered around and I could just shoot. Their dress sense was good, their attitude was good. So, it was a very easy thing to do. They were very photogenic. I was looking for authenticity, if you like. I was looking for the right background. So, wherever there was barbed wire or graffiti or something like that, I would try to get the band in the shot, juxtaposed with whatever else was in the background. I was conscious of that.'

In 1976, the band had used their art school backgrounds to accessorise old clothing with slogans and paint splatters, referencing the likes of Jackson Pollock. The Sex Pistols were at an advantage in that Vivienne Westwood and Malcolm McLaren created their fierce couture. The Clash began using two seamstresses, Alex and Christina, but were also styled by Sebastian Conran and his emergent Upstarts brand. The *NME* writer Nick Kent dismissed the result as 'pop star army fatigues'. On the afternoon of October 20, this look caused some alarm during a brief visit to Downtown Radio in Newtownards, just outside Belfast, when Joe and Mick were mistaken at reception for paramilitaries. Now, here they were, in their zippered combat pants on the Crumlin Road, having small talk with Keith, a moustachioed squaddie from the Midlands.

'Joe did mention in the van that he was very worried being photographed next to soldiers,' says Adrian, 'although it was actually him that walked over to the soldiers and had a chat with one of them.'

Peter Aiken drove them to the Shankill Road and the Falls Road. There was also an opportunity at Springfield Barracks, in front of a confidential phone number on a large sign outside. They stopped outside the Henry Taggart Police and Army Base at the intersection between the Protestant Springmartin and Catholic Ballymurphy estates. This was a brutal fortification with corrugated iron, link fencing, chains and cement. The towering defences were there for good reason. This had been one of the scenes of the so-called Ballymurphy Massacre in August 1971, when 11 civilians died. In May 1972, the Battle of Springmartin had taken place here, a crossfire of aggression from the Official and Provisional IRA, the British Army and the UVF West Belfast Brigade. It was the most intensive battle of its time, with 400 strike marks on the Springmartin flats alone. Seven people were killed in two days of violence, four of them teenagers.

The Clash entourage arrived here in the blue college bus with the NIPSU logo on the side. Immediately, the military came out and wanted to know why people were standing outside the fort. At which point, Peter introduced himself. In addition to his college role, he was a part-time member of the Royal Ulster Constabulary. He had his security service warrant card.

'I very specifically remember some of the army guys coming out – "You can't park here, you can't stop there", and again it was a warrant card and, "That's okay". So, the photographs were allowed. But otherwise you wouldn't have got some of those photographs. There were a lot of locals who came out to see what was going on. "What's this and what are all the photographs?" Because Adrian was very much there and he was positioning people and doing his bit. I remember being able to turn around and say, "Look, these guys are alright and I'm vouching for them".'

The final images of the afternoon pictured the band on Donegall Place in the City Centre, entering the ring of steel, each taking a body search as they came through the security cordon. Adrian was first through and so he documented the others being frisked before standing at the top of the avenue. Behind them, an Ulsterbus headed out of the city while a heavily armoured Saracen vehicle steered forward into Donegal Place. Civilian transport and the tonnage of the British Army.

'You can look back at the pictures now,' says Adrian, 'and think, "Oh, great, it worked out well". But at the time, no one expected much more than just a quiet photo session – "Let's use the time usefully". So, the fact that the pictures turned out the way they did, it was more to do with Belfast at the time than the Clash. I could have wandered around the streets without the band and shot pictures and it would still be quite dramatic. It was a dramatic backdrop.'

A week earlier, the Sex Pistols had released their fourth single, 'Holidays in the Sun'. It was a manic account of shifting economics and tourist gluttony. The narrator wants an alternative to the usual Mediterranean beach package. He's thinking about the Berlin Wall and a divided city. He wants history. He wants to visit *the new Belsen*. A visit to a concentration camp will give the visitor some bragging rights. Johnny Rotten is several decades ahead of the concept of Dark Tourism. And while there is no obvious judgement passed in the body of the song, the vocalist squalls a critical line in the record's opening bars: *a cheap holiday in other people's misery*.

It is perhaps the most moral line in the punk story. In each journey, in each encounter and in every transaction, there is a personal responsibility. The Clash members were not untouched by this guideline during their Belfast visit.

'I just felt like a dick,' said Mick Jones. 'The best time was when all the kids were in the photos with us. That was the only time it was human and real. The kids thought we were dicks. We asked some, "Do you want to be in the photograph?" and they said, "Bollocks" on the Ballymurphy Estate. I thought the group stuck out like a sore thumb.'

None of this had registered with the fans at the Ulster Hall. Many had arrived early and were enjoying the pre-gig ceremony as they queued along Bedford Street. The Ulster Hall had been designed for the working class of this industrial town – a place to enjoy the arts cheaply. It had opened in 1862 with Handel's *Messiah*, and had hosted Charles Dickens and Lord Randolph Churchill. Paul Robeson had enjoyed his visit in 1936, remarking: 'I've been made to feel you people understand me, the warmth of your welcome has gone to my heart.' Led Zeppelin would not return after the premiere of 'Stairway to Heaven' in 1971. Rory Gallagher kept playing blues there to the faithful. The venue had no previous experience with punk rock and the attendant subculture.

Maureen Lawrence was a punk enthusiast and the advertised Clash gig was important:

'That gig did give us the sense of normality. The anticipation was unbelievable. Up until then, we went to the local punk gigs with Rudi. The Outcasts were the local band that we followed all around East Belfast and beyond. But the fact that, all of a sudden, the best band ever was going to come to Belfast – it was affirmation that we were now part of the scene. Up until then, we just thought we had our own little thing going on. Maybe about 50 of the core group of people went to the gigs. We didn't know there was anybody else there.

'To go along, turn the corner, and see all these people who we didn't knew existed, it was just fantastic. There was actually a movement going on. I think that night became a movement. Because it was not just happening in our back yard, it was happening right across Northern Ireland.'

Jake Burns had just made the transition from singer with rock band Highway Star to punk contender. 'I suddenly realised that it wasn't just the four of us, that there were a lot of people out there who actually were listening to this sort of stuff.'

Caroline Coon remembers that the convergence outside the venue was unexpected. 'It was a shock to the band. We didn't know at this time how far punk had spread. We were astonished because the kids that were coming to us were self-identifying as punks. And that was astonishing because when you're in your own bubble, you're not quite sure how far it is spreading out.'

The Clash also provided an intellectual charge, as Ruefrex songwriter Paul Burgess recalls:

'In a Northern Irish context, what was even more important for somebody like me was that the community I came from, I found myself trapped into a world of sectarian politics. And what the Clash did for me was, it actually liberated me to have a valid interest in politics and a political process that wasn't coloured or painted by the place where I lived. It enabled me to relate to, at some level, class politics; that simply wasn't on the agenda of Northern Ireland in regard to the conflict here. So here was an opportunity and a voice to engage with political commentary though popular culture.'

Gavin Martin was putting together a fanzine, *Alternative Ulster*, with two of his friends in Bangor, County Down:

'I'd come from Bangor with some people. A few months before, punk would have been an anathema to them, but all through the summer of '77 with the Silver Jubilee, the Queen arriving in the bay at Ballyholme at the same time that 'God Save The Queen' was released, the royal yacht arriving there – it was a mounting thing. This was like the first actual big punk gig. The Feelgoods had been here. They were brilliant but the Clash were fantastic. They were coming to Belfast. I couldn't believe that it was going to happen. And it *didn't...*'

After soundchecking at the Ulster Hall, the Clash were informed that since the insurance cover was no longer valid, the gig could not take place. But there was an alternative, a chance to restage the event at Queens University, a mile away. Peter Aiken was alerted.

'It was very much a question of trying to keep as much under wraps as possible. Even to the extent of the soundcheck taking place. I remember standing on the level looking up at the boys onstage and doing the soundcheck. And then it was, "Right, there's definitely no chance, let's move".'

Austin Smith, the entertainments officer, realised that it was nonnegotiable: 'The insurance company said it was because there were outstanding claims arising out of Clash concerts.'

Outside the Ulster Hall, there was confusion and hearsay. There were face-offs with the security. Bedford Street was blocked for a time by punk rockers. Some of them lay down on the road. Three windows were broken at the Ulster Hall. People were running over to the hotel, two blocks away. There were five arrests: three males and two females.

'Everybody talks about the riot,' says Paul Burgess. 'But in terms of Belfast riots, it was about two out of ten. There was a bit of to-ing and fro-ing with the cops. People were working themselves into a bit of a frenzy. So, when somebody said, "Oh, they're not letting the Clash play" – that was the key thing. There was no talk of insurance certificates or anything. It was, "They're not letting the Clash play" – which would play out in the anti-authority scheme of things. And then a small group of people broke away and were running towards the Europa Hotel, shouting over their shoulder, "Joe Strummer's been arrested at the Europa". So, massive misinformation and confusion.'

Jake Burns was party to the chaos. 'There were a lot of people milling around and causing a disturbance outside the Ulster Hall and what amazed me was not the fact that they were causing a disturbance – because, after all, it was it was Belfast – but the number of people that was there.'

Barry Young, who was 15 at the time, had a Kodak Instamatic with him to take some snaps of the band and he started photographing the police in an altercation with some girls. This was provocation enough, as Barry's brother Brian recalls. 'Next thing we knew he was hurled into the back of a meat wagon. We only got him out after they'd smacked him about a bit and taken the film out of his camera.'

This had a lasting effect on Clash guitarist Mick Jones. The band had provoked a riot by accident. This was band mythology being actualised. And yet he was dejected afterwards. 'The most horrible thing was the way the kids were treated. They were pushed around. They didn't have a chance to understand what was happening, so they were disappointed in us. We ain't an army, we're a rock and roll band. It's like the band against the Army and the Ulster Constabulary.'

The band had decamped to the Europa, where Bernie Rhodes reviewed the options. Joe and Paul stepped outside the perimeter fence and explained to some fans that the show was happening up the road. Gear was being shifted to the Queen's University Student's Union. They put up equipment in the small bar. The capacity was 400 yet there had been 800 advance sales for the Ulster Hall. There were rumours that punks would be excluded, but Joe came out and reassured them that this would not be the case. Still, it was problematic. Eamonn McCann, the Social Secretary, wanted it to happen but his superiors said no. The band offered to cover any potential damage, but this was declined. The band exited from a side entrance into a series of Ford Cortinas on order from Fonacab.

The fans deserved a statement and this was the duty of Kyle Leitch, who worked the counter at Caroline Music on Ann Street. 'At the request of the band I had to stand up on a chair inside the Students' Union and tell a lot of angry punks that we'd failed and that refunds would be available from my shop the next day. Someone threw a bottle, which smashed against a nearby light, and then we all scarpered.'

Some of the fans made it back to the Europa and found a welcome or sorts. 'When I arrived at the hotel,' says Gavin Martin, 'Mick was holding court on the bed. Joe had lost his voice. He was unable to talk.'

Next day, the band took the train to Dublin, set for two shows at Trinity College. But it was the Belfast experience that was reported at length in the music papers and the Adrian Boot shots that became emblematic of a band in a political crossfire.

'When I got back to London,' says Adrian, 'the record company was very upset with me. I thought I would never work with CBS again. They said I was irresponsible and immature and that I shouldn't have considered risking their band in places like Belfast. But of course, the same picture of the band with the soldiers appeared in *Sounds*, *NME* and the *Melody Maker*. So, the anger shifted from CBS to the music papers, who were very pissed off that I had supplied the same picture to all the papers. It wasn't me who supplied the pictures, incidentally, it was CBS. They had sent out three or four pictures, as they used to do those days, and of course they had all chosen the same picture, coincidentally.'

At the time, Brian Young was playing in Rudi, the first proper punk band in town. His expectations were also tested. 'The Clash media people turned it into a trip to a warzone – staying in 'the most bombed hotel in Europe' when it was actually the most luxurious. But we did get to meet them. They were genuine enough people. And at least they tried to play, that was the main thing. And they did come back and play. Their McMordie Hall gig (December 17) was one of the best I ever saw in my life.'

In 2002, Joe Strummer was contacted by the authors of a punk book, *It Makes You Want to Spit*. They asked about his impressions of Belfast in 1977 and the importance of music at that particular moment. He responded with a quote in November. It was one of the last public statements he made before his passing, a month later:

'The punks informed us they were the only integrated people in the whole country. Let the child teach the man! When punk rock ruled over Ulster, nobody ever had more excitement and fun. Between the bombings and shootings, the religious hatred and the settling of old scores, punk gave everybody a chance to LIVE for one glorious, burning moment. Let it provide inspiration.'

YOU AIN'T NO FRIEND OF MINE

A formative moment for Belfast punk happened on July 13 1975. Marc Bolan was returning to the UK Top 20 with the strange boogie of 'New York City' and a new line-up of T. Rex. Their first live show was the Palace Lido in Douglas, Isle of Man and even though Marc's era of intense adulation was tailing off, it was still an occasion. The show coincided with the Northern Ireland holiday period of the Twelfth Fortnight, the centre of the marching season when the shipyard and many other large industries closed down. Douglas was a popular resort for these workers so the ferry trips were busy and the bed and breakfast trade was at capacity.

Four boys travelled together on the Steam Packet boat for the show. Brian Young was 15, from East Belfast and a Bolan fan since he'd watched a performance of 'Jeepster' on a kids' TV show in 1971. He was also into Bowie by this time, with cropped hair and some early hints of a rebel character. His mates were Leigh Carson, Marty Stitt and Gary White and shortly after arriving they discovered that Marc and his entourage were staying at the hotel beside the venue. These sleuth followers tuned into *Manx Radio* in the afternoon, heard the singer talking in the studio and worked out that the soundcheck was imminent. So shortly after 4pm they got to meet Marc, his singing partner Gloria Jones plus bassist Steve Currie at the back of the hotel.

Bolan wore orange strides and a harlequin-style blouson with purple lapels. He was remarkably friendly and every famous encounter afterwards would be an anti-climax for Brian. There was time enough for photos and conversation plus an invitation to chat further at the hotel bar. Bolan gave him a T. Rex songbook. He said that some of the chords in the book weren't correct and so he wrote out the proper ones. Gary was given a signed tambourine, which he sold on to Graham 'Grimmy' Marshall, another mate who was over on holiday with his parents. They got talking to the new T. Rex drummer Davy Lutton and found out he was actually from Belfast. He had played in the group Eire Apparent and his brother worked in the shipyard with Grimmy's dad John. All of this was encouragement enough. Rudi was formed soon after, named after a song from the stylish bovver band, the Jook.

Brian became a connoisseur of rock and roll – prepped on glam before discovering the New York Dolls and the fall-about cool of guitarist Johnny Thunders. He exchanged letters with other Thunders fans such as Steven Morrissey in Manchester. He got his guitar tuition by playing along to Chuck Berry records and, in time, Rudi managed a version of 'Pills' from the Dolls' repertoire. Later, they discovered it was a Bo Diddley original, but they told people in Belfast it was one of their own. Who would guess?

Rudi got extra encouragement in May 1976 when Brian, Grimmy, Marty and Ronnie Matthews travelled to see Bowie during the *Station to Station* tour at the Wembley Empire Pool. 'We were a year older,' Brian remembers, 'but much less wise. We found a lot more ways to get in trouble on that trip.' Their first gig was a house party during that summer, tolerating a local hood who insisted on singing 'The House of the Rising Sun' at intervals. But they were not risk-averse. 'We used to break into a youth club to practice – anything that we had to do. We were 16 and just didn't know any better. We had no limits.'

Semi-pro bands tended to stay in their own areas in Belfast, playing the working men's clubs and social nights. Rudi were curious enough to take part in a talent contest at the Cozy Club in Dundonald but the winner was a drunk who stood up and sang 'The Wild Side of Life'. The band needed a strategy.

'We decided we'd just do our own thing. We'd been going to the Glenmachan Hotel at the weekends. It was notorious and underage – the most violent, horrible place – but we had nowhere else to go. We used to book private parties and then say, "Oh, there's a band playing". The band would be us. We played the Glenmachan and the Girton Lodge, which had a similar reputation. That was where we honed our chops. We would be playing maybe an hour and a half or two hours. It was a weird mixture – 60s garage, whatever Bowie and T. Rex we could figure out and a lot of old rock and roll songs.'

At the time, the English punk style was evolving out of bands with attitude, sometimes draped by clothes merchants on London's King's Road. The look was also influenced by soul clubs like the Lacy Lady in Ilford and Crackers in Soho. It was nurtured in London's gay venues like Club Louise on Poland Street and the Sombrero in Kensington. The equivalent for Northern Ireland was in the seaside town of Bangor, County Down. Maureen Lawrence remembers her first night at the Viking:

'Eileen McCausland was wearing a black bin bag, all ripped. This would have been late '76, early '77. Fishnet tights, hair all back-combed, heavy black eye-liner and stilettos. She was dancing with Jeff Hughes who was a very stylish guy. He had a salmon-coloured bin liner on, with braces and high-waisted, pleated trousers and winklepickers.

'I can still remember what they wore. Paul Stockman was looking fantastic. White spikey hair, pink mohair jumper, black leather trousers, white winklepicker shoes. Some of them had gone to London, bought all the clothes and come back. We knew some of the older people who went. It was John Allen, Joss Cochrane, Greig Keyes, Alan and Alana Lovell. Punk was coming through. The DJ was playing the Stranglers. But it was always a soul club. Maybe one or two punk records at the start of the night and that was it. And then back into Earth, Wind & Fire and the Brothers Johnson.'

David Bowie was an energy source for this scene also, a meeting for glamour, androgyny and 40s chic. His 1975 album *Young Americans* was an essay in faded retro, looming disco and plastic soul. He was creating a 'gouster' persona, with vintage zoot tailoring, a wedge haircut and a melancholic, lost demeanour. The look translated to Belfast and Bangor, with some eager adopters at the Viking. Maureen, from Belfast, had firstly experimented with clothes and attitude at the Stables, a crumbling block in the grounds of the Glenmachan Tower Hotel. This Italianate pile, dating back to 1862, was at the Craigantlet Hills on the eastern outskirts of the city. In this rough setting, also frequented by Brian Young and his mates, under-18s were tolerated in spite of the licensing laws.

'It wasn't the greatest place,' Maureen remembers. 'People used to dance when the rain was coming through the roof and the umbrellas were up. We were into the granny sandals and the *Young Americans* look – the dirndl skirts, scarves around the neck, just to make us look different. We were into Roxy Music and the Bowie stuff. You could feel that was coming through. The guys were starting to wear drainpipes, a lot of that came through from the Viking. We used to see the older ones walking around town and we wanted to be like them. Our aim in life was to get to the Viking, really. When 'Anarchy in the UK' was released, we got the DJ at the Stables to play it. Halfway through the record he lifted the needle off, handed it over and said, "Don't bring that back". I think we knew at that stage it was time to move on.'

In 1977 another venue in Bangor, the Trident, became outsider-friendly. Now there was a fresh option on High Street. 'A certain crowd left the Viking to go to the Trident, but everybody still danced to soul music and were dressed in punk clothes. They would have played a few punk songs and then we all got up and danced to Donna Summer's 'I Feel Love'. Nobody minded, but we still knew we needed to have something. It still makes me angry that we were from the only city in the Western world where teenagers couldn't go into the city centre. And then Brian Young delivered punk rock to my doorstep.'

Brian draws a distinction between the Rudi generation and those regulars at the Viking and Trident:

'Some of them would have gone to Malcolm McLaren's shop and seen the Sex Pistols. But they weren't really into the music. There were a lot of people into the shop-bought manufactured fashion, which was fine. But for me, the important thing about punk was the DIY thing. Like the girl at the Clash riot who had a kettle for a handbag. People who were running about with six-inch nails in their pockets. That's the important stuff, because in 1976, punk started and there were punks here. They looked more like grown-up schoolboys – they were still at school, but that's what they looked like. The blazer, safety pins and paper clips, stupid plastic glasses, jelly sandals.'

Brain razored and spiked his hair. Grimmy, who worked with a clothes wholesaler, sidelined some nylon boiler suits. They hacked off the sleeves and wrote song titles and word-jams on the fabric with house paint: 'Pop Star' and 'New Commerciality'. Ronnie Mathews also sang and played guitar. In late 1977, Gordy Blair became the bass player after the band cut his hair and sourced extra-tall overalls, ready for the Trident on November 17. They had a light show and an unassailable feeing that that were the best. Unlike those old hippies at the Pound…

'It wasn't about being above everybody, but it was to differentiate yourself for the local bands who all wanted to end up being Light or Sk'boo, who we detested. We thought they were just dinosaurs. At the time, I thought when you were in your 20s you should stop playing. You were too old to be in a band. People came to see us and then once punk broke, people identified us. It sounds corny, but there was something in the air. You thought you were the only people who were into this stuff; you didn't realise that two streets away, there's two other people reading *Sounds* and *NME*. It was all working away. A lot of slightly younger people would have got into punk through reading the music papers and buying the first Ramones LP.'

Brian was apparently the first local to buy the Ramones album, on import from Caroline Music, a record shop that had been opened on Ann Street by Lawrence John in 1973. This was where Robin Brown and Kyle Leitch served up enthusiasm and knowledge, sourcing Tom Petty and Johnny Thunders imports, Sire pressings, whatever. For a time, Kyle was the *de facto* Rudi manager and an important connection for customers who wanted to hear about critical releases and local gigs. Other shops included Rocky Mungo's on Linen Hall Street plus Unicorn Records in Bangor and the four shops from the IT Records chain. Gigs by Dr. Feelgood, Graham Parker and Eddie and the Hot Rods quickened the idea that music was getting sharper and more emotionally direct. And in 1977 there was a new location at 102 Great Victoria Street, a three-storey terrace site that offered music, words, sedition, community and nourishment.

Richard Watters was on the ground floor with Sassafras Wholefoods, shifted from his old location at 24 Donegall Street. The building was suffused with the smell of his spices and herbs. Dave Hyndman installed a print workshop on the top, running off community papers, posters, poetry and fanzines. Terri Hooley was in the middle floor with a record shop, Good Vibrations. He took the name from a Troggs version of the Beach Boys song and there was a wry humour in the title: 'It was a joke – we were seriously insane.' They had spent several years as an abstract idea called the Co-operative Craft and Cultural Society Ltd. They aiming for funding and looked seriously at a property on 12 Lower Crescent. Their plans had included a restaurant and community TV business, but funders were not convinced. So, this leftfield collective got a free lease period on the derelict building on Great Victoria Street, put in new windows, fashioned up shop fittings with wood hauled from skips and painted the toilet seat red ('so that it would look nice in case some girls turned up'). Then they had a big party.

After years of talking up the idea of the Belfast Arts Lab – bringing strands of the cultural revolution into a single location – Terri had arrived. In the old 1971 attempt, he had created energy and gathered potential allies. 'Then they set up a committee,' he muses, 'and voted me out.' Undeterred, he had leafleted with the Music to Belfast Campaign and protested about the civic planning that was set to cut off the west and north of the city with a traffic system that functioned as a *cordon sanitaire*. He had dug in while many of his free-thinking friends moved away and The Tribe was effectively scattered. He had approached the Peace People for funding help in 1976 but they had also rebuffed him. Terri remained stubborn and contrary at a time when many of his peers had been beaten by circumstance.

So, it was a mixture of brute will and folly that had brought this endeavour to a street that was bomb-strafed from incidents around the nearby Europa Hotel. His record business had grown out of a lucky outcome when a batch of second-hand vinyl from *Exchange and Mart* revealed some valuable stock. He was selling from his house and then put out his stall at markets in Belfast and Ballymena. It was David Hyndman who persuaded him to set up in a permanent city location. Great Victoria Street was on the other side of the city centre to Caroline Music and so music fans created their Saturday afternoon rituals, passing the hours between each shop, stopping at Cornmarket en route, loading up on singles and badges, picture sleeves, fanzines and solidarity. They came on bus rides from Derry, Antrim and Fermanagh.

'The shop was a real meeting place,' says Terri. 'It was like an oasis in the middle of this cultural wasteland. I had to laugh when people later called the area the Golden Mile – there was nothing golden about it. We hadn't a clue what we were doing, really. I was just this mad, ex-hippie. The energy of punk in Belfast gave me the chance to relive my youth again.'

In the early 70s, Terri had worked in the processing department of Kodak on Corporation Street. One of his tasks was to create funeral mass cards from the photographs of the dearly departed. Like many citizens, he was losing his own friends in the conflict and two of them died horrendously in 1974. Gerard McWilliams had been living in England for six years and was only back a few days when he decided to walk home to Andersonstown after a night in Lavery's Bar. They found his body on the morning of September 26 off the Donegall Road. He'd been stabbed and beaten with a blunt instrument. He was 25. Another good soul, Ivan Clayton, had been working on the door of the Club Bar on University Road when he was shot in the stomach by two UDA men who ran off into Sandy Row.

Terri himself had become a potential target when he defied the Ulster Workers' Council Strike in May 1974, a Unionist bid to wreck the power-sharing assembly, outlined by the Sunningdale Agreement. His boss at Kodak created a pretext to take him away to Blackpool on business. Later, he survived an abduction attempt when three gunmen tried to bundle him into a car as he left work. By chance, two people he knew were passing and he managed to escape. Afterwards, he wasn't going to slacken up on fun and mischief. 'I decided that I'll just have to go out and party and live life because I could be dead tomorrow.'

Media outrage in the UK press about the Sex Pistols and the irreverence of 'God Save the Queen' gave Loyalists an extra reason to dislike the local punks. When Rudi played at the Strathearn Hotel on October 11 1977, a threat was received that the Holywood UDA was planning to arrive, heavy-handed. 'Thankfully,' says Brian, 'they didn't show up.' Young's meeting with Terri was an important connection across two dissenter traditions. The guitarist made a visit to the shop soon after it opened and Hooley noticed his 'Back to Mono' badge, the discrete emblem of a Phil Spector fan. The pair of them had a mutual love of the Ronettes. Another regular visitor was Gordy Owen, a teenager from Sandy Row who had bad teeth and a home-made Iggy tattoo on his left hand. He was a punk evangelist and was never at school, as Brian recalls:

'Me and Wee Gordy used to haunt his shop. We used to just sit and talk about music. Terri wasn't interested in punk at all – it wasn't on his musical radar. But what was important was that Terri was selling second-hand and then getting lots of stuff from people in England so he had a lot of the more obscure punk singles. We just thought he was this old hippie. He used to fancy certain people in certain bands but that was Terri. He liked to wind people up.'

Gordy had met the Clash at the cancelled gig in November '77 and crashed out with them at the Europa Hotel. He invited Brian to meet them the next day and the energy of events translated into Rudi rehearsals. They used a Loyalist band hall on Glenmore Street, off the Albertbridge Road. Early Rudi songs had been about drinking and youthful thrills, but 'Cops' was a response to the thwarted Clash concert and the minor riot that ensued. The chorus was a flat declaration: *'we hate the cops'*. The verses conveyed some of the turbulence that had happened on Bedford Street and the black uniforms of the Royal Ulster Constabulary:

'Standing at the Ulster Hall, black bastards having a ball
Punks are different, punks are strange, but we ain't got no time
to change.'

Most remarkable of all was a chant that opened and closed the song. 'SS RUC' was a long-standing feature of football terraces, political protests and aerosol work on gable walls. It drew a comparison between the police force in Northern Ireland with the *Schutzstaffel* of Nazi Germany, entrusted by Heinrich Himmler to enforce security, terror and genocide. It was startling to hear this in a song and when Rudi played it live, their lighting guy Marty Stitt set-off the sirens and flashing lights, recreating the anxiety and over-stimulation of a Belfast night.

Rudi played 'Cops' for the first time at Jordanstown Polytechnic on December 13. When the bar staff heard it during the soundcheck, they told the band that on no account must it be performed during the gig. 'We played it as our last number anyways,' Brian says. 'No wonder they never asked us back!' It was also in the set for the first punk night at the Pound on January 12 1978. Terri was in the audience, driven there by Gordy's repeated demands. The Outcasts were also on the bill, and the punk-wary venue was tested by some new customers. Lights were smashed, the police came and returned with the Ulster Defence Regiment and so 'SS RUC' was played out by the band and seconded by the customers. It was the first local punk song about an actual event, naming the law enforcers and inciting the audience. Terri was thrilled. He liked their fierce version of '96 Tears'. The music reminded him of favourite garage bands like the Standells. Mostly, he was taken by the generational change. 'That was the night I realised that the punks had no fear. I was really impressed by that. The anarchy of it all.'

There was talk of pressing up a flexi-disc and maybe mounting it on a fanzine so Terri helped Rudi with the costings. It was 11 pence per unit, but excitingly, the cost of an actual seven-inch single at the EMI Ireland plant was 17 pence. So, with another impetuous move, Good Vibrations Records was created and the band had its first professional session booked for February 7. This was the Templepatrick Studio, home to the Emerald Records stable of showbands, folk and parlour songs. The producer was George Docherty, who had also worked with the likes of Clubsound (and became a future co-conspirator of Jive Bunny). The backing tracks of 'Big Time' were recorded live and vocals were added afterwards in an assured rush.

It was magnificent. The sound of teen petulance and a truth attack on a posing scenester who never bought the drinks. Brian's guitar was basic fare – an Antoria SG copy – but it went through an overloaded Carlsbro Stingray amp with the 'suzz' switch on full. His schooling in Chuck Berry and Johnny Thunders riffs was vividly reprised. A few weeks later, when Terri picked up the delivery of the pressing in Dublin, one of the ladies who worked there asked if she could keep a copy. Vindication. The sleeve was an A3 design printed by Dave Hyndman and folded, origami-style, to house the record, which had the heft and delicacy of a dinner plate. So, the label showed instant character and ingenuity. 'Big Time' was the first in a series of vital releases by Victim, the Outcasts, the Undertones, Protex and Ruefrex. It was a channel for unique voices and the unfiltered thoughts of a generation. Furthermore, Good Vibrations had a moral code, as Brian notes:

'Terri wasn't in it for any cynical reason. Like, Stiff Little Fingers made their single to get a record deal. That was the purpose. A lot of bands did. That was the way it worked. It became a bit of a cliché very quickly with punk bands who put out their own single and if it got picked up by A, B or C, then the majors would step in.

'That's how quickly punk was over. The truth is, when the Clash signed to CBS, when the Pistols signed to EMI, they were no different to the Bay City Rollers. It happened to Elvis with Sun Records and RCA. It's been the same down in history. 'Big Time' was different. It showed that anyone could do it.'

Terri's role in the story has been questioned over the years, but Brian is emphatic:

'His importance can't be over-estimated. He encouraged people. He was a great ideas man. Before that, people just laughed at you – "stupid kids, you'll grow out of it". But he took us seriously.

'We were just these teenage trouble-makers. Terri had that bit more suss. Plus, he can be eloquent and entertaining. He could walk into the BBC and talk to people. And he had enthusiasm. He wasn't in it for any cynical motive. He had the contacts, the knowledge and the experience to go ahead and do it. All we knew about the music business was *Stardust* and *That'll Be The Day*."

Even when the Undertones released 'Teenage Kicks' on Good Vibes in September and John Peel played it frequently and record company interest was piqued, Terri had no intention to monetise his efforts. The band's bassist Michael Bradley recalled it thus:

'The great thing about Terri was that he had no intention of saying, "I have a valuable property here". Anyone who knows Terri will know that making money is not at the heart of what he does. So, he really just introduced the record company guy to us. We then signed a record deal with Sire. Terri was there at the first meeting. Then Terri says, "Bye bye".'

After the jubilation of 'Big Time', few people noticed the disappearance of 'Cops' from Rudi's set list. The chief reason is that they were writing better songs. It was not a complete break from politics or comment. Rudi's style was variously joyous, camp and cynical. They sang about solvent abuse on 'Overcome by Fumes', an account of teenagers sniffing the stain remover Thawpit. Rudi wrote about cheating lovers and vacant DJs and also challenged the killjoys with monotone expectations. Songs like 'Excitement' and 'Time to be Proud' had a revolutionary import. Later lyrics like 'Toytown' and 'Crimson' painted up Belfast as a repressive city, declaring that *chains are strong, only to the weak*. But 'Cops' had been problematic on a few levels for Brian and the band:

'We wrote 'Cops' about one specific event; it was never meant to be a corny blanket condemnation of the cops. By then, punk was drowning in dumb sloganeering of the very worst kind. We used to argue with English journos who insisted we knew nothing about 'the Irish situation' as we weren't singing about tanks, rubber bullets and 800 years of British imperialist oppression.

'I think it's only fair to mention now – though we certainly wouldn't have mentioned it at the time either, for pretty obvious reasons – that closer to home, too many of our extended family members were members of the security forces. And coming from East Belfast it was pretty obvious what foot we kicked with. Certainly, punk enabled us to escape from being pigeonholed in the main – and playing to punk audiences was never any hassle – but the reality of life here was still that when you played outside Belfast, and often inside Belfast too, some people would sidle up to you and ask you what part of Belfast you hailed from. And back then your answer could have a very real impact on your well-being.

'We were run off the road and almost killed coming home from a gig in Castlebellingham, simply as some locals took offence at the part of Belfast they perceived we came from. We barely escaped with our lives. It was fucking scary – they rammed a car into the van at high speed tearing a huge rent into the side of the van. That was the day-to-day reality of life back then.

'We played a gig in Hunter's bar in Bangor in '78 and a huge crowd of paralytic squaddies besieged the venue, determined to give all those nasty punk rockers a good hiding. Grown-up men out to beat up a room of spotty teenagers – how brave! Thankfully the reviled RUC turned up in significant numbers and saved us all from a literal bloodbath. We never played 'Cops' again after that.'

Belfast still needed a home for punk. The social infrastructure was broken, as publican John McElhatton explains:

'In North Belfast there were 32 bars bombed out or burnt out in the early part of the Troubles. All these bars became waste ground or they became clubs – these social clubs that they all ran, in their own areas, where you had these bands mostly playing cover music. So, the original bands had no outlet. That was the problem. It was a result of the madness. In East Belfast it was something similar. There were a few bands like Baraka, with Rab McCullough, who had a major following in the West.'

Wes Graham and his cousin Colin 'Ziggy' Campbell were also veterans of the T. Rex gig in 1975 and had recently formed a band called Victim. The lack of a regular venue for new music in Belfast was a bother to them and so they walked through the city on a midweek afternoon in April 1978, looking for chances. Wes had enrolled on a journalism course at the College of Business Studies. Colin was a year below him, still at RBAI (Royal Belfast Academical Institution), a decaying place with high pretentions that was becoming a rock and roll high school, infested with members of Rudi, Protex, Victim and later the Zips, Acme, the Tinopeners and Pig Awful.

Their mission was to secure a willing venue with some kind of a stage. They tried a bar around Castle Lane, but since they were putting on strippers and doing fine, live music didn't interest them. The search moved onto Ann Street and again there was no success, but the musicians were advised to try a less obvious location, north of High Street, where Skipper Street became Hill Street. This was a dingy area that had once serviced the waterfront of the Farset River, a 17th Century stopover for maritime workers and the poorest residential area in town. Later, it had been developed into stores and bonded warehouses for the distillers and blenders.

Journalists from the *News Letter* and the *Belfast Telegraph* drank at the Duke of York at Commercial Court and Gerry Adams served them pints. There were rebellious echoes back to the 18th Century when Henry Joy McCracken and the United Irishmen had schemed around these alleyways and were hanged nearby. The Belfast Harp Festival of 1792 had convened a few hundred yards away at the old Assembly Room, when Edward Bunting had transcribed and preserved the airs of a dying breed. In 1978, the narrow, cobbled streets had not been challenged by modernity. The area was badly lit and the bad reputation was warranted.

According to locals, the Harp Bar on Hill Street had once been called the White Horse. Customers came from the New Lodge and Divis areas. In mid-August,1975 a sub-machine gun was fired into the bar, injuring one person. On August 30, around 8pm, a Ford Cortina pulled up and shots were fired at a bystander. One of the gang entered and threw in a bomb that killed a 30-year-old labourer, Denis McAuley, and fatally injured Sean Doherty, a docker and footballer who had played for Crusaders. The car was later abandoned at Dee Street and the UDA claimed responsibility, although it was suspected that other parties had also been involved.

The drinks trade, dismissed by the *Protestant Telegraph* as 'the hell-soaked liquor traffic', provided Catholic entrepreneurs an opportunity to develop and Belfast was served by families such as the Laverys and the Roddys. This was an option for Patsy Lennon, who ran a builders' yard on Hill Street. He took over the Harp Bar, believing that it might provide a cash flow for the business. Early security measures involved six oil drums, filled with cement, ranged outside. By 1978 there was scaffolding and chicken wire and a security camera, allowing the bar staff to screen activity on the street. Other bars were using pre-constructed cages around the entrances, but the Harp stockade was adequate.

Importantly, it had a stage upstairs. One of Patsy's business initiatives had been to fly strippers in from Birmingham at the weekends. This was where they performed. Wes and Ziggy Campbell spoke to the bar manager, Maureen Cunningham, and asked her if they might put on a gig. She brought over the barman Tony Douglas and she asked the two visitors what kind of music they played. Wes picked up on the conversation.

'We initially said we were a punk band but their jaws dropped so we swiftly changed tack to say that we were a new wave band, and that didn't really sit too badly with them. We didn't feel we were betraying punk because one of our favourite bands was the Jam, and they sort of described themselves as new wave. So, we were alright with that. I guess they just didn't know what new wave was, so they said yeah. It was an absolute dive but it had that all-important stage that we were chasing after and I remember it had one of those big glitter disco balls hanging from the roof and a little dance floor. So, it looked tacky but we both loved it. We were looking after our own interests. But soon after I remember telling Brian Young about the place.'

Victim played the Harp Bar on April 21 1978, billed in the *Belfast Telegraph* as a 'New Wave Rock Group'. The support act was the Androids, featuring Joe Moody. As agreed, the bands took the door takings, and around 30 people turned up. Punk finally had a focal point in Belfast and, for teenagers like Maureen Lawrence, it was an immense reckoning:

'The Harp Bar, it was pretty much hardcore punks. That was the way it was meant to be: our club, our movement. The early days were great, especially when you had bands like the Outcasts and Rudi, the Androids, Stage B, Ruefrex… every one of those bands was different. The best nights you could possibly have.

'And if we went out, we all went together. We knew people came from all sides of the city and eventually they started coming from parts of the country. Nobody asked too many questions. The idea was, you made it, you got here, we don't need to know any more than that. You had to fight your way through different people in your areas that didn't particularly like the way you dressed – there was a certain amount of respect went along with that. You still took your life in your hand walking across town or getting on the bus.'

Joe Moody from the Androids had a gun pulled on him in the toilet of the Harp. He was wearing a soldier's beret: 'A para gave it to me in the early 70s when I was a schoolboy. He was from Manchester, stationed at the bottom of Percy Street. He knew I was a Man United fan, so he gave me a beret. I thought it would be cool to wear it at gigs.' This wasn't a view that was shared by the regular drinkers downstairs, many of whom were Republicans. It was rumoured that the Harp was frequented by 'Stickies' – the Official IRA. So, there were face-offs and some violent exchanges. When Ruefrex were performing the Sham 69 song 'Ulster', a gun was also pulled. But if the regulars downstairs were intimidating, then the punks upstairs could also have rough-house tendencies. The daily aggression of Belfast life was reflected in the upstairs bar, even if it wasn't about religious sectarianism. Pretty Boy Floyd and the Gems (formerly the showband Candy) were abruptly treated and two members of the Tearjerkers were given hospital treatment and stitches after failing to impress the Harp politburo.

Terri and others were involved in the Punk Workshop, which brought over acts like the Fall, the Mekons and the Monochrome Set. When London-Irish combo the Nipple Erectors prepared to play, singer Shane MacGowan called in advance and asked if he should keep his head down. 'Just learn to keep your drink down,' Hooley advised. There was also a general rule that you did not cross the Outcasts.

Greg, Martin and Colin Cowan became the Outcasts in 1977 after being refused entry to a series of bars and clubs. Unlike the Ramones they actually were brothers. Guitarist Colin 'Getty' Getgood was their longstanding guitarist and they had travelled to see Alice Cooper in Liverpool and Bowie at Wembley. They had a bristling, bad-boy dynamic, living at speed, adopting the manner of Brando in *The Wild One* and released their debut single 'Frustration' in spring 1978. This was on the IT label, a Portadown-based enterprise that had previously released 'Big City' by Speed and 'Punk-Rockin' Granny' by the Duggie Briggs Band. The Outcasts had a firm presence at the Harp, and on one occasion they returned a PA system to Harry Baird's rental shop with human teeth embedded in the speaker cabinet. The pattern of uproar had been established at their very first gig in August 1977, at Paddy Lambe's bar in Ballyhackamore, East Belfast.

'At the end of that first gig,' Greg remembers, 'the guy walked into the dressing room and said, "Who's playing the National Anthem?" And Getty, God love him, reckoned he could struggle his way through it. He went out and he got pelted, absolutely pelted, with coins and everything. 'Cos they thought he was doing it to take the piss out of them. It was horrific. We had this mentality of us against the world. And the violence – I like to joke now that it was cartoon violence – it was not fucking cartoon-like when you were getting beat up by us. If something did kick off, the Outcasts made it worse.'

The Outcasts were happy to play outside Belfast, where the audience might not be appreciative. In April 1979 they were part of a Good Vibrations package tour with Rudi and the Tearjerkers, playing the likes of Ballymena, Cookstown and Omagh.

'It was Terri's idea to play around Northern Ireland. You would turn up even somewhere like Dungannon, and there was no nightlife. Police stations looked like military encampments. Cinemas were all bombed. You've no idea how bad those towns were and we'd turn up and play a showband hall that maybe held 400 people with a 100-watt PA and a 35-minute set, and the whole town would come. There were always wee guys with badges and big coats standing at the side of the stage. It did work for us. That's how we got our following. We played anywhere that would have us. We played in the middle of the Creggan in Derry, we played Crossmaglen, we played Strabane. I think we genuinely helped towards the political situation in Northern Ireland without being political. I think we did go some way between breaking down that barrier of only mixing from your own area. That's my proudest legacy.'

In Dublin, they became friends with a street gang, the Black Catholics, who famously hated U2 and disrupted their early shows:

'The Black Catholics adopted us. They were rough. U2 had a reputation of being middle-class boys in Dublin. Even though we were middle-class boys from Belfast, we got away with it. They adopted us to the stage that we were then banned from playing anywhere in Dublin for almost two years. We didn't realise that Dublin was a far more deprived city than Belfast.

'We played McGonagle's in Dublin and halfway through the second song, there's this fight in the front row in the crowd. And there was no noise. I'm standing on stage on my own watching the rest of the Outcasts in the front row, fighting everybody. I'll always remember the *Hot Press* review after that saying, "I've been to gigs where there's been trouble, but never where the band would drop their instruments and start beating up the front row half way through the second song". I mean, it did happen.'

The Outcasts name-checked the Harp Bar in a later song called 'Gangland Warfare':

'The words tell a story. The Harp was like a little haven but to get to and from it was a nightmare. We used to do a walk to and from the Harp when the Midlands opened and you walked along York Street and that was like something out of *The Warriors* film. There really were gangs that were waiting for you coming, to prey on kids. The guys who went to the Harp were real, they were from Rathcoole, from the Antrim Road, they fought their way down, fought to be punks in their own areas. You didn't fuck with those guys.'

Back at the Viking and the Trident in 1977 there had been a high ratio of females and a tolerant attitude towards the many gay regulars. This was less apparent at the Harp where machismo became an issue and only a few females performed in the bands. Maureen Lawrence considers this:

'I have been asked about the female role in the Northern Ireland punk scene. Yes, it was a serious time in a way, but more importantly we were just teenagers having a lot of fun during a very dark period. We were rebelling as teenagers do against authority, parents, and the political climate at the time but, alongside that, with an explosion of rebellious, energetic music that changed our lives. That's how I remember it. It was very much a boys' club to begin with. A group of females were involved from the early days and did that journey, but by the time we arrived at the Harp Bar a lot of girls had fallen by the wayside and stayed with the tragic disco scene.

'I 'screamed' in a band for a while along with Kerry McIlwaine (keyboards, Urban Bitch) and there were a few other girls fronting bands too – Alison Gibney (Family of Noise), Barbara Greer and Alison Mason (Déjà Vu) also Hilary Midgley (Skum) – but that was quite a rare thing in Belfast. Then again, when you've got someone like Siouxsie Sioux with a strong stage presence, in my humble opinion nobody could top that. Now, I would say well done to any girl who fronted a punk band back then. For me, Siouxsie had it all. She led the way and we all aspired to be her and, in our minds, we were her – young, creative, strong-minded teenagers with a DIY punk attitude to life. So irrelevant of whether we were in a band or not. We all played an important part in that scene.'

Film director John T. Davis took his early inspiration from the sight of D.A. Pennebaker in 1966, hoisting a camera on his shoulder, walking backwards out of the Grand Central Hotel on Belfast's Royal Avenue. The American was shooting Bob Dylan for his *Eat The Document* tour film and this combination of music, art and frayed circumstance had a great bearing on John's own method. Based in Holywood, County Down, he would also use hand-held cameras and wait for the rough illuminations. He applied this ethos on *Shellshock Rock*, a piercing documentary of the Northern Ireland punk scene.

He managed on a budget of £7,500, aided by a great deal of professional favours. He worked over the winter of 1978-79, showing a city in the doldrums, soundtracked by a Salvation Army band and the rolling tonnage of military armour. The poor light accentuated the grain and the feeble wash of Christmas illuminations. It was important to put in the setting because the music and the liberated faces of the music fans were so alert.

He shot the Undertones, declaring 'Here Comes the Summer' in the pure dinge of the Pound. There was footage of Stiff Little Fingers and 'Alternative Ulster' at the University of Ulster – a moment that was almost missed until Derek the soundman fixed a plug with a soldering iron just 30 seconds before showtime. John edited comedic music into the narrative from James Young and when he followed Rudi to a storm-lashed Orange Hall in the Craigantlet hills, he inserted 'Rhythm of the Rain' by the Cascades, sweetly love-sick in California.

The potential of punk constantly lights up the participants. Terri holds up a copy of 'Big Time' like a miraculous relic. The Outcasts struggle in Wizard Studios, a mess of swearing, rough musicianship and inarticulacy. Eventually, they win. Protex sing into the distorted night of 'Strange Obsessions' and the Idiots make playful havoc out the Dion fave 'A Teenager in Love'.

There's a scene at a youth club in Andersonstown where a kinder-punk band called the Parasites are doing their own song called 'Society'. They lack the cool references of the older acts around town. The music is a received clatter of two chords and rote phrases. Yet, they too are open to a provocative strain of thought that is reaching out from discerning record collections into housing estates and Third Form dinner breaks. Elsewhere in the film, 18-year-old Eugene Goldsmith rides through the city in the back of John's black Simca station wagon and articulates a descending truth:

'It's things like this that are gonna spark it off, y'know. Everything's gonna change sooner or later. It happens in small forms like music and crap like that. It starts changing, slowly, but it'll all change eventually. When people will kick in the whole way to live and just start from scratch again.'

It was a smart idea, that the punks were leading the peace process. Certainly, the best of them were setting an example. The reality was perhaps more nuanced, as Brian Young figures:

'At places like the Harp most people left their politics and sectarian baggage at the door. Then, once people got to know each other better, they soon recognised that they had much more in common with each other than they had with everyone else in the boring outside world. Sheer self-preservation was also important too, as punks were a very visible target. So even simple things like all walking round to get the last bus home together from the Harp or the Pound offered a modicum of protection and helped engender a feeling of camaraderie.

'It's also wholly inaccurate when people state blithely that all punks were non-sectarian. That's simply not how it was. We all know several very well-known punks on both sides who were anything but non-sectarian – and, similarly, there were many psychopaths and determined sexual predators too amongst the punk fraternity, whose behaviour seems to have been conveniently overlooked at the risk of disturbing the homogenised happy-clappy version of NI punk history.'

Further into the punk story, right-wing elements would employ the music for their own causes. Similarly, in Republican communities, some felt that punk was part of their language, their particular struggle. Máirtín Ó Muilleoir, growing up in Andersonstown, had no issue with this:

'The narrative is that the only people who loved punk in Belfast were apolitical, when in fact, that spoke to us. I spent all those years from 1976 to 1980 on protests, every Sunday at a different H-Block protest. And yet our theme music going down to that would be the Sex Pistols, Siouxsie and the Banshees, Buzzcocks, the Stranglers, Talking Heads and the Ramones. Was it because it was the language of protest? Or was it just that we were kids who wanted to be different?'

A Sense of Ireland was a six-week cultural programme in London, starting February 3 1980. There were over 90 events in 44 venues, involving Seamus Heaney, the Chieftains, the Abbey Theatre plus Rory Gallagher at the Venue on St Patrick's night. Directed by John Stephenson, the aim was to present a confident and evolving review of the island. There were political and artistic representations of the North at the Action Space on Chenies Street. The Men of No Property were now in the listings as the People of No Property. Good Vibrations was invited to put on a showcase at the Venue on Victoria Street, March 16. Terri brought over Rudi, the Tearjerkers and the Moondogs. It was a positive story but not everyone was pleased, as Hooley recalls:

'I had been told that my bands shouldn't play this festival because it didn't represent what was happening in Northern Ireland – the strip searches in Armagh, the boys in the Kesh and things like that. And I said, "We're going. You can shoot me, but don't shoot the bands." At the press conference in London, a woman said, "We have Terri Hooley, who has been threatened, but has decided to bring the bands over". I thought, "Thank God it's late in the afternoon and the *Belfast Telegraph* has gone to press and nobody's gonna pick this up". I didn't want this blasted over the newspapers. I was certainly afraid of these people but there were many times I stood up to them. I'm a natural born coward, but I did it. I used to get threatened all the time. Very serious threats from some quarters. And years later, I got apologies.'

Good Vibrations went bankrupt in April 1983. Terri's tax reporting had been erratic and his debts were £20,000. He argued that his assets were worth that amount and his accountant, Brendan N. Lynn set out a case for an appeal. There were extenuating circumstances, such as the separation from his wife, a period of worsening problems with his eyesight and vinyl stock that had been unaccounted for during his time away from the business. The Good Vibrations record label, stated Brendan, was an 'unprofitable diversification' and that contracts with successful acts were not binding due to his client's 'soft-hearted approach'. Finally, there was one creditor who had a long-standing and significant account with Terri, who might have enjoyed a future business relationship if the relatively small debt was somehow managed and extended. Was there a concerted push to take Terri out of business, hence, the demand for immediate payment? Unfortunately, this debt was a deal-breaker and the company folded. Terri had anticipated his demise in an interview with *Melody Maker* in 1979:

'We'd rather be failures than be owned.'

ALTER YOUR
NATIVE LAND

Brian Faloon, Henry Cluney and Jake Burns are copping an attitude in the back row of the school photograph. They are disgruntled members of Form 6C at the Belfast Boys' Model School on the Ballysillan Road, North Belfast, 1974. Brian has the centre parting, a basic feather cut and a large knot in his tie. Henry stares upwards and away from the camera, half of his face hidden by a sloping fringe. Jake wears rimmed spectacles; his arms are folded high on his chest and he looks into the lens with contempt. They reassure each other's misfit condition and they will not smile on demand.

By an accident of birth, they have been born into a part of the city that is a mess of territorial corners and flashpoints. The Welfare State has gifted them the chance to sharpen their minds and the school has let them rehearse inside with their band on the weekend. Jake is a Rory Gallagher fan – he first saw him when film of the farewell Taste show at Queen's University Belfast was broadcast by BBC Northern Ireland on New Year's Eve 1970: 'I was transfixed from that moment on and that was what I wanted to do.' The three players are also keen on Led Zeppelin, Black Sabbath and Deep Purple and a song by the latter act will be their stage name when they perform in November 1975 as Highway Star.

Gordy Blair, another wayward Boys' Model pupil, plays bass with them until late 1977 when he reappears with Rudi. His replacement is Ali McMordie, from the same side of town but educated at Belfast Royal

Academy. The work ethic of the showbands has also coloured the local rock scene and so Highway Star learn to play a two-hour set with an interval in the middle. They include tunes by ZZ Top, Bachman-Turner Overdrive plus 'Ohio', a song by Neil Young about the killing of four Kent State University students by Ohio's National Guard in 1970. This had taken place at an anti-Vietnam rally and while the song is politically inflamed, Highway Star are not so engaged, according to guitarist Henry:

'Not a clue! The only reason we played it was, we could play it. It was E minor, D and A. We knew that it was about politics, we knew what the situation was, but it wasn't done for that reason. We didn't think, "That's a political song, let's cover it". We just liked the tune.'

That said, they had their own experience of civic unrest. Drummer Brian Faloon lived at Glenbryn Parade. 'We were right on the interface of Ardoyne. Every so often there would be gun battles. The Army would be on one side and there would be conflict back and forward on Alliance Avenue'.

Henry was from Torrens Avenue, half-way up the Oldpark Road. 'One side was a Protestant side; the other half was a Catholic side, and as years went on the Protestant side was sort of an enclave. We lived almost opposite the police station. And there would be people shooting. So, we used to sleep underneath the beds with the wardrobe up against the window, just in case. It seemed normal. We ended up having to move because you just couldn't live like that anymore and it was just getting a daily occurrence. We left there in 1972 and moved down to the Shore Road. People tended to move to areas where it's either one religion or the other. You don't tend to move from one flashpoint to another, you know? Pointless.'

They realised that music was starting to refresh itself. Jake with his Rory affections could see the value in Dr. Feelgood, especially the choppy blues and stop-time of guitarist Wilko Johnson. Henry was enthralled by Eddie and the Hot Rods, notably their roaring version of 'Get Out of Denver'. Naturally, they sought out the new music at Caroline Music in the city centre.

'Always,' Henry affirms. 'Kyle Leitch used to make me laugh 'cos I'd say to him, "Well, what have you got this week?" And, you know, Kyle can be really demonstrative and I would sometimes come in when he was ruling the papers for the charts and he'd start saying, "We got this… we got this…"

and he'd start swinging the ruler around like a sword. I might have come in for a specific single or even an album but he would say, "Oh, you have to hear this…" So, a lot of the stuff that I would have ended up buying would have come from him. And sometimes Terri Hooley.'

Likewise, with Ali McMordie: 'The penny dropped when I heard the Ramones' first album, which we rushed down to Caroline Records and 'shoplifted' straight away. I remember Kyle keeping a quare eye on us to make sure that everything was paid for. It was on import 'cos we had to get it straight away. It inspired us to stop listening to Deep Purple and Black Sabbath, tuck in the flares and cut the hair.'

Jake reckons that Henry was most emphatic on the take-up. 'He went straight out, cut his hair, tore holes in his T-shirt and bought every available record he could. I took a bit longer to be convinced.' In the meantime, Henry was sulking in the middle of Highway Star gigs at Mooney's bar, sitting down on his amp during the old rock numbers and irritating the management, who wanted him sacked. Instead, he changed the band's centre of gravity:

'I thought, "This other music is so much better, so much more energetic and so much more fun". And it was then that I started bringing the music to Jake. I used to have to walk up to his house – it was two miles, walking up from the Shore Road. I'd bring them round and say, "Listen to this". He was resistant at the start. I basically just kept beating him over the head with the stuff.'

Thus, they became Stiff Little Fingers, named after a Vibrators' song in preparation for their first gig at Lambe's Lounge in East Belfast, August 16 1977. Brian Young from Rudi was one of the few paying customers (Henry insists there were 18 of them) and he noticed that while the band had made some concessions to punk style, Jake's slogan-stamped shirt was still made of cheesecloth. There was also a private dilemma when it came to their performance of the Sex Pistols tune, 'God Save the Queen'. Should the band aspirate the mention of 'H-Bomb' in the lyric like Johnny Rotten, with his Catholic Irish roots?

'It was like, what do we sing?' Henry remembers. 'Do we sing 'haitch' even though we don't say it that way? It became ridiculous – what do we do here? Because if we sing '*aitch*' are people gonna say, "That's not the right words...'"

When Colin McClelland moved to the *Sunday News*, he was known as an entertainment writer. That was a role that had carried him though *City Week*, *Spotlight* and occasional features for the *New Musical Express* as its Irish stringer. He had been involved in club promotion at the Marquee in Belfast and he had managed a showband, Chips. With this in mind, his News Editor Jim Campbell determined to toughen him up.

'He sent me out to the worst markings every day, into really deep Provo areas with no contacts. Into riots and murders. I had to think on my feet all of the time. You have to go to people's doors and there's blood on the doorstep where somebody's been shot and you try to get a photograph of the deceased. And the photographer is pleading with you to get out because the neighbourhood is turning hostile and the army and police have pulled out. You're the only people left and there are no streetlights. It was Dante. It really was horrific.

'The paper went to bed at 2am on a Sunday so anything that was happening around midnight or even 1am, we could still get it in the paper. So, we'd sit there and Jim would have the radio tuned into the police frequency. We'd be thinking, "Please don't pick me". And he's saying, "Could you get to the junction off the Falls Road? There seems to be a bit of trouble going on up there." That was two baying mobs trying to kill one another and you were in the middle of it and the houses were on fire.'

There was still time to write a social column, and Colin responded to readers' invitations and PR events with a deal of affected *ennui*. Sometimes he would take the rise out of tiresome letters and then there were moments that made him curious. 'Jake Burns started to write to me, typed letters, saying, "I don't know what you're talking about" – and he would name a particular band I had mentioned. He'd say, "I have the best rock and roll band in the world and you have to see us before you can write about anybody else". I thought, "Who is this guy?" He said he was typing at work on a stolen typewriter. He intrigued me because he was so persistent and so clever with the words and I would mention him. I'd say, "Here's what he wrote to me and if he's as boring onstage as he is in print, he'll probably go far".'

Another journalist arrived in town in December 1975. Gordon Ogilvie was from Stockport, south-east of Manchester. Just ahead of his graduation with an English degree at St Andrews University, he had been recruited as a trainee journalist by the Thompson Regional Newspaper Group. He worked at the *Aberdeen Evening Express* for three years during the oil boom and his stories of this era saw him recognised as Young Journalist of the Year, 1974 at the IPC Awards.

In 1975, he saw a position advertised in the *UK Press Gazette*. A national newspaper was looking for an unmarried person to work in their Belfast office. He applied for the post and then Stanley Blenkinsop, Northern News Editor of the *Daily Express*, invited him down to Manchester for an interview. They had already vetted him by the time he arrived and so they discussed terms and a salary. Stanley advised him that Belfast 'was like Glasgow, but with a war on'.

Part of Gordon's training at the Thompson Group had concerned the journalistic position, neither involved nor detached. 'I remember one of the tutors saying to me, "Look, it's like being a doctor – if you faint at the sight of blood, you're no damned good as a doctor. But if you don't care about the people that you're operating on, then equally you're no damned good." He said, "What you need to be able to do is to be professional enough that you can get the job done and then you go round the corner and throw up. Or have a stiff drink because of what you've seen."'

This was useful advice for the Belfast posting. Gordon was a few weeks into the job when he was sent to cover the Kingsmill Massacre, January 5 1976. Ten Protestant workmen were lined up against their minibus and shot. One of them survived. The killing was later identified as an IRA operation. 'When I got to the location,' Gordon says, 'all the bodies had been removed from this this country road. It was in darkness but there were literally puddles of blood on the road and bullets riddled down the side of the bus.'

There were three journalists in the Belfast office of the *Daily Express*. They worked the schedules so that each could take off a long weekend every third week. Gordon took his motorbike over on the ferry, visited his partner in Glasgow and then travelled to Edinburgh to meet friends. Recreational time was spent there in the record shops around Princes Street, where prices were much cheaper than Belfast.

'Compared to what I'd been earning in Aberdeen I had a huge increase in salary, so that's when I started buying albums by the fistful. I got into buying punk rock, having been tipped off by John Peel in the first instance. What excited me about it was it was new and it was different. Dylan was huge hero of mine. I was always as much into lyrics as the music. It had to mean something. The minute I heard the first Clash album I said, "That is a really important, landmark album".

'I remember saying, "If kids in London or Manchester think their life is rubbish, why isn't this happening in Northern Ireland? There must be something going on in Belfast, surely?" Subsequently, that's what I found out to be the case.'

Gordon and Colin became friends, talking about music and books, and the visiting journalist revealed his punk affections. Colin recalls it thus: 'He said, "Northern Ireland should be the place that punk rock comes from – because the kids are disaffected. My God, they're run into the ground here." And I said, "Funny you should say that. I've been meaning to go up and see this guy – he has a band called Stiff Little Fingers". He said, "Where?" I said, "Friday night, they're playing up at the Glenmachan".'

It was November 14 1977. The roof of the Stables was still leaking. Stiff Little Fingers had some drama getting their backline to this, their fourth gig. They played their cover versions and the two journalists were startled, as Colin notes:

'I'd say there was about 20 people there. And they were a bit shoddy looking on stage and there was a bit of feedback. But then when they started to play and they really got into their groove, if you like, Gordon turned to me and said, "Well, if this is a garage band they must have spent a lot of time in a fucking garage". We had a sort of an Epstein moment – "Shit, these guys are good…" – y'know. I'd managed bands before so I knew a bit of what to look for. Gordon was basing it on what he had heard in the punk rock genre. So, we met the band after the gig and they said, "What do you think?" We said, "We're very impressed".'

They set up a meeting two weeks later at the Shaftesbury Inn on the

Antrim Road. They talked about helping the band with PR. Gordon had an additional surprise. When he'd returned home after the Glenmachan gig, he had written his first ever lyric. Just as the Clash had taken their name from a headline in London's *Evening Standard*, so Ogilvie was thinking of an impactful phrase that was used often in Belfast journalism. Small, incendiary bombs were often placed in city centre stores, hidden in clothing or behind shop fittings, timed to go off after closing time to destroy the premises. These were suspect devices.

'Gordon always had this aspiration,' Colin says, 'to have his name on a Top 10 single. He turned up at the next meeting, unbeknown to me – I didn't know he was doing this – and he gave Jake some lyrics. It was 'Suspect Device'.'

In the lyric, the young person has become the violent weapon, primed and manipulated by the warmongers, wired into a system of fear and obligation. The conflict has been perpetuated in this way, causing the death tally to reach 2,000. The anguish in the song is due to a moment of self-knowledge. At least one voice has become aware that the game is fixed and the cards are marked. '*It's time the bastards fell*,' is the determination. And if a mind can be engineered to inflict damage then it follows that the harm can be directed back to the perpetrator. Like a bomb with a faulty timer, it can explode in the user's face.

'In a way,' Gordon says, 'it's a pacifist song, written in a very aggressive style. A lot of the problem was because kids on either side of the divide just followed on and did what their parents told them to do. I've always had a great respect for teenage rebellion. The lyrics are essentially saying, don't be a kid caught up in this. Don't perpetuate it. Find some way to stop it happening.'

This was the proposition that was delivered to Jake near the close of 1977. At the time of the meeting with Gordon and Colin, the death total from the conflict was 1,978. By the time the song had been recorded and released, the toll was 2,012. The notion of writing about the Northern Ireland situation has been discussed on the night of the Glenmachan show. Now there was a script.

Jake was enthused. 'To say that a light came on in my head would be an understatement. Whole bloody firework displays went off.' He had already written a song on the subject called 'State of Emergency' and the band had supposed that they had used up all their Troubles material. Now Jake felt he had been given 'permission' to go further.

'I'd been playing in cover version bands and been singing songs about bowling down Californian highways when I'd never been further west than Galway in my life, and it just didn't connect to me. To hear the Clash singing about growing up in West London suddenly struck a huge chord with me. So, when Gordon suggested writing songs about where we grew up, I jumped on it because I thought, "Yes, this is exactly what we should be doing".

'I was a bit concerned that it probably wouldn't have an audience outside of Northern Ireland. But at that time, I didn't really much care because I felt that there was enough going on around in my life, and obviously in the lives of everybody who was living there at the time, that it merited actually singing about. Because, apart from us, what the hell else did I know about? I don't really know what sort of reaction we were expecting. We were hoping that it would ring a bell with people at home and if nothing else make them sort of stop and say, "Aye, that is actually what living here is like".'

Critics of the band suggested that they were coerced or exploited by their media-savvy handlers – something that Jake consistently denied. Gordon argues instead that the working partnership was mutually respectful. 'I had nothing whatsoever to do with the music. The first time I heard it, I thought, "This is gonna rain down. People are not gonna forget this." He first played the music he wrote for 'Suspect Device' at a rehearsal and within seconds he played 'Wasted Life', which he'd come up with totally off his own bat. And at that point I thought, "OK, this is happening but also, this is serious and this is these kids' lives and I'm certainly not gonna be any artist's Svengali character, just trying to rip them off and then disappear". To that extent it was a serious project.'

'Suspect Device' was recorded at the Downtown Radio eight-track studio on February 4 1978. Some vocals were added three days later. Business was handled by Rigid Digits, the management company and record label, administered by the two journalists who took a sixth of the income each.

Gordon was salaried as a war correspondent, so he had the cashflow. Colin had the showbiz contacts. He booked out-of-town gigs and arranged a single launch at the Glenmachan. For a limited run pressing of the record, he consulted Billy McBurney at Outlet Records, the man who had taken Barley Corn and 'The Men Behind the Wire' to the top of the Irish Charts in 1972. A Dublin pressing plant was hired for the job.

The flip side of the single was 'Wasted Life', another stormy denial of the paramilitaries and their recruiting officers. This was a Jake lyric, written about a local incident. He was also thinking of 'the roadblocks, the riots, the constant hassle, in fact the sheer paranoia of everyday life and how you almost felt suffocated by it'. So, the outburst of *'stuff their fucking armies'* is hoarse advice and it was heeded, as Ali McMordie explains: 'We met a couple of kids after a show who'd said that because of the influence of the band and the lyrics, they had thought twice about getting involved in the local paramilitaries. All party politics aside, that could have been a couple of lives saved.'

At the Shaftesbury Inn meeting, Gordon had shown Jake some sample artwork. It was a picture taken by a *Daily Express* photographer at a police press conference. The RUC had intercepted a cache of IRA bombing equipment, and they were on a table for inspection – rows of suspect devices. Gordon took the image and made it into a rough inlay card, slotting it into a cassette case. He gave it to Jake along with the song lyrics: 'we could market it like this.'

This became the single sleeve, delivered on March 17 1978 ahead of the Belfast launch gig 12 days later. Most media contacts were sent the vinyl for their consideration, but a few were sent the tracks on cassette, packaged with the mock-up explosive image. There was also a press release that stated: 'This is one terrorist incendiary cassette that will not go off in your face, but we reckon the music inside will still blow you away'. They were sent to media agencies and record companies in London. There was talk of panicked reactions in music business offices.

'I think it was Gordon's idea,' says Henry. 'Putting them in the cassette with the wiring printed and things on it, obviously it's a publicity stunt. But coming from Belfast at the time we thought, "It's either gonna get you noticed or it's gonna get you into trouble". So, we thought, "Well, what have we got to lose?" Looking back on it now, okay, it's a bit corny, but it was like, you gotta use what you've got that you can use. And that's what we did.'

Colin McClelland concurs. 'Nobody would be stupid enough to look at it and think, "Oh, this is a letter bomb". And I think it gained a bit of purchase. We said nothing to contradict it, 'cos it seemed to be getting a bit of publicity and we just let it go.'

'There weren't more than half a dozen,' Gordon says. 'They were only sent to record companies. They employed a black and white photo of an incendiary device that the IRA were using at the time. Now, I've heard stories about how this caused panic in EMI or wherever, and people dropped them into buckets of water and stuff, but that has to be complete and utter bollocks. Because, quite clearly, it was a black and white photo. It was clearly packaging.'

John Peel played the record on his BBC Radio 1 show, mentioning the Belfast context and the subject matter. This was an important boost as the band felt overwhelmed by the volume of singles and the many sleeves they needed to put together, as Jake recalls:

'Five hundred records doesn't sound like a huge amount but you try sitting in a room with them, you know. It's like, "How the hell are we going to get rid of all of these?" Obviously, the idea was to sell them but we weren't businessmen; we'd no idea at all. So, we fired off copies to the likes of John Peel who, God bless him, played the record something like ten nights in a row.

'By that stage we had arranged to send copies across to Bruce's Records in Edinburgh, and to Rough Trade. At the time, we were basically cutting out photocopies of the sleeve, sticking it together, putting these records in the sleeve, putting them back in boxes and then packing the boxes on to a bread van which was doing a run from an Irish bakery across to Scotland. They went across on that to Edinburgh and then on down to London. The demand really went through the roof after John started playing the record and the little cottage industry of making the sleeves and re-bagging the record had reached fever pitch. We were doing this in the evening, listening to Peel's programme and it did actually get to the stage when we were sat, up to our eyes in Pritt Stick and bits of torn record sleeve, and he would play the record and we would literally all be screaming at the radio – "*Stop playing the feckin' record!*"

Up to this point, the band had been getting their critical feedback from local fanzines. The likes of *Private World, Alternative Ulster, Nine to Five* and *Laughing Gravy* served the scene with pithy invective, humour and a sense of connection. *Alternative Ulster* was jointly produced by Dave 'Angry' McCullough, Roger Pearson and Gavin Martin. The latter explained his position in a Radio Ulster punk documentary called *Year Zero*:

'The great thing for people who weren't able to make music about punk that was that there were so many other opportunities. You could write and make your own magazines. People were motivated to get together for something bigger than themselves – looking for a community outside the restrictions that every institution, political party and paramilitary had administered as being the way. No – *this* is the way things are, and the fanzine culture was very important to disseminate this. This was a bush telegraph.'

Alternative Ulster had asked Jake for a song that they might use as a flexidisc (a similar proposal with Rudi had mutated into the first Good Vibrations single release, 'Big Time'). Jake obliged in February, using the fanzine title to imagine an empowered, shared space, the punks united against the bigots. Jake says he was chiefly the author of the song, although Gordon had provided the wordplay of '*alter your native land*'. The song was declined by the fanzine but Stiff Little Fingers had another flaming tune in the songbook. Also, they were working on their version of Bob Marley's 'Johnny Was'. Some liberties were taken with the words, Henry says:

'I think we were up in Gordon's flat and he was playing the album *Rastaman Vibration*. We knew the Clash had done [Lee Perry's] 'Police and Thieves' and we liked their version of that. And it was like, you know, it would be good to put a cover on the album. The original version we did on a demo changed the names. It was like, '*Paddy was a good man*', '*Frankie was a good man*', '*Billy was a good man*' – we changed the names all the time. And then we just left it to the original.'

'Alternative Ulster' was released in October, delayed by a frustrating experience with Island Records. They had stepped back from a deal, apparently because the label boss Chris Blackwell didn't see their international potential. A new independent imprint, Rough Trade, agreed to put it out as a 50/50 business split. Again, the artwork for the record was provocative. The single cover showed a British soldier on patrol on the Springfield Road, pointing his rifle around the side of a battered, concrete pillar. His crouching position was directly across the road from the Henry Taggart Memorial Hall, a military base and one of the sites of the Ballymurphy killings in 1971. A little boy in a parka jacket looked down from the top of the post, laughing and unafraid. The image was the work of *Daily Express* staff photographer Milton Haworth and had been taken in 1974. The five-year-old child was later identified as a local, John Brannigan. Milton describes the photographic moment:

'The picture was taken when I got wind of shots being fired at an army patrol. I raced to the area and stationed myself behind a wall, parallel with a couple of soldiers as the army searched the area. As I focused on one of the squaddies, up popped this cheeky young scamp and started mugging for the camera. It isn't a montage. It's exactly as shot.'

Gordon had co-opted another memorable image. He was not inhibited by the Northern Irish sense of caution, as Colin explains:

'He had a broader view of what you could do. We were incredibly parochial when I think back on it. We'd never think of sending something to a well-known name in England. That was just unheard of. Or even Dublin. But Gordon didn't see anything wrong with that. It wasn't that he initiated anything, he just made us feel comfortable with the idea: why not?'

'Alternative Ulster' had started as a squalling tantrum about the lack of social amenities in Belfast, but the lyric carried extra weight and the band and its audience invested in its meaning. It became their most important song. Brian Faloon considers this:

'It did become an anthem. Yes, we might have pushed it a little bit in terms of our anger. There were people who were far more repressed than we were; for example, in our area we weren't getting nightly visits from the British Army, kicking in doors and stuff. That was happening on the Falls Road, or in the New Lodge or Whiterock or wherever. But we realised that was happening, that there's a level of repression going on which outweighs any conscionable action.'

And in Belfast, he notes, Stiff Little Fingers were attacked by the community papers on both sides:

'I remember reading both the *Woodvale News* and *An Phoblacht* on the other side. And both of them criticised us quite heavily for the stand that we took. We thought, "We must be doing something right if they're both pissed off at us". Because the stand was, you've got nothing to offer anybody, other than sectarianism or death or imprisonment or a life of fear, which you also subject the rest of us to. So, lyrically and musically, we had no truck with them; so equally, we were criticised. That was great.'

A 28-date 'Out of the Darkness' UK tour with the Tom Robinson Band put Stiff Little Fingers before an audience that was young and receptive. Tom was singing about sexual politics (notably, 'Glad to Be Gay') and fronting the Westminster establishment. So, if his Belfast support act was also tilting at prejudice and systemic failure, there were many ears prepared to listen. Even so, Brian Faloon was surprised. 'We'd get 17-year-olds coming back, full of enthusiasm for what we were doing – both musically and in the context of what we were trying to say. That took us aback.'

Tom Robinson had promoted his *Power in the Darkness* album with a 12-inch stencil, packed into the album sleeve. It had been designed at the Socialist Workers' Party print shop in London and it depicted the Gay Liberation fist, a variation on the Black Power salute. There was a proviso that 'this stencil is not meant for spraying on public property'. It was an integral part of the singer's branding, and there were no qualms about taking this image to their gig at the Whitla Hall in Belfast. In the city, Ian Paisley and his followers in the Free Presbyterian Church were still railing against the partial liberalisation of homosexuality in the UK and had presented their own campaign, Save Ulster from Sodomy, in 1977. They had attracted 70,000 signatories. Tom Robinson was pleased to note that not everyone had signed up and also that the stencil was doing its work:

'When we went to Belfast, Catholic kids took us on a guided tour of The Falls. And there was the fist, on the ends of buildings.'

Stiff Little Fingers were invited to play at the second large-scale Rock

Against Racism event at Brockwell Park, Brixton on September 24 with Elvis Costello and Aswad. They took a place on the bill after Sham 69 had received death threats from right-wing elements of their fanbase (Jimmy Pursey did, however, make a speech at the gig). This was a significant event for SLF since a right-wing minority continued to view them as anti-IRA and, therefore, on their particular side. There was also a deal of confusion over the anti-racist lyrics of 'White Noise' when the bigoted name-calling was sometimes taken at face value. 'People would Sieg Heil at a few shows,' Jake remembered, 'and a couple of times it descended into punch-ups. Any band that was perceived as punk was fair game.'

There were issues with Loyalists at the Merville Inn in Belfast and an IRA threat when they played in Drogheda. 'The local boys had warned the promoter that he should not be putting this band on,' says Ali. 'The promoter was actually persuaded by the fact that the show was packed out by quite a few punters. To see what all the buzz was about.' Still, satire was a problematic weapon, and this issue followed the band on a later song, 'Fly the Flag'. It was a send-up of patriotism, but Henry remembers a few instances when the irony was missed:

'We used to get people throwing things at us when we played it in Dublin. I don't think they got the point of it. 'Fly the Flag' used to get to people, for years, when we played in the Republic. Obviously, that's a generalisation because there were a lot of people who did understand it, of course. But, yeah, it got us into a few scrapes.'

The debut album *Inflammable Material* was released on February 2 1979. While there were some vocal critics at home, the band was warmly recognised by writers such as *NME*'s Paul Morley. Again, it was the independent label Rough Trade that managed the release and the astonishing logistics of getting a DIY record into the UK charts. 'It was definitely the first completely independent to ever break the official UK Top 20,' Jake says. 'It went in one place higher than Barry Manilow's *Greatest Hits*, which I was always really proud of. It actually did go into the charts on my 21st birthday so that was the best present you could have ever hoped for.'

Also, there was 'Barbed Wire Love', a star-crossed conflict ballad with a doo-wop breakdown. Somewhere between Shakespearian tragedy and the maudlin schlock of vintage weepers like 'Leader of the Pack'. Stiff Little Fingers, with the assistance of a bottle of vodka, had written themselves out of a depressive state (freshly rejected by Island Records, Brian had announced his departure) by loading up on terrible puns and mocking their own seriousness. Henry was teetotal, but he was happy to participate:

'There's 13 tracks on that album and I think five of them were about Northern Ireland, which people sort of tend to overlook. But they were all very serious. So, we thought, "Is there a way we could do a light-hearted song about the Troubles but not be offensive?" It was basically a case of sitting down and coming up with the most ridiculous lines – *'you set my Armalite'*. The whole point was to say, "Okay, it's bad, it's dark times, but people still live and have fun", and I think that was the whole point. We got people who would say, "Is it about drugs? You set my arm alight?" People don't know what an Armalite [assault rifle] is, which is fair enough – why should you?

'A few weeks ago, we [Henry's current band XSLF] were doing a gig down in Drogheda and a guy came up to me and he said, "When you guys came out, I was one of the guys walking around with black flags and during the days of the Troubles I would have signed up for the IRA… and I heard *Inflammable Material* and it really made me think." He actually said to me, "I want to thank you for that". It can sound corny but it's nice to hear. I'm not one of the ones who says that *Inflammable Material* changed everybody's life – but it changed some people's.'

Jim Reilly was their new drummer. The band had transitioned to a major label, Chrysalis Records, and a series of *Top of the Pops* appearances. The lyrical outlook broadened, but still there was attrition in tracks such as 'Tin Soldiers' and 'Piccadilly Circus'. Henry had decided to remain in Belfast while the others had decamped to London. He wrote 'Gate 49', a reference to the departure gate at Heathrow Airport and his personal exit strategy.

The band split in 1983, but reformed with popular assent in 1987. The line-ups have changed – Henry and Jim play separately as XSLF – but the band has a valued place in the punk pantheon. 'I don't think anybody can accuse Stiff Little fingers of jumping on the bandwagon because they never jumped off,' Brian Faloon reckons. Colin McClelland has also thought about the legacy:

'They were articulating what an awful lot of the kids felt. Because they didn't have a voice, there was nobody representing anybody under 20, except musicians. Those things filter out from a core. There are the adherents, the punk rock fanatics who know every word and that becomes their philosophy. But the philosophy does tend to spread out into non-punk areas. I think the impact was that in the absence of basic rights – that the conflict had imposed upon people – this was a voice, somebody to support, talking on your behalf.

'What effect did that have? It certainly didn't change what the politicians were doing. It didn't change what the paramilitaries were doing. But I think that if you're looking for a flag to assemble under, they provided a flag, and gave people just a sense of identity, that you're not alone. It's hard to take it any further than that.'

CASBAH ROCK

Feargal Sharkey's father Jim had wired up the Radio Free Derry equipment in Rossville Flats back in 1969. He was an officer in the Electrical Trades Union, he had served in the Irish Army and was a member of the Derry Labour Party. When he took part in the Civil Rights Association marches, he wore a shirt and tie, like many men of his generation. His wife Sibéal was the Registrar of the *Féis Dhoíre Cholmcílle*, otherwise known as the Derry *Féis*. This took pace in the Guildhall every Easter Week, a feverish contest of Irish singing, dancing, verse, storytelling and drama.

Feargal helped out in the weeks before, delivering the competitor tickets across town on his bicycle on the promise of a fish supper from Duddy's chipper. During the *Féis* itself, Sibéal was completely taken up by the event so Jim took the week off work and cooked up a quantity of stew for the family. Feargal was a competitor also, taking singing lessons from James McCafferty and his uncle Sammy Burke, and was often rewarded in the categories of Boys Solo and Duets, alongside Mary Simms. His rendition of 'How Soft Upon the Evening Air' apparently left an adjudicator in tears. He also featured in the St Peter's CBS Choir that he'd joined to avoid school hurling practice. Feargal was an exceptional singer in a city like no other.

'On a daily basis, there was an awful lot going on,' he says. 'I remember walking to the Creggan estate from the Christian Brothers' School and seeing these palls of smoke everywhere. Derry was a working-class city.

There were high levels of unemployment and a lot of disruption. There was the Civil Rights movement and the right to vote. But you saw all that as normal. The remarkable thing about the human spirit is that you just get on with it. Especially if you're 15 or 16, and you're interested in music and you're with these other teenagers who want to form a band.'

The Undertones had bought their gear with credit vouchers from an instrument shop in Raphoe, Donegal. They learnt songs by the Rolling Stones, Cream and Fleetwood Mac and after they'd sourced records from a mate, Domnhall McDermott, they were up to speed with the Stooges, the New York Dolls and the Ramones. They finessed their set during an 18-month residency at the Casbah in Derry, a basic venue at the corner of Orchard Street and Bridge Street, set over a bomb site. The Casbah had no stage and punters were forbidden to pogo because it played havoc with the drinks shelves. If the young punks tried, Big Tony the barman would flick them with wet tea towels.

'It was a dinky and lovely place,' Feargal reckons. 'It was basically a Portacabin. I believe it was dropped on top of the remains of the previous build. There was a lot of remodelling going on in Derry on a daily basis. It was an alternative to town planning. The outside of the Casbah had been covered in chicken wire and cement and was made to look vaguely Moroccan. There were two people at the first gig we played there (February 24 1977), but the barman let us back because he thought we were funny.'

Feargal was keen on Led Zeppelin and worked with Radio Rentals during the 1975 boom when Derry switched to colour television. He had the use of the company van and he made basic PA speakers that he could sing out of. The Undertones bickered plenty and, by early 1978, they were on the verge of splitting and had to persuade Sharkey to stay for what they believed might be a legacy release. A series of English labels had already rejected their demo tracks and when John O'Neill heard the second Buzzcocks album, he felt that his band was after the event. They were not even sure about the merit of Feargal's tremulous voice, according to bassist Michael Bradley.

'It wasn't until people remarked on it that we realised that it was a very distinctive voice. But we used to have problems with him singing. I remember the early demos, and the singing was exactly what you would

ABOVE On the road to Derry, January 1969 (*Northern Ireland Civil Rights*). BELOW Juke Boy Bonner during rehearsals at the Albert Hall, London, October 3 1969 (*Val Wilmer*).

ABOVE LEFT *Melody Maker* cover story on Rory Gallagher in Belfast, January 8 1972. ABOVE RIGHT The Abercorn, Castle Lane, Belfast. BELOW Radio Free Derry, Eamon Melaugh wears welding goggles for the camera, 1969 (*Open Reel Productions Ltd.*). OPPOSITE John Lennon and Yoko Ono on the *Oz* March, London, August 11 1971.

ABOVE The Miami Showband, May 1975: Tony Geraghty,
Fran O'Toole, Ray Miller, Des Lee, Brian McCoy and
Stephen Travers. OPPOSITE The Clash on the Crumlin
Road, Belfast, October 20 1977 (*Adrian Boot*).

ABOVE Terri Hooley outside the original Good Vibrations
shop, 102 Great Victoria Street, Belfast. OPPOSITE Brian Young
from Rudi at the Pound, Belfast, 1979 (*Alastair Graham*).

ABOVE Jake Burns from Stiff Little Fingers at the Pound,
Belfast, January 1979 (*Alastair Graham*). OPPOSITE Feargal
Sharkey from the Undertones at the Pound, Belfast,
December 1978 (*Alastair Graham*).

ABOVE Greg Cowan and Colin 'Getty' Getgood from the Outcasts in the Crown Bar, Belfast, 1984 (*Alastair Graham*). BELOW Ruefrex at the Harp Bar, Belfast, 1979 (*Alastair Graham*). OPPOSITE Elvis Costello live at Maysfield Leisure Centre, Belfast, June 3, 1983 (*Alastair Graham*).

ABOVE Bananarama at the funeral of Thomas 'Kidso' Reilly,
Belfast, August 12 1983 (*Pacemaker Press International*).
OPPOSITE Bono at the King's Hall, Belfast during the
Joshua Tree Tour, June 24 1987 (*Alastair Graham*).

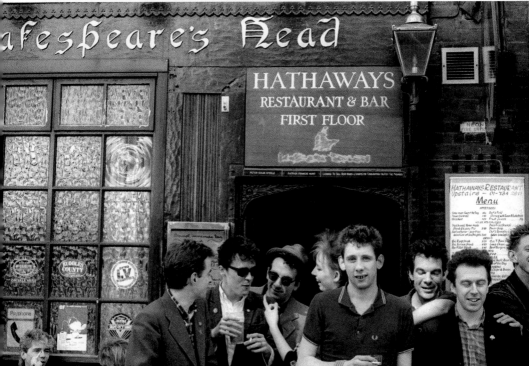

ABOVE Sinead O'Connor and Christy Moore, Olympia Theatre, Dublin, July 17 1988 (*Derek Speirs*). BELOW Christy Moore meets Special Branch in Dublin, May 5 1981 (*An Phoblacht*). OPPOSITE, ABOVE That Petrol Emotion, 1987 (*Steve Double*). OPPOSITE, BELOW The Pogues, Elvis Costello and Alex Cox during the video shoot for 'A Pair of Brown Eyes'. Carnaby Street, London, 1985 (*Alastair Graham*).

ABOVE David Trimble, Bono, John Hume, Waterfront
Hall, Belfast, May 19 1998 (*Pacemaker Press International*).
BELOW 'Please' artwork for the U2 single, 1997.

hear on the first LP, but Billy [Doherty, the drummer] said it was terrible. You basically went along thinking your band was awful.'

Billy had begun to phone in and write to John Peel, who would read out dedications. The band would tape the show and then play out the messages before the gig started on a Friday evening. Meantime, a Derry associate called Bernie McAnaney was at Queen's University in Belfast and campaigning for a Good Vibrations release. He said the band was going to break up if they didn't get a decent chance. Terri Hooley, in a typically random moment, promised an answer by the time he had crossed to road to Lavery's Gin Palace on Bradbury Place. Sure, he said, they were on the label.

The studio budget was £200. Terri was outraged when they tried to charge him VAT. The Undertones had played the McMordie Hall in Belfast on June 14 with Rudi, the Outcasts, the Idiots and the Detonators – a fundraiser for the anarchist project, Just Books. Next day, they set up in Wizard Studios, a modified clothing warehouse above Commercial Court. Four tracks, essentially recorded live, with an allocation for mixing a few days later. Davy Shannon set up the controls. Brothers John and Damien O'Neill constantly asked for their individual guitar levels to be raised until the fuzz quotient was perfectly overloaded.

They had worked through their Beatles records into girl-pop originals by the Shirelles and the Marvelettes, into soaring productions by Phil Spector with the Ronettes and the Crystals. John O'Neill was a fan of the songwriting partners Jerry Leiber and Mike Stoller. Their tunes had been put to use by Elvis but it was those lyrics with the Coasters, like 'Charlie Brown' and 'Yakety Yak' that best captured the aches, scrapes and frustrations of youth. The guitarist also loved the soundtrack to *American Graffiti*, released in 1973. All this had a bearing on 'Teenage Kicks'. The titled hinted at 'Route 66'. Likewise, 'Teenage Lust' by the MC5. And then Feargal took the heartbreak to another, overwhelming level.

'We had already made cassette recordings in Mrs Simm's shed,' says Sharkey, 'and then we'd made a demo on a four-track studio at Magee University in Derry. So, when we got to Wizard Studios, we weren't particularly overawed about what we had to do in four hours. By the time we did that session, we were pretty good.'

The release date was August 31. Hooley had taken a box of records to London but the industry was not impressed. He got a copy into John Peel's pigeonhole while the band worked other connections to the DJ. Within two weeks Peel had broken the broadcasting codes: playing all four tracks on a show, cuing 'Teenage Kicks' twice in a row. Peter Powell made it his record of the week and when Peel heard it played during that slot he pulled the car to the side of the road, weeping uncontrollably.

Seymour Stein, boss of Sire Records, caught the record on the Peel show and dispatched his charge, Paul McNally, to Derry to sort out a deal. Terri Hooley was out of his depth and largely uninterested in the finances. Eventually, he settled for £1,000 while Feargal and Mickey tried to negotiate a deal for the band in London, claiming that Derry's finest were on a par with the Clash and the Rich Kids. They walked away with a worse deal than the Bay City Rollers but they were on *Top of the Pops* within weeks and John O'Neill had plenty to offer yet. Again, there was appreciation for Terri. This time it was John who put a value on his contribution:

'He was like Neal Cassady, without the amphetamines – he had the energy of a speeding train about to go off the rails and, at first, I found it quite overwhelming. However, when we discussed music, you'd tell straight away he knew what he was talking about and how much passion he felt about it.'

Feargal had a dalliance with plastic trousers but the Undertones essentially wore the regulation issue of corner boys: leather bombers, straight jeans, Wrangler jackets and the snorkel jacket by Lord Anthony, outfitter to the working class. Footwear was black brogues or the famous boots with bouncing soles. 'They were just boys from the Bog,' says the actress, singer and admiring neighbour, Bronagh Gallagher. It was street credibility, though perhaps not as London scenesters knew it.

'It did mark us out from the dour, God-love-us punk bands,' Bradley reckons. 'Also, we were in a good position in that we came from a *bona fide* place where it was hard. It's not like we came from the leafy suburbs of some English town. I'm from Creggan, Feargal's from Rosemount and John and Damian are from the Bog. So, we didn't have to tell people about it because it was fairly obvious.'

Interviews with the London media were difficult in that many of the journalists could not understand their accents, and blithely stated so. The band members were frequently written up as gauche outsiders. They tended to be inward-facing, talking about girlfriends, homesickness and their low opinion of the music business. They were never fans of Stiff Little Fingers though, even writing the vindictive 'Whizz Kids' as a gesture to the Belfast band and stressing that they would be measured for the music, not the context. 'We don't want people to feel sorry for us,' John repeated.

They tried to explain the city geography to the music press, how the few Derry venues were on the west bank of the Foyle and that some Protestants across the river on the Waterside preferred to see the band when they played Portrush, 40 miles away. 'They're too frightened to go along in Derry,' Sharkey told the *NME*. 'Once they're inside, wherever we're playing, the reaction is exactly the same.'

Feargal was resilient, even though he was often abused in Derry. 'People would actually run across the road to spit on him,' Terri recalls. The singer told another writer that 'most of the young people over 16 despise us. I haven't a fucking clue why.' Then again, it was not just recent form. 'I was slagged all the time back in secondary school. I had a real tough time just 'cos I wasn't one of the boot boys. It was all wrecking things and vandalism and I wasn't one of the boys.'

The Undertones were also wary of how they would be marketed by Sire Records, as Michael relates:

'I remember a record company ad, a radio ad, which we managed to stop. It was a voiceover for the first LP that said, '*they fought their way from the war-torn streets of Derry*'. We just laughed. We were smart enough to realise, nah, don't do that.'

There was another form of escape, afforded by Derry's proximity to the border. John saw his first live band on a summer holiday in Donegal. 'We were only 20 minutes away from beautiful beaches, gorgeous countryside and a normal environment. My first experience of hearing live music was in a bar in Bundoran when I was about 13. The band was playing a mixture of traditional Irish tunes and rebel songs. That was what inspired me to first learn to play the guitar. My point here is that, even though we were living through some horrific and politically unsettling times, I still have great memories of long summers in Donegal and I suppose that helped me gain a less negative perspective on life that definitely seemed more prevalent in Belfast.'

His brother Damian remembers the flip side of the experience. He had missed the Civil Rights march in Derry on Bloody Sunday, 1972. Instead, he was at home at 22 Beechwood Avenue, watching the TV highlights of Chelsea and Arsenal games on *The Big Match*:

'You heard the shooting from our house. You can see down the Bogside, quite a distance. You saw lots of people just running for their lives and then my dad came up about 40 minutes later, white as a sheet, saying, "Where's your mum, where's your mum?" He didn't know, she hadn't come up. So, he went flying back down again 'cos he had lost her when they'd ran. All that affects you, you know? And I remember writing a diary about it. Unfortunately, I threw the diary out because after Operation Motorman [a large-scale military operation in 1972 to enforce law in 'no go' areas], we thought if the army raided your house and seen some diary, they'd arrest you – and I was paranoid. So I burnt it. I wish I kept it to this day, just to see what an 11-year-old thought.'

The TV presenter David Frost put together a report on Bloody Sunday, broadcast on London Weekend Television, February 6 1972. *The Frost Programme* talked to people on the Bogside in Derry and also on the Shankill Road in Belfast. John McKeague had been active with the Shankill Defence Association and in 1972 he was developing a new paramilitary organisation, the Red Hand Commando. On the TV programme, he stated that 'Bloody Sunday was a good Sunday'.

'I remember being outraged,' says Damian. 'I think Bloody Sunday politicised me. About being a Catholic more than anything – the injustice, second-class citizenship thing. And then, later, the British Government propping up Stormont and how wrong that was.'

On August 11 1979, the *NME* news pages announced an ambitious Derry gig, featuring the Clash, the Undertones, the Boys, SHAKE (with Jo Callis, ex-Rezillos) and new local act the Moondogs. The date was Saturday, August 25, the location was outside the Templemore Sports Complex and admission would be free. The Undertones had played four nights at the Marquee in London (August 1-4) to raise the finances to make it achievable. There was a quote in the paper from Feargal who was understandably positive. 'There's so little live rock in Derry, so we want the festival to be accessible to everyone in the community. We hope it will be a trouble-free day for everyone.'

There was even a press shot of the band and their London headliners outside Wessex Sound Studios in Highbury, north London where the Clash were recording *London Calling*. This bold proposition might attract upwards of 50,000 people, the organisers hoped. When the Boys pulled out, they found a better replacement with the Damned, so now there were two seminal punk acts and no admission charge.

A week later, an *NME* courier delivered a letter to Wessex Studio for the urgent attention of the Clash. The newspaper's Editor, Neil Spencer, had written a cautionary note at the front of it: 'I don't know if this is serious, but you should have it.' The attached letter was dated August 14. It was hand-written in red ink in block capitals, over three pages. The author was S.V., Commanding Officer, Londonderry Battalion, Red Hand Commandos (*sic*). It was essentially a death threat against Clash singer Joe Strummer, pertaining to be from the Loyalist paramilitary group.

During the UK election season that May, Joe Strummer had taken part in a political vox pop for the *NME*. When he was asked what his agenda might be if he was the elected national leader, he stated that Troops Out was on his manifesto. This is what the letter writer was objecting to.

'WE HAVE THEREFORE COME TO AN AGREEMENT THAT THIS MAN... JOE STRUMMER SHALL BE EXECUTED IF HE ENTERS ULSTER WE SHALL NOT PERMIT NO MAN TO ENTER OUR COUNTRY IF HE CONDEMNS OUR CROWN AND HERITAGE AND OPENLY BACKS THE IRA.'

There was an option in the note, stating that Joe's sentence might be lifted if he was to make it public that his statement was 'A GROSS MISTAKE' and that troops were indeed needed in Northern Ireland. The note continued:

'WE ARE SORRY TO DO THIS AS WE WELCOME ALL BANDS WHO COME TO ULSTER TO ENTERTAIN OUR BRETHREN... BUT NO MAN SHALL PERFORM IF HE CONDEMNS THE PROTESTANT RELIGION AND HELPS THE IRA WAR MACHINE.'

In closing, the letter noted that the festival was being held in 'AN IRA

SECTOR' and signed off with the admonition, 'TAKE HEED THIS THREAT IS FOR REAL'.

Johnny Green, Road Manager and trusted fixer with the Clash remembered that the singer's face turned white when he read it. The other band members also looked over the note and the consensus was that the gig plans should be pulled. They rang the *NME* offices and Neil Spencer supposed that the warning might be legitimate. They showed it to Elvis Costello, who was on a passing visit, and he was alarmed. However, Joe asked Johnny to look into the logistics of the day and to see if potential danger could be eliminated. They examined ferry routes and thought about travelling in disguise. Johnny got site plans and figured out whether the band could be brought in by helicopter. But space around Templemore was limited, and besides, there were windows overlooking the site and the stage where a sniper could take up a position. Reluctantly, they decided that the gig was potentially fatal.

Joe, Mick Jones and their manager visited the Undertones at Eden Studios in Acton where they were recording. Joe stated their position.

'He was a wee bit embarrassed about it,' says Michael, 'because he says to us, "Look what I've got", and showed us the letter. We kind of looked at the letter from somebody claiming to be from the Red Hand Commando – it was written in fairly bad kind of writing – and we said, "It's not genuine". Don't know if we asked for a code word or anything but we kind of went, that's probably not genuine.

'We were so naïve that we said, "This concert's in Shantallow, so the Red Hand Commandos will not come there". We realise now it was a very parochial thing to say. But it wouldn't wash with them, so we had to cancel. It brought home to Joe that it's OK posing in the *NME* with a H-Block T-shirt, but when you come to Northern Ireland, people will take grave offence and may wish to injure you.'

The Undertones were invited to America with the Clash on their 'Take the Fifth' tour. Damian reckons they got the offer due to Clash guilt over the Derry cancellation. 'I think they offered us the tour because they felt really bad about it.' Michael remembers being elated. 'I suppose like any first time in America it was it was absolutely brilliant. They had just finished recording *London Calling* but it hadn't actually come out so they were playing the songs live and we heard them for the first time. We were sitting there, just awestruck with them. They were really nice to us, they talked to us when we did soundchecks and they were great.'

The tour ended on September 26 in Toronto. The Undertones heard that the Clash were going to have a party in their honour.

'We thought, "We need to get them something, a present", so we got them Mike Nesmith hats with the bobbles and all and we got them toy guns. I don't know if they took it in the way it was intended – maybe they just thought we were really stupid – but we started to give them all this stuff to gently take the piss out of them.'

'At the time,' says Damian, 'they were wearing their gangster chic – their trilbys and their big coats – so we thought, "Right, let's buy them toy guns".'

Ironically, as Stiff Little Fingers were moving away from political comment, the Undertones became less comfortable about their own style. By the time of their third album, *Positive Touch*, songwriter John O'Neill was feeling pressured to reflect the Derry experience in his lyrics. 'Crisis of Mine' was a meditation by John about his inability to write about the conflict:

'I suppose we were conscious of getting reviewed about coming from the north of Ireland, but we weren't writing songs about it and Stiff Little Fingers were the band seen to be doing that. I remember we played this club in Derry called Oscar's and it was like a matinee thing and the fella came up to me afterwards and he said, "Why do you not write songs about the war?" And I was going, "Well, Stiff Little Fingers do it really badly", which is what I felt at the time, and I found it very hard to write songs specifically about a particular topic, but it did get me thinking.

'I was trying to listen to more and more other forms of music and really getting into soul in a big way and discovering *What's Going On* by Marvin Gaye – coming from Motown and being a pop singer and then writing this kind of socially aware record. So, as I was trying to become as good a songwriter as possible, this was also going on in the back of my mind. Basically, that's what 'Crisis of Mine' was about; it was the crisis of trying to write a song about what's going on around you but not being good enough to do it.'

Another album track, 'You're Welcome', concerned the return of a Republican prisoner to his home in Derry. 'He was the first person I had ever met that had been inside and got released... I'd known his girlfriend had stayed with him the whole time he'd been inside.'

On April 28 1981, Joe Strummer interrupted a Clash gig in Madrid to make a speech that he'd written and learned in Spanish. He was wearing a black armband and wanted his audience to know about the Republican hunger strikes. Prisoners at the Maze in Northern Ireland were refusing food and demanding special category status, including the right to wear their own clothing, as befitted political prisoners. In response, the British Prime Minister Margaret Thatcher presented an unflinching public face. Joe had tested his speech in advance with a member of the touring party, Jock Scot. 'He told them about Bobby starving himself to death in a prison,' Jock later told the writer Chris Salewicz. 'He did his homework, he read up on it. He felt he had to have an opinion.'

A week earlier, the Undertones had released 'It's Going To Happen!'. It was a co-write between Michael and Damian, who had earlier delivered the most successful Undertones song, 'My Perfect Cousin'. The two writers have different recollections about the intent behind the 1981 release.

'Basically, it was me that came up with the tune,' Damian says, 'and the chorus was alluding to the hunger strikes. In fact, I did write some verses because I was really, really angry. I wish I'd kept the lyrics. They must have been really bad. It's so hard to write a political song without being contrived. So, I gave it to Mickey – "Rescue this please, do whatever you want". And he turned it into a pop song. He kept the chorus, *it's gonna happen all the time*. Without the meaning.'

The bass player says he was not aware of any such content in the song:

'If you're gonna write a song about the Troubles, it needs to be very, very good, subtle, to work on so many levels and be fantastic. That must have been in the back of our minds. It's easier to write an averagely good song about boy-meets-girl than it is about people losing their lives. I just know that Damian came up with the chorus. I don't remember seeing a verse, but I do know that he handed it to me and I thought, "I'll do something about some vague, paranoia type thing". It was only later on that Damian said it was going to be about the hunger strikes. Which sort of caught me on the hop. I don't remember him ever discussing it with me.

'Possibly, the pressure to write about the Troubles may have got to Damian and John. But I wouldn't know where to start writing about the hunger strikes. Because we still lived in Derry. You knew the tension was building, but the idea of writing about it wouldn't have had any impact on me. I know that if I was asked to write lyrics for a song that Damian had written about the hunger strikes, I would have said, "No, you're got the wrong man". People get a second-hand version of that story. They think, "Oh, that's the song about the hunger strikes". Sometimes, life is too short to explain to people.'

The band was invited to perform the song on *Top of the Pops* on May 5 1981. Bobby Sands died early that morning after 66 days without food. Damian wore a black armband during his performance:

'I only decided on the day and probably an hour before we were due on. That's probably why the rest of them didn't do it. I remember thinking, "That's fine, but I'm gonna do it". With hindsight it's just as well – for my professional career – that it didn't get spotted, because it could have got us into big trouble. But it was a big statement. Foolish but brave. I've said in the past that I've regretted it, but at the same time, I don't regret it. I really was fucking angry. We all were. Seething about the whole thing. About Thatcher, really. She was gonna let these people die over prison clothes.'

The Undertones split in 1983. According to Michael, the singer had further ambitions:

'During one of our many tedious meetings, the subject came up about a record. If a record came out and it wasn't a hit what would we all feel? I said to Feargal, "If it got a good review in the *NME* would you not be happy with that?" I remember Feargal saying, "Nah", and then I thought, "Right, that's the writing on the wall there". So, whenever the next record came out and it wasn't a hit I suppose we were just counting down to Feargal leaving. He had greater ambitions. He thought he could do better himself and, as I've said many times, he was right. Within a couple of years, he was a worldwide superstar.'

Feargal returned with 750,000 sales of 'A Good Heart'. He was top of the charts in 1985, mates with Dave Stewart and Jack Nicholson. He wore shirts by Yamamoto, co-wrote a bunch of songs, took lessons at the Actors Center, Los Angeles and was not concerned that *NME* gave him Worst Haircut in their annual awards. The success carried into a second album, with a guest appearance from Keith Richards. The Derry boy was preparing for a substantial record launch when a writer for *Record Mirror* randomly asked him about the U2 song, 'Sunday Bloody Sunday'. Sharkey's mood flipped:

'It really pissed me off. I was there at the time and I couldn't understand how Bono, sitting in his comfy house in Dublin, could pass comment on what was going on in my mind and in the minds of the other 25,000 people on the march that day when British troops opened fire on us. I always find it extremely arrogant for people who've never lived there and never really experienced it, to start writing songs about it.'

And while he was taking in the cloudless Californian skies, Sharkey had also been moved to write a lyric about partition in Ireland and a mythical quote – ascribed to both Edward Carson, original mainstay of the Northern Ireland state, and Ian Paisley. The Feargal song was called 'Blue Days':

'I got it from the Reverend Ian Paisley who said, "We will not forsake the blue skies of Ulster for the grey skies of an Irish Republic". I wrote that song because I believe, at the end of the day, despite sectarian differences, nobody is happy with what's going on in Ireland.'

That Petrol Emotion also arrived in 1985, featuring John and Damian. There was no holding back when they spoke to *NME*. They gave Stiff Little Fingers another bashing and promised to present Irish issues 'more explicitly'. John was already setting out the territory:

'The typical English view is that both sides (Protestant and Catholic) are as bad as each other, but really nothing will change in Northern Ireland until the Unionists give way – they are the bigots. In 20 years of Troubles in Ireland the Unionists haven't budged one iota. They are the reason why the IRA exists – and there would be much more violence without the IRA – and they are also actively supported by British political parties of both persuasions. Until the ordinary Protestant realises that, the Troubles are going to go on and on.'

IT'S A PROFESSIONAL CAREER

Elvis Costello is on *Top of the Pops* **in February 1979, miming to 'Oliver's Army', his biggest ever hit.** The tune is pretty, the chorus is memorable and Steve Nieve is a keyboard wonder, his right hand splashing and stabbing around the melody. He plays piano cascades, triple-timed in the manner of Abba's 'Dancing Queen'. This is a kind of punk heresy, yet the record is number two in the charts and their TV performance is loaded with wit and spite.

Costello and his band the Attractions have indeed been listening to Abba on the tour bus, washed down with alcohol and other substances. The line between sincerity and sarcasm has become messy but his new songs are able to flip between so many contrary positions. This keeps a lot of the new wavers on-side, endears him to the radio programmers and expands a few minds.

'Oliver's Army' might sound like a swooning pop song but the content is twisted and there's some history for anyone who cares to unpack it. The title refers to Oliver Cromwell, the Puritan leader who signed the death warrant of Charles I and then waged war in Ireland, a source of enduring hatred there. His campaign on the island (1649-53) caused massive civilian casualties, a combination of New Model Army brutality plus disease and famine. Upwards of 20% of the Irish population was lost, followed by deportations, land acquisition and anti-Catholic Penal Laws. For some, Cromwell was the ultimate folk devil.

Elvis Costello was born Declan MacManus, part of the Irish diaspora. His great-grandfather had moved from County Tyrone to Birkenhead, Merseyside. He died at a young age and his son Patrick joined the British Army as a teenager, was wounded in the Great War and was later stationed in Dublin, just ahead of the 1916 Rising. He was advised to keep his head down in advance of the Easter upheavals, a useful forewarning. Patrick's grandson Declan would later write up this story in a song called 'Any King's Shilling'.

The words to 'Oliver's Army' came together during the singer's first visit to Belfast when he played the Ulster Hall on St Patrick's night, 1978. On his way to the venue he saw some British soldiers on patrol. 'They looked like little kids,' he remembered, 'but they were little kids holding machine guns. You knew they'd come from towns that really looked no different from Belfast.'

He had finished the song by the time he arrived back in London. The lyric deals with armies abroad and the imperial wars that have taken them there. In his rough notes for the song, he wrote out locations such as Johannesburg, Hong Kong and Salisbury. He remembered the Control Zone security notices from Belfast lamp posts and he scribbled 'Mister Churchill' on his pad also. Early in the process he came up with the line, *'have you got yourself an occupation'*. It was reference to the Armed Forces recruitment drives that promised to give the unemployed a career and a skillset. For the unfortunate countries that were patrolled by such soldiers, the occupation meant another thing entirely.

And so 'Oliver's Army' was sweetly seething – the work of a third-generation Irishman who knew his history and who realised that the underclasses of Liverpool, Tyneside and London were going to be enlisted and then dropped into trouble spots. Civilian fatalities were just an inch of trigger away. 'They always get a working-class boy to do the killing,' Costello explained.

Around the same time, while Stiff Little Fingers toured the UK, a young recruit from Edinburgh called Alan began appearing at gigs. He inspired a song called 'Tin Soldiers', as Henry Cluney remembers: 'Him and a group of friends would follow us and come to every gig and they'd sleep in bus stations and the usual sort of thing and we got talking to him and it turns out he was AWOL, which was not a good thing. And that song came from him, it's specifically about him. He told us that whole story – about how he thought he was joining for two years and then they said, "No, your time doesn't start until the first two years is over".'

'He told me his tale one night on the road,' says Jake. 'The track was scheduled to be played on *Top of the Pops* and we had gone through the Musicians' Union thing of 're-recording' the day before or so only to be told that the lyrics 'were too real and might dissuade people from joining the armed forces', which of course was the whole point. As the record was a double A-side, the Beeb decided to go with 'Nobody's Hero', even though that meant miming to the actual record, something they were supposedly 'against' in those days.'

The Clash had a similar message in their song 'Tommy Gun' but David Bowie had prefigured them all in his 1972 track 'Star'. He sang about how the old street gang members had dissipated. Bevan got into politics, Rudi stayed home to starve and Johnny went to fight in Belfast.

Kate Bush had her say in 1980 with 'Army Dreamers', in which a mother waits for the corpse of her teenage son to arrive at the airbase. She mentions '*BFPO*' or British Forces Post Office, a service that is returning '*mammy's hero*'. She has a posy of purple flowers to mark his passing and she sighs that his life has been a waste. Like the foot soldiers in 'Oliver's Army', this boy has lacked the education or the finances to do anything else with his life. The song is written in waltz time and the recording mixes in parade ground commands and the sound of rifles being cocked. Talking to *Zig Zag* magazine, Kate explained the song's vocal intentions:

'The Irish accent was important because the treatment of the song is very traditional, and the Irish would always use their songs to tell stories, it's the traditional way. There's something about an Irish accent that's very vulnerable, very poetic, and so by singing it in an Irish accent it comes across in a different way.'

'Ruby Don't Take Your Love to Town' had been written about a veteran of the Korean War, but when Kenny Rogers had his hit with the song in 1969, his listeners supposed it was an anti-Vietnam protest. The story's development became stranger in 1981 when Gary Holton, stumblebum rocker and actor, took the song to another conflict. '*It wasn't me who started this old crazy Irish war*,' he bleated in the recording, which also featured keyboard player Casino Steele. In the video, he wandered around an urban riot zone with a rifle and flak jacket, more *Dad's Army* than Murder Mile. It was number one in Norway.

When the British Army arrived in Derry and Belfast in 1969, they had attempted to charm the locals with musical entertainment. This only increased the rivalry between the soldiers and the local males. Future political leader Gerry Adams protested against the army-run discos at the Henry Taggart Memorial Hall in 1970, setting up a picket at the Ballymurphy venue with the Sinn Féin women's branch. It was, he remembered, his first opportunity to organise the public opposition to the troops, focused on their 'attitude to womenfolk'. He later claimed that these actions ended the discos. By the summer, there were posters in West Belfast that underlined this message with the diktat, 'Don't Fraternise'. There were similar tensions in Derry when soldiers began socialising at the Embassy Ballroom.

On November 9 1971, Marta Doherty from the Bogside was shorn, tarred, and feathered for accepting the marriage proposal of a soldier. She was tied to a lamp post while a crowd shouted 'soldier lover'. Several other women received the same treatment, including a girl on the Falls Road in Belfast. There was to be no tolerance shown. Earlier, on March 10 1971, three Scottish soldiers were the first to die after socialising in Belfast, encouraged out of a bar and shot while they relieved themselves on a remote spot off the Ligoniel Road. City centres were essentially off-limits.

The flip side of the 1970 Clubsound record 'Belfast, Belfast' was called 'The Professionals'. Written by ex-serviceman Tommy Thomas, this was a comedy skit, introducing soldiers to their first tour of duty in Northern Ireland. A Brummie fusilier is confused by the language and the mannerisms but an interpreter is at hand. Later, there's a courtship scene at a home in Donegall Pass. The amorous soldier discovers an anti-handling device in the woman's underwear. She is worried about future consequences and complains to her lover: '*It's English fellas like youse 'uns that'll be getting me a baldy head.*' The serviceman offers to send her a wig from his next posting in Hong Kong.

The author Stuart Griffith sets his autobiographical *Pigs' Disco* in a later stage of the conflict. He is in the 3rd Battalion, Parachute Regiment, stationed at Palace Barracks in Holywood, County Down. Recreation is now almost wholly confined to the camp. The narrator ingests LSD and magic mushrooms in an attempt to cope with the stultifying conditions. Soldiers are watching German hardcore porn and Vietnam films such as *Apocalypse Now* – the latter is thought essential by the senior members of the platoon. There is a mural in the base that celebrates the recent killing of joyriders: the Vauxhall Astra has been 'built by robots, driven by joyriders, stopped by A Company'. Northern Ireland, he says, is described as the 'Live Training Area' and the combatants are 'barbaric and violent'.

Stuart, from Manchester, is detached from his fellow soldiers. He is listening to Pink Floyd and rave music and has some limited contact with the locals via a Sunday evening disco in the NAAFI Bar, also attended by vetted girls who have been given security clearance. The scenes are claustrophobic and brutish. 'It is, for many, an excuse to get violently drunk, naked and fall about in urine and vomit, while local girls dance around their handbags wearing the fashion garments of the day: tightly permed hair, padded-shoulder cocktail dresses and white stilettoes.'

The rest of the army battalions call them bird shit. 'There are only two things that fall from the sky,' they say, 'Paratroopers and bird shit.' Yet they seem to revel in their status. 'Crap hats' is their name for other military. 'You need this warped sense of elitism to get you through a theatre of war'.

There was a 1972 song about one of their own. Sergeant Michael Willetts from 3 Para was killed by an IRA bomb in the reception area of Springfield Road police station in 1971. He had died shielding civilians from the blast. The song, 'Soldier', was written by Harvey Andrews, who, like the deceased, was from Birmingham. Written in a folk vernacular, it tells of the subject's recruitment, his military journey and the posting to Belfast, *'another bloody chapter in an endless civil war'*. Across seven verses, Harvey sets up the serviceman's dilemma of being in a room with a bomb and with few options. The song is not patriotic. The soldier is described as a *'pawn lost in the game'*. Near the end of the piece, he suggests that the soldier's body had an abusive exit from the station.

> *'And the crowd they clapped and cheered and they sang their rebel song*
> *One soldier less to interfere where he did not belong.'*

'I was expecting a reaction,' says Harvey, 'but the continuing controversy has been beyond anything I could have imagined on the day I wrote the final word of the lyric. Over the years it has led to me getting some wonderful gigs and making lasting friendships as well as costing me work and causing me to be shunned in some quarters.

'I wanted people to realise that a soldier, just because he's wearing a uniform, does not suddenly become a non–human being. In this world, so many people are in situations they don't particularly want to be in. it's how you respond to that situation. And that what 'Soldier' was about – how he responded.'

There were passionate discussions about the song in the pages of *Folk Review*, starting with Leon Rosselson, who rebuked its 'catastrophic naivety', and supposed a flawed political outlook, 'which is, simply, that the role of the British Army in Ireland is, and always has been oppressive, is not, and never has been, to save the civilian population from terrorist bombs'. Others, such as Dick Gaughan, compared it unfavourably to another of his songs, 'Hey Sandy', about the killing of an America student at Kent State by the National Guard.

Conversely, soldiers paid Harvey compliments and he later worked at Combined Services Entertainment events. 'What they liked about it was I'd realised they were just blokes who wanted a job. A lot of them had enlisted before the Troubles started and then they found themselves up to their necks in this mess and they couldn't understand most of it.'

It was released as the B-side of a single, 'In the Darkness'. A record shop on the Shankill Road flipped it over and played 'Soldier' out of a loudspeaker on the street. According to Harvey, it was selling 25 copies a day but the distributor struggled to meet demand as interest became exponential. Eventually, the sales total for the one shop exceeded 5,000, while other outlets also serviced the demand.

'The story of the song in Northern Ireland is a complicated one,' he says. 'It seems that it was taken to be a pro-Loyalist song, which was never my intention. Years later it was released as a bootleg single by a Loyalist band and I have been told it was sold in pubs and out of car boots at the Glasgow Rangers ground to raise money for paramilitaries. I was strongly opposed to this but was powerless to stop it. A song I had originally intended to once again mirror man's inhumanity to man has somehow become a vehicle for more of the same, something I regret.'

There's a related theme in 'The Dying Soldier', written by Ger Costello from Limerick and recorded by Christy Moore in 1983. It presents us with the desolate thoughts of a wounded infantryman. He goes from surprise to panic and then resignation as the blood drains away. He hears the sound of people nearby but there is no compassion, not even at the end.

'Stop the shooting
Don't you see I'm dying?
Someone kneel and say a prayer.'

In the 60s, Nick Stewart had attended Eagle House preparatory school in Berkshire with the future song-writing legend Nick Drake. In 1980, he signed U2 to Island Records in his position as an A&R man. During the time between, he was a Platoon Commander with the Coldstream Guards. He served twice in Northern Ireland.

'Belfast in '72 was a bit of a Wild West show,' he says. 'Then when I went back in 1976 to Londonderry, I was there on a slightly different role, which was PR and community relations. When I arrived in September, the two Women for Peace, Mairéad Corrigan and Betty Williams, walked across the Craigavon Bridge and I thought, "Hey, this is great, we're gonna see the end of this". It wasn't quite like that.

'It was still pretty dangerous. Bombs were going off, people were being shot, there were political assassinations. The shoot-to-kill policy was in full flow. Belfast was dangerous and in elements of places like Strabane and Londonderry, it was still pretty wild.'

In local newspaper offices, they were tuned in to the security forces' short-wave radios. In his barracks, Nick Stewart was listening to John Peel:

'I used to listen to that show religiously. There wasn't much television in those days so I used to listen to that show. When I arrived, he was playing Robin Trower and Boston. He played Side One and Side Two of *Songs in the Key of Life* by Stevie Wonder and then something extraordinary happened.

Virtually within a week he started playing the Ramones and the Damned and suddenly there it was, this explosion of music. Which was part political, part social anger. And it's like he threw away his record collection and started again. So, I was right in at the start of all that. I thought, "This is raw".

'And, in my travels into Londonderry, I could see this happening. I went into the Brandywell estate at one point, into a pub, to meet a contact, and there was a band called the Undertones. And they were playing 'Teenage Kicks'. I sent a note to my friend back in London, saying, "I've got this very charismatic band fronted by this young kid. The Undertones, are ripping it up in Londonderry." It was a fascinating time to be listening to music and that's when I decided I wanted to get into the record business.'

After signing U2, were there conversations about the Northern Ireland situation?

'I don't remember specific conversations about the North versus the rest. The band was clearly aware that I had been a serving soldier in Northern Ireland and I think there were a couple of sessions in bars, or whatever. I was very reluctant, particularly in Ireland, to talk. For me, my time in Northern Ireland was the reason I left the army and ceased to want to be a professional soldier – not that I ever *was* a professional soldier. And I wanted to move on and move out. It was a depressing experience being there. And I realised I wasn't cut out.'

Later, Bono would sing 'Sunday Bloody Sunday', seemingly about the actions of the British Army:

'He always said that it was nothing to do with Bloody Sunday, but it's clearly something to do with the conflict. Bloody Sunday is one of the five most ignominious episodes in the history of the British Army. There aren't many, but that's one of them.

'I was keenly aware that there was injustice. You've got to remember that the British Army, when they went out there, were welcomed in the Catholic enclaves with open arms. We were there because we had come to protect them from Protestant outrage. And the Irish Republican Army used that as a way of moving the thing on. Then we found that we were, in the words of Howard Devoto, shot by both sides.'

A REBEL I CAME

He slipped away from his clerical post at the National Bank and moved to England in 1966. Christy Moore was variously employed on building sites, oil rigs and in folk venues. He got to know Rochdale, Bury and Halifax and he stayed with the singer Mike Harding in Manchester for six months. Sometimes he played in RAF camps and Army bases, taking requests for 'The Patriot Game' and 'Kevin Barry'. It was strange that they wanted to hear a lyric about British soldiers being shot by an Irishman. 'Give us an old rebel song, Paddy,' they said. And so, he obliged.

'Things were very different then.'

His youth in the garrison town of Newbridge, Kildare had been interrupted by Elvis, Billy Fury and Chuck Berry. But the really momentous instant was when the 17-year-old saw the Clancy Brothers and Tommy Makem at the Olympia in Dublin in 1962. The act had already starred on the *Ed Sullivan Show* and their ballads were adored in New York but this was their first Irish tour. During their American exile, they had added some swagger and drama to the native come-all-ye.

'That was stunning,' Christy says. 'I've never experienced anything before or since that was as exciting as that. It was a realisation for a whole generation of people that we had something in Ireland that we weren't aware of. It was the way they presented it and what they did with it. Pure excitement and magic, just four guys with one guitar up there, tearin' it out. Really moving people with songs we'd heard bits and pieces of growing up, but never presented to us in this way.'

The Clancys led him towards the music of Joe Heaney, Sarah Makem and the piping of Séamus Ennis. Also, there were ancient, mesmeric songs by the tinsmith and the settled traveller John Reilly. 'The Well Below the Valley' was biblical and murderous. Christy had made use of that prolonged bank strike in Ireland as the incentive to play for a living. He befriended Billy Connolly and he was astonished to hear Hamish Imlach singing 'Black is the Colour' at the Manchester Sports Guild. He met Luke Kelly one evening in 1967 when he was busking at the queue of a Dubliners gig. He woke the next morning in a strange room with an empty whiskey bottle. The band had already checked out. 'I thought, "Jesus, I hope somebody's paid the hotel bill".'

Importantly, he came to know Ewan McColl and Peggy Seeger and the Singers' Club, where music was enmeshed with social action and commentary. Ewan was central to the folk scene and a member of the Communist Party. 'I realised the importance of songs,' says Christy. 'They could be meaningful in a contemporary context.' When he heard the American dustbowl rouser Woody Guthrie on some scratched records in a squat in Finsbury Park, he was inspired by the man's simple, direct expression.

In 1969, he was working with Dominic Behan. The latter was a Dubliner, the brother of playwright Brendan, and had authored many songs, including 'The Patriot Game' – a song about Feargal O'Hanlon, a teenage IRA casualty from the 50s border campaign. This had a major influence on the Bob Dylan release 'With God on Our Side', a song that in turn swung back to Ireland and protest events in 1968, when the Derry marchers changed Bob's lyrics to 'the North-West' instead of 'the Mid-West'. Christy and Dominic had met the year before at a Civil Rights fund-raiser in west London. Now, the famous writer was going to produce Moore's debut album. Unfortunately, it was a mess of ideas, session musicians and patchy focus. It was recorded in six hours and *Paddy on The Road* is not fondly remembered.

It included 'The Belfast Brigade', a ballad about the Irish War of Independence (1919-21) that he'd picked up in a Shepherd's Bush folk session. The words hailed the exploits of the IRA in the North, battling the Black and Tan forces and vowing not to settle for the compromise of the Free State, partition and 26 counties. His anti-treaty vocals were thin and disengaged. 'I was still singing songs without paying any great heed to what they were about. It wasn't really where I was at.'

In the same year, Dublin balladeers the Wolfe Tones released their fourth album, *The Rifles of the IRA*. The title track was another backwards glance to the War of Independence, as perceived by Dominic Behan. Once again, there was damage caused to the Royal Irish Constabulary Special Reserve – the 'Black and Tans' nickname had referred to their ill-matched uniform. Winston Churchill had been involved in their conception; they were recruited from Britain and they had a reputation for extreme violence. Many of them were killed by IRA bullets.

On the cover of the record, the Wolfe Tones celebrated this historic payback by wearing trench coats, black brimmers and ammunition belts worn Sam Browne style, accessorised by vintage rifles. Christy Moore was not impressed. 'I equate that particular record sleeve with Foster & Allen, dressed up as leprechauns. It was the very same thing. It had the same significance at the time.'

After his five years away, Moore returned home to form Planxty with his Kildare friend Dónal Lunny. The music was deep into the tradition but also artistically bold. Songs and traditional tunes were bolted together in ground-breaking ways. They gained from the searing *uilleann* pipes of Liam O'Flynn, the acoustic precision of Andy Irvine and an influx of young, keen listeners. On the 1973 self-titled *Planxty* record, Christy sang 'Only Our Rivers Run Free', a song that Fermanagh writer Mickey MacConnell had written as a teenager. In this lyric, the natural world is seemingly damaged by an artificial border. There's some hope in the refrain that harmony can be restored to the land. It was a breakthrough moment for Christy. He was digging into the emotional centre of a song – political but not hectoring. And rather than being retrospective, he could sing in the present.

His first stint with Planxty was over by 1974. He continued to vocalise about the North in his solo gigs, but admitted later that he knew Manchester and London better than Belfast or Derry. He was drinking excessively and eating hash on occasion but in the second half of the decade his social awareness was lit. There was a swelling protest about the likelihood of a nuclear power station at Carnsore Point in County Wexford. Christy headlined a three-day festival in August 1978. They carried the message of the Anti-Nuclear Roadshow to 12 towns, steering environmental issues to the mainstream. The festival returned in 1979 and for several years after. It was the 'Irish Woodstock'. But it was also blazingly current and they had managed to create a new public conversation. The plant was never built.

Meantime, there were changes in British policy at Long Kesh prison, now rebranded as the Maze. New buildings, named H-blocks because of their architectural design, were installed on the former airbase site. Some older prisoners remained in the Nissen Huts but the regime was intended to create a criminalised climate inside. Political status was going to be stripped away. The system was endorsed by the Secretary of State Roy Mason and activated in 1976. Incoming paramilitaries would not be regarded as prisoners of war. There was a series of restrictions but in particular the issue of compulsory uniform incensed the new inmates. Kieran Nugent refused his State-issue apparel on September 16 1976. He covered himself with a blanket and was not permitted to leave his cell without clothing. Other prisoners who mounted the 'blanket protest' also lost their remission for this transgression. Furniture was removed after violent altercations. Later in the year, Francie Brolly from Dungiven wrote 'The H-Block Song'.

> *I'll wear no convict's uniform*
> *Nor meekly serve my time*
> *That Britain might brand Ireland's fight*
> *Eight hundred years of crime.'*

In 1977, Christy was asked to write about the protest and was then invited to visit Brendan 'Bik' McFarlane in prison. It was transformative, as he recalls:

'I was actually quite shaken by all of that. I've visited a lot of prisons since then but this was a time in my life when I was moving away from being a Stage Paddy to being more serious about my work. What I did then was

I arranged to meet three young guys and to find out what it was like and wrote the song as a result. The song '90 Miles from Dublin' was about the apathy in Dublin towards the dirty protests, which lasted four years and culminated in the hunger strikes.'

Christy used a familiar melody, 'The Homes of Donegal'. He told the account of a prisoner who had been interrogated in Castlereagh Holding Centre in Belfast, sentenced without trial by jury in a Diplock Court, subject to forced washing and cavity searches using a mirror. The inmate hears that there is American interest in his condition, but there is less curiosity from the south of Ireland: '*Though it's 90 miles from Dublin, it seems so far away.*' He released 1,000 copies of the song independently. Later, there was an album, *H-Block*, with musical contributions from Matt Molloy and Mick Hanley. The actor Stephen Rea read out contributions from prisoners including several pieces from IRA prisoner Bobby Sands.

'I had actually heard from Bobby Sands,' Christy says, 'and I had some of his writings from about 1978. He used to send out his writings under the name of Marcella, which was his sister's name. I still have a couple of the poems he wrote. One is called 'A Retort' and the other is 'Prisoner of Conscience'. I have the actual writings on Her Majesty's toilet paper. Both those poems were on the album.'

There was a press launch for the record at the Brazen Head on Lower Bridge Street, Dublin. The event was raided by the Special Branch who took names and confiscated the albums. Years later, a retired officer asked Christy to sign a copy that he'd kept. This act generated publicity but, during the following decades, Christy and his associates were heavily monitored by the State.

The first hunger strike in the H-blocks started in October 1980 and ended in confusion in December. The prisoners planned a more concerted second protest and, on March 1 1981, Bobby Sands refused food. A series of strikers joined the protest at regular intervals and so the tension and political pressure was designed to last for many months. Their demands were focused on wearing their own clothes, being absolved from prison work, free association with other prisoners, remission restored and planned recreation. They wanted Special Category Status.

Christy was playing the Baggott Inn, Dublin with a new band, Moving Hearts. They rehearsed on the top floor, played pool on the middle floor and gigged downstairs on Monday, Tuesday and Wednesday nights. The bar management was pleased because these were normally the slack evenings. Now they were busy. Moving Hearts, like Planxty, were ready to stimulate the Irish tradition, this time with jazz and electricity. Christy remembers that the process was essentially 'heads down, knobs to the right'.

It was important enough that unemployed music fans were admitted for half price. Moving Hearts took the method further again. All the band members and their crew were on the same wage. Keith Donald, a Belfast jazz veteran and former psychiatric social worker, played alto sax. He recalls the act's constitutional mettle:

'We had an agreement amongst ourselves that anybody had the power of veto over the lyrics of a song. That was from the get-go, from the very first rehearsal when the very first song was presented. It was, "Can we sing this?" Anybody in the band – and crew – had the power of veto over the lyrics of the song. And that stayed on.

'It was very immediate and very intense. There was a lot of love and respect between the audience and us, which I had experienced a bit through jazz but nothing to that intensity. The music was very fresh and new because of Dónal Lunny's and Declan Sinnott's arranging abilities, the rock and roll rhythm section, the jazz from my sax and the Irish trad from Davy Spillane and Dónal. It didn't sound like these things were artificially grafted together. It actually did work well.'

They sang about nuclear meltdown, slum landlords, US foreign policy in Latin America and they imported the dread of Jackson Browne's 'Before the Deluge'. Also, they rolled out their commentary on Irish history at an extremely turbulent time.

'Eamonn McCann called us the political wing of the Wolfe Tones,' says Keith. 'We were seen as being critical of the way the British Army treated certain sections of the populace in the North. And here I am, a Belfast Protestant, talking about this. We were seen as being in support of people who were against the colonisation of the North of Ireland. But we never preached violence.'

One of the remarkable songs in their set was 'No Time for Love'. It had been written by Jack Warshaw in 1976, an American architect and draft-resister who had settled in London. The original title, 'If They Come in the Morning', came from a book title by the activist Angela Davis. Jack's song told of dawn raids, death squads and repressive acts in Santiago, Chicago, Boston and Belfast. It mentioned the Black Panthers and delivered a short history of industrial action. Soon after Jack recorded it, the piece was adopted by the Men of No Property on an album, *Ireland – The Fight Goes On*.

Christy heard it at Carnsore in 1978 and tried it out on a later version of Planxty. But it was the defining song of Moving Hearts, who 'went to war on it'. It was rousing and literate from a left-wing viewpoint. It echoed the protest voices of Guthrie and Dylan. In 1981, Moore took some liberty with the tumbling lines, adding the names of hunger strikers Bobby Sands and, eventually, Patsy O'Hara. In the Warshaw lyric there was also mention that '*the fish need the sea to survive just like your people need you*'. It seemed to echo Chairman Mao's strategy for guerrilla armies, harboured by the populace. All this was highly emotive. Keith recalls the song's introduction to the band's setlist:

'The reaction to it was phenomenal, immediately. So, I suppose we then realised that it was an important song. It meant a lot to different sections of society. When we were travelling around Ireland at that stage, it felt extraordinarily edgy and difficult. Black flags on the lamp posts. Especially in the North. It was very, very tough. Terrible times.

'When we came out of hotels in the North of Ireland, we'd have to hang around for a few minutes while the band looked in the engine compartment, looked underneath the vehicle, and so on. We only once didn't travel north when we got a serious threat with a code word attached to it, and our publicist rushed to the band meeting saying, "Don't travel north today". Otherwise, we did.'

Bobby Sands died on May 5 1981. The British Prime Minister, Margaret Thatcher, noted that: 'Mr Sands was a convicted criminal. He chose to take his own life. It was a choice that his organisation did not allow to many of its victims.' A photographer took an image of Christy on that day in Dublin. He was wearing a short black jacket, a woollen hat and jeans. A Special

Branch officer had stopped him in the street and was searching his pockets. Moving Hearts were under surveillance. The police cars were easy to spot as the weight of the bulletproof panels weighed down the suspension. The singer also believed that their phones were being tapped. Concerts provided an outlet for the anxiety.

'It wasn't like it had ever been before,' Christy remembers. 'During the anti-nuclear movement of the mid-70s, there was a time when the music was an important part of the movement. But though that was a very big issue, hunger strikes are different. I don't think I'll ever experience anything like that again. I hope I don't. There's all kinds of emotions flowing around – the helplessness. Yet you're singing about it. And because of some people's attitudes towards songs, some people might even think it's disrespectful or bandwagoning. It was a difficult time for everybody.'

On July 13, Moving Hearts were set to play the Community Hall in Collooney, Sligo when they heard that Martin Hurson was the sixth hunger striker to die. They made a live recording that evening of 'On the Blanket', a Mick Hanly song that had featured on the *H-Block* album. Mick sang most of the vocals with contributions from Christy. '*If we stay silent, we're guilty,*' they chorused. Loose and emotional, it was released on the major label imprint, WEA.

Keith Donald recalls the unrelenting tension: 'I certainly had no optimism that Margaret Thatcher was gonna back down. My own personal feeling was hope, that it wasn't gonna come to deaths. But when the first death happened, I was appalled. That period of months when they were dying on a regular basis was just sick, horrendous. You'd be clutching at straws, like, so-and-so is going in to see the prisoners – maybe a religious person or some kind of mediator – and then you'd get hopes dashed on the rocks of reality.'

The hunger strikes ended on October 3. Ten men died on the protest and 61 people were killed across Northern Ireland in heightened violence during those 217 days. Christy left Moving Hearts in 1982 and his solo music continued to deal with the prison story. He released an independent album *The Spirit of Freedom* to raise funds for the families, buying them a bus for prison visits. The music was stark and it was the beginning of reassessment and mythology. He sang two lyrics that had been written by Bobby Sands.

He had come across the first of these at a house session on Chamberlain Street, Derry, and the second after a show at a GAA club:

'It was really weird. In two successive nights I had two concerts. The first one was the Rialto in Derry and afterwards I met the guy who gave me the song 'Back Home in Derry'. He'd been in the hospital wing during the hunger strikes and he'd learned the song in there and was a bit of a singer himself. So, he sang that to me. The next night I'm 60 miles away in Bellaghy and after that I met this guy, Colm Scullion, who'd been in the blocks and he sang 'McIlhatton' to me.'

The title track of his 1983 album *The Time Has Come* was written about Patsy O'Hara, the fourth hunger striker to die in 1981. Moore approached the song from the position of the family, at the moment when the prisoner would lapse into unconsciousness and the relatives would have the legal option to call in medical assistance and intravenous feeding. This issue had been discussed at length in the H-blocks, and parental pledges of non-intervention were secured:

'That's what inspired it, not so much the hunger strike itself. That song was written more for the families of the hunger strikers, for Patsy's mother and also the family of Francis Hughes. I stayed in that house and spoke with them and I also spoke to Patsy's mother Peggy and along the way; I met other families as well, but specifically those two families. Their dilemma during the hunger strike was what I was attempting to describe in the song.'

These three songs became immovables in the Christy songbook, performed without introduction or context. Most of his audience understood. Ballads had been part of the late-night exchanges between the prison cells at the Maze, when the inmates would sing older songs like the famine ballad 'Skibbereen' and 'Sean South', which commemorated a 1957 IRA death. Individuals like Bobby Sands and Brendan McFarlane were creating new lyrics. 'Back Home in Derry' was developed from a Sands poem, 'The Voyage'. An Irishman has been taken on a convict ship to Australia for his part in the Irish Rising of 1803. The song describes the fatalities on the journey, the rough conditions of Van Diemen's Land and the resulting homesickness. The words were spliced to the melody of Gordon Lightfoot's 'The Wreck of the Edmund Fitzgerald' and thus it entered the tradition.

Christy also sang about hangovers, powerful romance and rogue football supporters, but conflict was a constant. He sang material about Armagh Women's Prison ('The Bridge', 'Andytown Girl'), about media censorship ('Section 31'), the Birmingham Six ('Scapegoats'), the Guildford Four ('Giuseppe') and a song that came together at a meeting of Derry families on the 21st anniversary of Bloody Sunday ('Minds Locked Shut'). There was a public exchange of words and lyrics when he took exception to a Paul Brady song, 'The Island'. Christy played to HIV Positive men in Mountjoy Prison and on the maximum security Provisional IRA landing at Port Laoise:

'Interestingly enough, I also had some letters from Loyalist prisoners in the blocks. Talking about the music, asking about chords and stuff and telling me about their songs.'

He sang with Sinéad O'Connor on July 17 1988. They were celebrating the 70th birthday of Nelson Mandela at the Olympia Theatre in Dublin and they performed 'Irish Ways and Irish Laws'. It was a song that dated back to the first Moving Hearts album and had been presented after one of their feverish Baggott Inn shows. John Gibbs had sung it to Christy and the lyrics were scribbled on the back of a Major cigarette box. They pictured Ireland under Medieval, Brehon law. Sinéad followed Christy's lead, singing it as a low-key lament and later took it on her own tours.

'If I have a hero, it's him,' Sinéad told *NME*. 'For his music. But even more so for the way he is and what kind of life he has. He lives what he sings about and he's real.' Sinéad also sang at a Troops Out rally in Dublin 1989 and made a series of comments in her early career about the armed struggle. These messages were sometimes contradictory but Sinéad later gave some support to the 'Peace Together' initiative led by Ali McMordie (Stiff Little Fingers) and Robert Hamilton (the Fat Lady Sings) in 1993.

She has used the 'The Foggy Dew' to evoke the spirit of the Easter Rising and has questioned the Republic's supposed drift from the principles of the 1916 declaration. On 'Famine', Sinéad challenged the mythology of the 19th Century mass starvation and the role of Empire in the outcome. The song uses the imagery of domestic abuse to make a point and blames the Irish reliance on alcohol and other substances on this abiding trauma. Part of the recovery, she insists is the act of 'remembering'.

There's a related idea on 'This is a Rebel Song', the notion that the two islands on the edge of Europe are like dysfunctional partners. She takes an initiative, offering her affections to the bigger island and tries to tease out an apology:

'I love you my hard Englishman
Your rage is like a fist in my womb
Can't you forgive what you think I've done
And love me – I'm your woman.'

Christy Moore began to question his own response to the conflict, particularly after the Enniskillen cenotaph bombing of 1987 that killed 12 people. There was further consideration after October 1990 when the IRA launched a series of human proxy bombs, strapping three civilians into trucks and forcing them to drive up to military targets. Many in Ireland were revulsed by the 1991 killing of Tom Oliver. The farmer had been abducted from the Cooley Peninsula, severely beaten and then shot by the IRA who falsely claimed he was an informer. The singer later explained to the *Sunday Independent* that such events had caused him to reassess his position. He talked this over with Joe Jackson from *Hot Press* in 1991:

'I find I've reached a point in my life where I can't fucking take it anymore. After Enniskillen, and now, I find I no longer can support the armed struggle. It's reached a point of futility. It doesn't seem possible to carry out an armed struggle against the enemy. It's an armed struggle in which too many little people are blown away…'

'There have been thousands of Republicans interned, hundreds locked up for possession of weapons yet we never had a British soldier charged for shooting children with rubber bullets. That causes deep confusion within me, and anger. I can't handle it. And as I talk to you now about it that old sense of hopelessness sweeps over me and I see no way out of it all. I understand why the struggle goes on but I can't see where it will end.'

He met Bono at Toronto airport in 1985 and they talked about collaboration. When they met again at a Dubliners TV tribute in 1987, Christy showed him a rough lyric called 'Hands Across the Lough'. He was writing about a man in transition, troubled to think he has little time remaining to reach out to his estranged neighbour. The voice in the song is awkward but he wants a connection, even an embrace:

'It was born of an awareness that in my travels around Northern Ireland I would only basically encounter, in the main, people from the Nationalist population. Very seldom would I encounter people from the other tradition. There were exceptions to that, people I knew across the years. That's what spurred the original concept for the song. I started the song long before I finished it.'

Bono worked with him to create a revised lyric, eventually called 'North and South of the River'. The yearning in the first draft remained. There was still talk of unapproved roads and the moral darklands around the border. The character is tired of looking over his shoulder for the incessant danger and he wants to empathise with the other. There's a delicacy in the new version and an admission that perhaps the old sureties are under review:

'There's an old church no longer ringing
Some old songs are not worth singing.'

'Bono kind of turned it inside out and upside down,' says Christy. 'He's a really interesting collaborator. He works in a way that I hadn't encountered before that I found really interesting. This song has survived and I include it regularly. Early on, it ruffled the feathers of a few. I like that. It's a great song to play. It can sound very different from night to night. Sometimes gentle. Sometimes it rocks.'

Christy released his version as a single in 1995, with backing vocals from Bono and Edge. A U2 recording of the song arrived in 1997 and Bono quoted from the lyrics in Belfast on the evening that the Good Friday Agreement was thrashed out, April 10 1998. They also performed it in the aftermath of the Omagh bombing. As listeners took stock of the words, Christy was questioned about the line, '*I've been doing this wrong all of my life*'. He maintained that this was a personal admission, not a wide-reaching statement about the conflict or Republican beliefs:

'There was nobody offended about it, as such, but some people were curious as to why I would write it. People who I would describe perhaps as diehards. Mostly ideological, but there are those as well who feel very much at a loose end. You know, they were so deeply immersed in the whole struggle – without it, they're a bit lost, I think. There are people on both sides who would have the same attitude – that the job is not done yet. There are people on the Loyalist/Unionist side who say the job will never be done when there's ever a possibility of a United Ireland. Both factions are there, still at it, you know.'

In the past, Christy was often labelled as a rebel. Rather, he maintains the right to be contrary, evading categories:

'It's something that keeps coming up. I don't mind what way I'm tagged or pigeonholed, because I'm not going into the pigeonhole. I'm going to do my own thing. Some people say that I'm a political singer – I don't accept that. Some people say I'm a folk singer – I don't accept that. Some people say I'm a wanker – I don't accept that either. I just do my own thing and hope it works out.'

On March 23 2017, Martin McGuinness was buried in Derry City Cemetery. He was variously described as the former Deputy First Minister of Northern Ireland and a former IRA Commander. Christy was at the graveside. He sang 'The Time Has Come':

'When I heard that Martin was very, very ill, I made contact and said if it was ever appropriate, I would certainly visit and sing a few songs for him – because he liked the songs and he used to come and hear my concerts and, sadly, that didn't come to pass. But having made the offer, then I was contacted and asked, "Would you like to come and sing for Martin at his passing?"

'A song was suggested and I just said, "I'd like to sing at Martin's funeral, but leave the song up to me". And I chose that song because it was one that he particularly liked. Martin would come to my gigs in Derry when time permitted; later years he seldom had time. The atmosphere throughout the city that day stays with me. It was very striking to see Arlene Foster [leader of the DUP] come into the church – even more so than the international attendees.'

Christy's touring schedules have been halted due to heart issues, fatigue and a mental breakdown in 1997. The drugs and the drink were foresworn a long time ago. He has returned to the stage, sometimes tentatively, often with new recordings and sentiments. His performances revisit the lightness, flippancy and rapture that have always coloured his shows. He also takes his listeners into those years of duress. The songs are not chronological. They flip across the decades, through emotions and associations. Certainly, there are cheers for the tough messages from the 80s, while others from his parish have made the metaphorical reach across the water. This must be a huge weight to carry as a performer:

'I don't feel that way. I certainly don't feel any responsibility or I don't feel any obligation or I don't feel any weight attached to it. I mean, I'm 72 now, I've been singing all my life – professionally since 1966. Even at the age I am now, I'm constantly seeking songs. The journey continues. And songs are my obsession and it's just part of what I do. I sing songs and about different aspects of what I see. It's an ongoing thing, you know. It just continues on.'

And what of the ambivalence at the live shows, the mixed expectations and reactions?

'My own mind is forever 'mixed'. If you felt people were of mixed minds, I'm happy with that. I like 'mixed audiences'. The more mixing we do the better. Maybe mixing is fixing.'

THEY TAKE YOU DOWN
TO CASTLEREAGH

When Ian 'Buck' Murdock passed his driving test he bought a purple Austin Allegro and put the title DEFECTS STAFF CAR along the sun-strip. The Royal Ulster Constabulary was not impressed. Buck was stopped often, sometimes every day. They didn't like the lettering and the spikey-headed passengers. They hauled the car over by the Ropeworks in East Belfast and put everybody against the wall, frisking the punks down on a Saturday afternoon while all the shoppers and the buses went past.

'It was very 'White Riot',' they say, remembering the cover photo on the first Clash single. 'They hassled us constantly.'

On another occasion, the police directed them down a lane and took the car apart. They removed the hubcaps and then the wheels. They put everything back together and told them to be on their way. Some of the enforcers had an attitude. 'Hey Musky, we've got some rock stars here,' said one of the cops to his mate. 'Here, look – "*SS RUC…*"'

The Defects had some history with the law and a song called 'Brutality'. It was on the B-side of their debut single, 'Dance Until You Drop' in 1981. The song was about an actual Defects experience at Castlereagh Holding Centre in Belfast. This was a fortified location in the East where paramilitaries were interrogated. It was the subject of concerned Amnesty reports and had received a mention in the Christy Moore song '90 Miles From Dublin'.

Buck was teetotal but other Defects members and their mates took part in teenage drinking sessions around the deserted houses at Burmah Fields. People from Sydenham and the Upper Newtownards Road were joining in, as many as 50 on the weekends, so the police would arrive to disperse the party people. 'They really did raid you,' says Buck. 'Land Rovers, dogs, big spotlights, the full shebang. All we were doing was sitting having a drink.'

The supposed troublemakers were taken away to the local station at Strandtown or sometimes Castlereagh. The band's drummer, Glenn Kingsmore, visited a few times. 'You were slapped about a wee bit, you know. If you retaliated sometimes it got a bit worse.' On the night that inspired the song, he was removed to Castlereagh with his friends Lugs and Alistair. There was an altercation inside the Land Rover and a policeman suffered a broken hand. The Defects' version of the story is that the RUC man was swinging a fist when it connected with the side of the wagon. Alistair was charged with assault and Glenn came back in a poor condition. Buck wrote the song.

'I remember writing 'Brutality' in Castlereagh Tech (Technical College). And it was actually about Glenn. I was smart and didn't drink but they always ended up in the back of the meat wagon. He came back the next day with blood all over him. I was sitting in Tech class and the teacher came over and checked the words and he wasn't too impressed.'

'Brutality' was also significant in that it included the "SS RUC" chant, previously scored into the Rudi song 'We Hate the Cops'. The Defects were next generation punks and they played it faster and harder. Their audience was partial to studded jackets and rough manners and so the song provoked rowdy scenes when they played it live. But there was an issue with Defects recruitment, as Glenn reports:

'The ironic thing is that Jeff Gilmore, our bass player, chanted "*SS RUC*" on the first single and ended up joining the police. Our second bass player, Gary Smith, chanted "*SS RUC*" on the remake of the track, and he ended up joining the police. That's very strange.'

There was little reputational damage when they played the Harp Bar in the city centre. At first, they were denied entry due to their under-age status, yet they spent Saturday evenings outside the Hill Street venue, just to experience the energy. There were sectarian stragglers around the back alleys who wanted to know everyone's religious background – to make sure that they weren't the wrong sort. The outcome of the answer might be painful.

'I remember walking down there,' says Buck, 'and someone shouted from behind me – "What are ye? What are ye?"'

'And I shouted, "I'm a *punk*!" And went into the Harp. And that was it. Closed the door, got out of the way.'

Beyond punk there was Oi! music, an issue in the late 70s. The music was basic by design, with echoes of skinhead culture and 60s beat groups. Oi! bands such as the Cockney Rejects used football terrace chants to make a point. Sham 69 were caught up in the tumult and received death threats when they supported Rock Against Racism (they also wrote 'Ulster', a futile song about the futility of the conflict). Oi! gigs became routinely violent and a 1981 summer bill featuring the 4-Skins and the Business ended in a street riot and the burning of the Hambrough Tavern in Southall. Some of the bands claimed that their gigs had been infiltrated by right-wing politics. Others acts made a willing connection.

Skrewdriver, from Lancashire, went past the frontiers of Oi!. Singer Ian Stuart Donaldson allied himself to the National Front, talked of race wars and supposed that the Holocaust may not have happened. 'Most Irish in England are Communists,' he reckoned. He called himself a 'British National Socialist', described Nelson Mandela as 'scum' and released a single called 'White Power' in 1983. There were two other tracks on this release, 'Shove the Dove' and 'Smash the IRA'. The latter song proposed that IRA members should be hanged, that the British Army might be given a free rein and that Loyalists in Northern Ireland should be appreciated for their service in two world wars. '*Support the Red Hand*,' he called.

A Belfast band, Offensive Weapon, adopted 'Smash the IRA' and other Skrewdriver songs. Based around the Lower Shankill, they were active for several years (1981-84), mainly playing drinking clubs and Loyalist bars. Brian Watson, the guitarist came up with the name. Sam "Skelly" McCrory sang and the drummer was Julian Carson. The bass player was Johnny Adair from Fleming Street, who had a series of juvenile convictions for disorderly behaviour and assault. They also tackled songs from the repertoire of the

4-Skins and Chuck Berry. When the National Front paraded in Belfast on September 3 1983 (known locally as the 'glue-sniffers' march'), Adair, McCrory plus their friend and occasional roadie Donal Hodgens took the route from Sandy Row to the Shankill, clashing with a CND rally, as planned.

Their own songs included 'Gestapo RUC' – based on another chant from the football terraces – 'Made in Ulster' and 'Castaways'. Their finale was often 'Bulldog', a call to *keep Britain white*. They played with the Outcasts at the Pound on October 5 1992 and recorded a 1981 demo with Greg Cowan.

'I always look at Johnny Adair's arms when he's on TV,' says Greg, 'because somewhere there's that Outcasts tattoo. I didn't think of them as political, but more as hoods, criminals. And all of a sudden there were stories of Johnny Adair. I have been in his company, I think, twice. This is the biggest regret of my life. I had this home studio and I recorded this six track EP, didn't keep any of it. I had to play the bass because Johnny couldn't play the bass in time. But we were quite naïve. As in not even realising what they were.'

They played a Rock Against Communism festival in Suffolk in 1984 with Skrewdriver, Brutal Attack, Buzzard Bait and others. Johnny Adair's musical career tailed off that year as he became involved in 'C' Company of the paramilitary Ulster Defence Association. He eventually became Brigadier and was termed 'Mad Dog' by the media while the body count escalated. Adair was convicted in 1995 for directing terrorism. Sam McCrory also became an inmate at HMP Maze.

The counter to Offensive Weapon was Stalag 17. Petesy Burns from New Lodge in North Belfast was the bass player. They had a song called 'National Front' that made fun of a racist youth they had met during their time at Boucher Road Government Training Centre. Now it was time to sharpen up their politics, as Petesy recalls.

'That was '80, '81, when the uglier side of the skinheads and people like Johnny Adair and Skelly came onto the scene. And we were doing a song called 'National Front' and we just thought, "That's a bit too ambiguous", because it was tongue-in-cheek. If you were listening to it, it could sound a bit like an anthem for the National Front. So we just changed it to 'Smash the Front'.

'I used to live in Cliftonville and I'd come down the Crumlin Road and I'd come past Johnny and Skelly all the time. They were almost like a part of the crowd to some degree, even if a separate part of it. They used to come to Paddy Rea's. And I'd be sitting there going, "What the fuck are you talking about, blacks stealing our jobs? What's that about? Where?" There was probably one black family in Belfast at the time. 'Smash the Front', for us, became more of a rallying call, for the ones who didn't think like that, the ones who wanted to resist that. They're insidious, they get in and then they start to just intimidate a wee bit, and then if they see they can get away with it, they just take over, and that's what happens. They started to get sucked into that world, which was less and less to do with music and more to do with nutting people.'

Later, there was a Stalag 17 gig at Drains Bay, outside Larne. A National Front paper had urged their supporters to turn up and cause trouble. Around 20 skinheads arrived and there was friction at the entrance to the hall. When the band started playing, the gameplay continued.

'It was the usual skinhead thing of throwing people about the floor and stuff, and we were saying, "Take it easy lads". They were just making their presence felt. And people were a bit intimidated. Because I was up at the stage I could see these fuckers were picking people off.

'So, at one stage I says, "Gimme that bass". Joe Carey had just joined us and he didn't know 'Smash the Front' and I just kicked into it and the band followed me. The skinheads all stood – about 10 of them anyhow – lined up against the front of the stage with their backs to us and gave the Nazi salute out at the crowd, during the song. And every fucking person, every punk in the room, just got up and formed a big semi-circle round them, looking at them. And one by one they skulked off, apart from their leader who stood to the end, just looking stupid, and people were laughing.'

The English band Crass offered another political outlook for the punks. The challenge was to make records outside the capitalist system, part of a resourceful, conscious lifestyle. They berated the Clash for signing to a corporate record label. Their own records were sold below the accepted unit price. Food and consumer choices were also part of the notion of personal responsibility. You could reject factory farming and grow your own vegetables. Animal rights was a basic. Squatting and communal living were options. For Crass, this was a reality at Dial House in Essex. They wore utility black and didn't follow leaders. Some called it anarcho-punk. They had something to say about the conflict across the Irish Sea and the apathy of the TV viewers in Britain. The song was 'Nineteen Eighty Bore'.

> *'The army occupy Ireland, but the boot will never fit*
> *Was it Coronation Street? Or was it Londonderry?'*

The Anarchist Collective in Belfast was a like-minded project, running a semi-regular feature in the Carpenters Club on Long Lane on Saturday afternoons. They hosted music, alternative poetry, art, served wholefood and put on a banned film every week. Glue-sniffing was tolerated at the Anarchy Centre for a time but the fumes were overpowering and the post-event clean-up was a much greater chore. Crass played for them on September 11 1982. It was a Saturday afternoon show. Petesy Burns was impressed:

'I just walked into the place and it had been transformed completely. They brought their own PA, they had their banners all round, they had the screens. And they're doing it because they want to do it – they're going to lose money. And we couldn't get that concept at the time. But what struck me more than all that was the actual people. The night before, Steve Ignorant and a couple of the others came round to Paddy Rea's just to have a pint with us. They wanted to see something apart from where they were staying in Belfast. And I thought, "This is brilliant" – the level of conversation you were having with them. They were listening.

'That's when I started to do my homework, finding out about Dial House and the whole hippie commune thing. And on some level, I thought, this whole thing is contrived because this is a project to them. But the other side of that is they're enabling. There's a band with them, Dirt, who were on their label. There's all these other bands then I'd never heard of, the likes of Conflict and the Mob, who've just taken the money from their own sales and put it back into a label. I thought that was a fantastic thing.'

There was a dispute during the Belfast gig and the police arrived. It was met with the Crass chant of '*fight war, not wars*' and the local rebukes. The UDR were called in and the alley leading out from the venue was heavily secured. This played out in music mythology as State suppression but according to one version of the story, a notorious skinhead had entered the venue through a fire escape and had stabbed someone. The law enforcers wanted ID from those leaving.

'They sealed off both ends of the street,' says Petesy, 'and they were up for a ruck. The Belfast Anarchist Collective, fair play to them, were going, "Don't take a rise – they're gonna try and hassle you. They only need one excuse to come in and beat all around them – don't give them it." And definitely, that was what it was all about – provocation. And why? Was it because it was Crass, an overtly political band? I dunno. It just so happened that, on this Saturday, the place was under siege.'

David Hyndman was part of the Collective. He had served his time as a compositor in the Northern Whig building and became excited by the change in technology that had been introduced with small offset printing. People could now create their own magazines with typewriters, cow glue and scalpels. He had been active in various locations around town, notably above Terri Hooley's shop on Great Victoria Street. They had been partners in mischief, but not without their differences. 'I was always saying to Terri, "Look you've gotta be more professional. This is your big moment, try and get it together."'

As well as printing fanzines for the punk authors, he worked with community groups and helped them to publish their complaints about housing and urban development. In June 1978, the money raised by Terri's Battle of the Bands night with the Undertones and Rudi had allowed David and several friends to set up Just Books, a home for political and alternative literature on Winetavern Street.

'I didn't know what politically I was. It took people to come along and say, "Well, you're the libertarians, you're the anarchists, you don't want political parties". And I said, "Well, I guess I am, because I wouldn't dream of supporting political parties". All the ideologies we had were all about self-management and organising and anti-State. The State was always interested in consolidating its own power and all the rest of it. But, again, anarchism is like 57 varieties of Heinz Beans – you've different types. In a way, I didn't really try and fixate. Anarchism is such a loose philosophy for a lot of people.'

Just as electronics had made the printing industry accessible, so David felt excited by cheap synthesisers and sequencers. Crass agreed to put out his music. He was the Hit Parade, he identified as P. Checkov (a 'P' Check was a police search on personal particulars) and his art was unfiltered and often apoplectic. The *Bad News* EP from 1982 was about unreliable media, State PR, plus 'Here's What You Find in Any Prison', a thunderous defence of petty criminals, the downtrodden, unwitting convicts and scapegoats. The track 'H-block' repeated the title at the start of each line. It was unavoidably harsh, a babble of machinery, Margaret Thatcher rhetoric and samples from angry street meetings.

'When I was writing it, I was sitting in the Lyric Theatre watching some play or other. I remember one bloke saying to me [that] in Germany they didn't mention the camps. I was thinking in the Lyric, "*Here*, they don't really mention the H-blocks". I'll do a song that every other word is H-block… I just felt a huge frustration in that within the media within Northern Ireland people didn't really talk about what was happening. They talked about what was going on but never the reasons.

'I used to do a lot of internment posters about interning mothers and used graphics about gay rights. I was always fixated about why the arts was not engaged with trying to raise these human rights issues. And even the music I felt was real lacking there, in trying to talk about the situation. I always describe it as the fascism of youth – you have a very blinkered view about what was politics and so on – but I just thought, "Where's the cultural people? Why aren't they engaging? Let's talk about what's going on."'

Nick Knack Paddy Whack was a Hit Parade release in 1986. The lead track is a clattering, imagined scene from a police interrogation room. Penny Rimbaud from Crass acted out a pleasant-mannered English officer while David became the aggressive local. This double act finished up by pressuring the suspect to agree a confession. 'Sign!' they constantly shrieked.

Many of the Crass releases were contentious, blasphemous, pushing the censors. The Hit Parade and acts like Flux of Pink Indians also caused havoc in records shops and there were legal actions in Manchester and Chester. The Obscene Publications Act was cited. There were other moments, David says, when Hit Parade records were removed from English shops. This apparently coincided with a visit to Westminster by Gerry Adams from Sinn Féin, when the tabloid newspapers were in outrage mode. He learnt this in a letter from Penny Rimbaud. 'They'd lifted mine, but just to be sure, they lifted all the Crass ones.'

The Anarchy Centre had been a useful experiment but Belfast punks wanted a permanent home. The Harp Bar had been remodelled as a Western saloon. There were positive times at the Manhattan Bar and the Labour Club. The café above Just Books was a place to be inspired and, in time, there was an affiliation called the Belfast Youth and Community Group. They set up on Donegal Street Place in 1986 before decamping up the road in 1991 to the old Plaza building, with a wooden sprung floor and space for gigs, rehearsals, a vegetarian café, poetry readings and interlocking parts such as the Warzone Collective and the Belfast Musicians' Collective. Most people called it Giro's in honour of the social security cheques that sustained many users. The bands were certainly outspoken and 'No More Sectarian Shit' by Pink Turds in Space is of particular interest. Ann Campbell roared with conviction. The venue closed in 2003 but in 2011 the Warzone Collective opened on Little Victoria Street, sustaining the alternative ethos. Petesy Burns remembers the early years with particular fondness:

'What the Anarchy Centre was trying to say to us at the time is, "You've got to create it yourself, because no one's going to create it for you". It was flying by the seat of your pants but to us it was brilliant. This is what we had always wanted to do. You could play to whatever time – when we got tired, we locked up. There were no restrictions. The cops had their hands fairly full. We worked as a collective because we wanted to do it. No one was employed, no one got paid anything. There were a few kickbacks – if you were in a band, you got your practice time, or you got fed in the café. So, over the years, what we managed to do was develop a real strong volunteer base.

'When you're in that world, you find like-minded people. There's no veggie or vegan place in town, so let's create one. And the politics around the whole thing, the hunts group just blowing horns at hunts every week. Just becoming very aware. The Animal Release Movement was just down the street – they had done stuff on a small scale until they met us. And we were filling vans every week, sending punks to go out getting the tactics and knowing what to do.

'You can look at practical things that it did. Not overnight, as is sometimes portrayed. Even within that, I lived in the New Lodge; I was still a New Lodger but there was something that made me a wee bit different – it didn't draw me out but it was *drawing* me out. I sometimes romanticise it, as if it plucked me out. That wasn't the case. You were extricated but you went back into it, with all that – back into what you'd been brought up with.'

ROUGH JUSTICE

Jim Reilly was another musician born into the shifting urban lines of Belfast. He was originally raised on Denmark Street, off the Lower Shankill, before relocating to the Falls Road, Divis and Turf Lodge. When he was 14, his mother asked him what he wanted for his birthday. He asked for a drum kit and a neighbour had a mail-order catalogue, so it was ordered up. 'She paid the first pound and that was all she paid. The Troubles started just after I got my drum kit and our area became a no-go area. So the tick men couldn't come in to collect the catalogue money. I got my first Premier Olympic drum kit for a pound.'

His parents occasionally sent him to live with his uncle in Sheffield. He was working there as a window cleaner when he heard that Stiff Little Fingers needed a replacement for Brian Faloon. He dialled London and made his bid. 'I said, "Cancel the rest of your auditions, 'cos I'm your new drummer". They thought I was very cheeky and they liked that.'

By his estimation, he wasn't a proficient player but he'd paid his dues in the Republican clubs and shebeens, in pick-up combos such as Paddywack. He'd already seen Stiff Little Fingers live so he bought 'Alternative Ulster' and learnt the parts. He passed the audition and was given an acetate copy of *Inflammable Material*, ready for an Irish tour, December 1978. He was happily employed.

'In my eyes, punks are very liberal people. They don't take fools gladly.

War is wrong and sectarianism is wrong and racism is wrong and bigotry is wrong. It was very exciting to be involved with a band that was writing about that. I just lucked on. I'll tell you the truth. See, all my friends I grew up with – they all ended up in the IRA and doing long years in prison. And simply because I was playing music that kept me away from that. If I hadn't played music I'd have been caught up with them. I'd just have been another prisoner.'

As he moved some of his furniture into a flat in White City, West London, he was questioned under the Prevention of Terrorism Act 1974. 'I did get a lot of shit for being Irish in London. It didn't matter if you were a Protestant or a Catholic – you were just a Paddy or a Mick. That was the time the IRA were bombing London left, right and centre. But it was a great time to be there, and a great time to be Irish, because you had the Undertones, the Radiators, the Boomtown Rats. We ran about with Phil Lynott. We were like a community and we used to all gravitate to the Marquee. It's a wonder we're still alive.'

When he came back to play Belfast in May they put him up at the Europa Hotel, where he'd once trained as a commis chef. He looked down on to Great Victoria Street and he saw his brother Thomas outside with his mate. They'd been stopped on their way to the Ulster Hall gig by the UDR, who had them against the wall. 'I said, "Fuck this" and I ran down. They said, "Who are you?" I said, "I'm Jim Reilly from Stiff Little Fingers". They said, "Ah, go ahead lads – can I have your autograph?"'

He met Siobhan Fahey at a Bo Diddley concert in the Lyceum in July 1979. In September, she started at London College of Fashion and, in the summer of 1980, they were in a Holborn flat with fellow LCF student Sara Dallin and Terry Sharpe (from Belfast band the Starjets) plus Keren Woodward and her partner Paul.

'When I was going out with Siobhan,' Jim says, 'we went to Jersey for the weekend and brought a tent. We both had Irish passports and were questioned by Prevention of Terrorism police at the airport. Then, about three in the morning, the tent was raided by the Special Branch. They stuck the gun through the tent, I stuck out my head and they said, "Put your hands up, turn around". They handcuffed me. Siobhan didn't know what was going on – she had an Irish passport because her parents were from Tipperary.

'They took me in. I says, "Look, call Chrysalis Records". And within half an hour I was freed. The cops that arrested me asked for an autograph. "Fuck off," I said.'

His brother Thomas was doing well with a music merchandising company called Bravado. His friends called him Kidso; he was passionate about Celtic and toured with acts like Depeche Mode, Altered Images, Fun Boy Three and the Jam. He was out with Spandau Ballet in the spring of 1983 as 'True' topped the UK chart. Gary Kemp was glad to have him on the crew: 'We soon became very fond of him. He was a good guy whose optimistic temperament encouraged others to fold their proverbial wings around him.' When Siobhan, Sara and Keren became active as Bananarama, he was also part of their support network. 'He was a great guy,' Siobhan remembered. 'He absolutely idolised Jim.'

Thomas was home in Belfast during the summer of 1983, staying at the family home on Ardmonagh Gardens in Turf Lodge. On the Monday he played football with his mates in the playing fields at St Aidan's Primary School near the Springfield Road. He was back there on Tuesday, August 9 and there was a disagreement with soldiers from the Light Infantry. He headed off towards Turf Lodge, bare-chested, wearing cut-off jeans and holding his T-shirt in one hand. He was shot from behind and died by the gates of St Aidan's.

'He was only over here for two days to visit my mum,' says Jim. 'And he was shot dead. Shot in the back, one bullet. The British soldier that actually killed him was Private Ian Thain. He was the first British soldier in 800 years of the British occupied Ireland ever to be charged. He was sentenced to life imprisonment and he was back in the Army within less than three years.'

Siobhan, Sara and Keren led the funeral procession. There were wreaths from Paul Weller, Depeche Mode and Claire Grogan from Altered Images.

'It takes strength to get through it,' Jim explains. 'The way I look at it, the guy was 18 years old when he shot him dead. Do you remember when you were 18? You knew nothing. To give 18-year-old men, who are working class, guns and then send them to another county to sort out other working-class kids, it ain't gonna work. I forgave him right away. It wasn't his fault, you know. He didn't sit down to shoot my brother. When you're 18 years old, you're still a child. He was just a triggerman. The guy who gave the order didn't even go to court.'

Bananarama released 'Rough Justice' in 1984. In the video, they interrupt a news programme to present their own slant on current affairs. They say some of the innocent have '*no time to smile before they die*'. Siobhan explained to the readers of *Smash Hits* that they were grieving for a friend. 'I know a lot of people say this after somebody's died but it's absolutely true. Thomas was one of the most truly good people you could ever meet. There wasn't a bad thing about him. It just seems like those people are the ones to suffer and evil people thrive.' She also revealed that the lyrics of the album track 'King of the Jungle' related to his death. 'The song is about how ridiculous it is that 18-year-old boys are given guns and are endorsed by the government to go out and kill people.'

Spandau Ballet played Maysfield Leisure Centre, Belfast on December 1 1984. Next day, Gary Kemp met up with Jim and they visited Kidso's grave at Milltown Cemetery on the Falls Road. The visiting singer witnessed the segregation of a city. 'What affected me most as we walked were the so-called 'peace lines' that blocked the streets branching off that Catholic thoroughfare. On the other side I saw people walking, dressed in a similar style, fellow citizens, no different from the people I found myself with on this side, but cordoned off by the barricades – they could have been on another continent.'

Gary was living in Dublin for a time in 1985 and reading *The Troubles: Struggle for Irish Freedom, 1912-22* by Ulick O'Connor. Gary remembers that he woke at 2am and wrote 'Through the Barricades' in one sitting. He quoted the 'terrible beauty' phrase from W.B. Yeats and his poem 'Easter 1916'. He put the lovers on either side of the divide and they met in the wasteland. A popular song that he later termed 'one I'm really close to'.

Fun Boy Three also used the idea of a rogue news broadcast for their 1983 video 'The More I See'. The song references Ian Paisley, Sinn Féin, grieving widows and young people dying on the pavement. The received wisdom is that it's really no concern of the English. The song works up a sense of alarm, a moral imperative:

> 'Belfast's only half an hour away
> Close your eyes but it won't go away.'

The Police had previously taken a Troubles song into the Top Ten in 1981 with 'Invisible Sun'. It marked the return of the Armalite assault rifle, previously referenced by Stiff Little Fingers in 'Barbed Wire Love', but it was the dreary video that caused the broadcasters to recoil. Sting had been married to the Belfast actress Frances Tomelty and writing new music in Roundstone, Connemara, at a time when English accents were not always welcome.

'It was during the hunger strikes in Belfast', he told *Revolver*. 'I wanted to write about that but I wanted to show some light at the end of the tunnel. I do think there has to be an 'invisible sun'. You can't always see it, but there has to be something radiating light into our lives.'

The video for 'Belfast Child' by Simple Minds continued the woebegone tradition in 1989: the monotone panorama from Cave Hill, derelict housing stock and children running in slow motion. Jim Kerr borrowed the melody from 'She Moved Through the Fair' and the lyrics were an apparent response to the Enniskillen Bombing. '*The war is raging, through the Emerald Isle,*' he observed. Top of the UK and Irish charts.

Very few Troubles songs were upbeat, but German producer Frank Farian had managed to vamp up a song by Drafi Deutscher and created a 1977 disco success for Boney M with 'Belfast'. A German language version of the song by Gilla was tested a few months previously, urging the listeners to clap their hands in time to the banal truisms.

Post-punk bands tried harder. Gang of Four from Leeds had Marxist sympathies, icy rhythms and a 1978 B-side called 'Armalite Rifle'. They invented marketing slogans for the weapon with some detachment: '*Breaks down easy fits into a pram / A child can carry it do it no harm*'. A year later there was 'Ether', a split-channel discussion about cosy aspiration versus colonial actions, the dirt behind the daydream. The counter-argument nags the listener about Long Kesh, H-Block, news censorship and white noise interrogation techniques.

The Au Pairs carried on the theme with 'Armagh' in 1981, this time a consideration of the female prisoners in Armagh Prison:

> *'We don't torture*
> *Alleged crimes withheld information*
> *She gets no sanitation*
> *dries her shit on her cell wall.'*

Johnny Rotten had summoned up the bogeymen of the UDA and the IRA with 'Anarchy in the UK' and after the demise of the Sex Pistols he reverted back to being John Lydon. His new project was Public Image Limited and on 1979's 'Careering' he presents a character from the wet, ambiguous borderlands, seemingly on a new mission. The lyrics are covert, but so is the main character. There are secret trade-offs and erased stories, a laundering of guilt and history. The band's bass player, Jah Wobble, explained it to *Impulse* magazine in 1980:

'Careering' is basically about Northern Ireland, a gunman who is careering as a professional businessman in London. Careering – isn't it amazing how one word can have more magic than an entire opera?

Secret identity was also a notion in the 1984 Madness song 'Michael Caine'. It was the band's 18th record in the singles chart, and one of the few featuring the vocals of Cathal Smyth, also known as Chas Smash. He had family connections to County Mayo (a grandfather had served in the Irish Republican Brotherhood), yet he was born in London. In 1971, his father's work took him to Coleraine, County Derry. 'I was the badly edited boy. In London, they knew I was of Irish descent because I said 'fillum' and then by the time I'd got the accent right I was getting the shit knocked out of me in Northern Ireland.'

He attended the Dominican Convent at Portstewart on the north-west coast but left three weeks later after persistent bullying. 'I was used to stealing Bazooka Joe bubble gum and my classmates were making copper-pipe bombs'. During their year away, the Smyth family took a trip to Belfast to visit some of his father's old college haunts, but they got lost. 'He was asking after a family and he got complete blanks. We ended up in a dead end and there was a burning car overturned and it was like, we better get out. It was obvious, no matter how he spoke, that there was a tinge of the Brit about us. I also remember in London, mum telling me that the Special Branch raided our house. Having an Irish accent wasn't good during the early 70s. And then it continued.'

In the early 80s, State policy involved the use of the supergrass – a paid informer or an IRA member who was granted immunity from prosecution if he led to the arrest of his colleagues. There was a high-profile instance in 1983 when Christopher Black's testimony resulted in 22 IRA convictions for a total of 4,000 years (many were later quashed). A year later and Raymond Gilmour was the sole witness in a trial of 35 suspects. This trial ultimately collapsed but Gilmour and others were given new identities and housed in exile under a witness protection programme.

'Michael Caine' draws on this feature of the conflict. The character in the song is anxious and startled by the sound of a phone. He wishes he had a photograph or a memento of his past life, but this is unsafe and not permitted by the programme. The name repetition is a technique to resist interrogation and by using Michael Caine (who obliged Madness with a voice sample) it references the dark espionage of films like *The Ipcress File*. The song also draws on Cathal's memories of Coleraine and Portstewart in 1971:

'Woody [Dan Woodgate, Madness drummer] sent me a cassette of the music and the lyrics came to me immediately. I don't know why. I thought of my time in Northern Ireland, you know, Bernadette Devlin, the people banging the dustbin lids on the floor, that comedy tune, 'Belfast, Belfast'. I remembered going to the shops and being frisked. I remember thinking back to when rubber bullets were being used, thinking, "Jesus…" It was general mood of suspicion and fear.

'At the front end of the song I said, "*we'll get the IRA and yah yah*", which was like, we'll get the IRA and shit, but I was too scared to be obvious. And then the concept of Michael Caine put a veneer over it, which made it feel like a spy film, like *Get Carter*. But it was totally inspired by Northern

Ireland. I was scared to be overt. I wanted a song to have a sense of the fear and the underlying suspicion that was prevalent. It was almost tangible in the air. You know, that thing of the right street, the right pub… the wrong street, the wrong pub.'

WRECKAGE DOWN ON MAIN STREET

'The Island' by Paul Brady takes a stand but it also aches for a way out. The absolute conviction in the centre of the lyric is that violence is not justified. There is tension in the song because Brady knows that what he is saying is out of line with many of his peers. The song is also conflicted because there's an impulse is to step away from the problem, to escape with his partner to the Atlantic shoreline, to make love and not fixate on the death toll, the screaming and the revenge attacks.

The song has been worked and studied until the language is clear and the thought patterns are simply laid out. Paul Brady spent a long time on the words but when he hit a recording deadline he had to literally write the missing parts at the microphone. 'The Island' does not have time to feel complete but that raw element lets the listener understand that here is a troubled soul and a voice you can trust.

The choruses are dropped in like apologies. He takes time out from awful events to appreciate the morning dew, the sound of the ocean and the joy of walking barefoot at the shoreline. All of his senses are alerted, he forgets his mournful ways and connects again with the elemental stuff. He yearns to go there, but some dutiful call brings him back to Desolation Row, where the TV channels have a feed from the latest atrocity and the home schooling is about blood sacrifice and martyrdom.

Paul Brady recorded the song at Utopia Studios in London, at the closing sessions for his 1985 album *Back to The Centre*. It was a wise decision not to crowd the song with players and production. Also, there was an impressive tone in his singing that had been conditioned by traditional music, by ballads and rhythm and blues. As a teenager he had sung Ray Charles and James Brown. He had connected to the folk boom as a member of the Johnstons, learning about social commentary in a lyric. In the 70s, he was a sometime member of Planxty, the decade's most legendary Irish folk act, and his solo work was adored by fans of traditional music, including Bob Dylan.

So, he was able to reach every nuance in the song, the stations of sorrow, dismay, anger and hope. And while there was a hint of acoustic guitar, the chief instrument on the track was Kenny Craddock, playing piano in a self-effacing, gospel style. In the parlance of Al Green, he was taking it to church. Which was absolutely fitting because, at the end, Brady is looking for a life beyond the wreckage of another car bomb on Main Street. Just like those Civil Rights marchers in their clean shirts and serious faces, he wants that moment of aspiration and action:

'As we go marching down the road to freedom.'

The song starts with an image of another dreadful act in the Lebanon, where multiple factions are clashing and thousands of civilians have died. The attention flips to Ireland, where Brady finds a painful analogue. Belfast landmarks are hung with banners and smeared with slogans and the Witch Doctor is making issue about a flag – an allusion to Ian Paisley's mob-rousing actions in 1964, determined to remove an Irish tricolour from a window in Divis Street. The singer shows his contempt for the ideals and death cults that have resulted in *'young boys dying in the ditches'*. Paul Brady clearly believes that such a mind-set is out of date. He makes his case as a quiet, hymn-like plea. It is not a rebel song.

'There's a perception that all Irish people can sing about are the most brutal and unsubtle kind of things,' he told *The Guardian* later. 'It is fashionable to think that all Irish artistic utterances are in some way rebellious and I've found that media in the UK are enamoured with the idea of Irish revolutionary fervour as long as it's kept to the other side of the Irish Sea.'

At home he was subject to criticism. Even though he made allowance in the lyrics to the notion that he was '*copping out*', Republicans felt that he had affronted the cause. Additionally, he had turned down many requests from the folk community to play political benefits, to support causes like the blanket protest. Brady had written about anti-Irish prejudice in an earlier song, 'Nothing but the Same Old Story', but that was a general complaint about an emigrant being abused in an English bar, suspected of being a terrorist. His colleagues in Ireland felt that he could do more.

'I was very isolated at the time,' he told Joe Jackson from *Hot Press*. 'Because the basic mood through the traditional musical world at the time was "Lads, fuck it, hunger strikes, fuckin' Thatcher, let's get together and help the boys". I used to get phone calls from musicians who had played on records and it was, "Paul, there's an H-Blocks rally on at Liberty Hall tonight. You're coming down, right?" And I'd go, "No, I'm not". And you could hear the silence on the phone. I was completely isolated because of that, really hurt.'

Much of this related to his own background, growing up in Strabane, County Tyrone. The border location was ideal because his parents worked as teachers on either side of the boundary. His father Sean, originally from Sligo, cycled to work across the River Foyle to a National School in Lifford. His mother Mollie was from Irvinestown and she taught school at Sion Mills. Paul had also attended this primary school, founded by Quakers. It was rare for its time in that Catholic and Protestant children were integrated. His summers were spent over the border in Bundoran, Donegal, a county he held in his imagination as a kind of paradise, the escape route in 'The Island'.

The most public rebuke to the song came from Christy Moore. His response was a song called 'The Other Side' in which he contended that some of the singer's old neighbours were unable to relax on Donegal beaches because they were detained in prison.

> '*In the Long Kesh the Tyrone boys are dreaming*
> *Of making love upon the strand someday.*'

Commentators saw this musical dispute as indicative of the schism between Nationalism and Republicanism, SDLP and Sinn Féin. Christy re-wrote the lyrics several times, toning down the criticism and re-recorded it in 2011 as 'Tyrone Boys'.

'Paul and I get on very well, these times,' says Christy. 'I've great respect for him, he's a fantastic artist. A great singer. I tried to cover one of his songs and I just couldn't do it. Once you take Paul and his playing and singing out of the song, I couldn't cover it.'

Thirty years after the song's release, Paul Brady gives dominion to the song, rather than the songwriter. 'I wrote the song to find a way through all the ambivalence and confusion. I'm never able to explain 'The Island'. It's a song that's bigger than me. People want to nail you down and I don't want that. I'd rather the ability to just float.'

One of the greatest comeback lines of 1985 came out of a *Melody Maker* encounter between Kevin Rowland of Dexys Midnight Runners and the journalist Barry McIlheney. They had met to discuss the new album *Don't Stand Me Down*, which featured some pointed remarks on Britain's attitude towards Ireland and the subject of national pride. Wolverhampton-born Kevin revealed he carried an Irish passport.

'But you were born in England?' Barry remarked.

'Just because you were born in a stable doesn't make you a horse,' said Kevin.

His parents were from County Mayo and they sometimes met with other ex-pats in St Theresa's, Wolverhampton. 'I was about seven or eight,' he says. 'They happened to be pretty much all Irish people in there. It was daylight, like a Sunday, and all the curtains were drawn. There was smoke and there was drink and they were playing 'Kevin Barry'. And my mum says to me, "Oh, this song's illegal in England". I said, "Why?" She said, "Well, it's about what the English did to the Irish". I remember thinking, "Blimey, we're living in England". So, it was a bit odd.

'If you'd say something about England my dad would go, "You need to learn about some Irish history". I remember going over to Dublin, going over to the West, probably in my early teens and my mum showed me the Post Office where the Easter Rising was. I was fascinated by it. And I liked it. It was a sense of belonging, you know?'

He used to go occasionally to the Shamrock Club in Birmingham and would watch Irish showbands like the Indians. He was taken by their brass sections, the stage moves and the way they would swing their saxophones and other instruments around. He got work in the Bullring commercial area and was employed there at the time of the Birmingham pub bombings, November 24 1971. IRA bombs killed 21 people at the Mulberry Bush and the Tavern In The Town.

'I was in Birmingham that night, yeah. I was in one of those bars the night before. I was working in a shop just around the corner from that pub. I remember every few hours after the pub bombings there'd be bomb scares, the shop I was in being evacuated. The Bullring would be cleared and I remember the police clearing us out and somebody coming up to the policemen saying, "There's a bloke round there with an Irish accent. I'm sure he's a duck egg." They started calling them duck eggs. Because they were thick. It wasn't very rewarding being Irish around that time, really.'

He was working at a hospital in Edgeware when he was 16 and he often clashed with one of the guys in charge. 'He was a very hard-going, English upper-class bloke and I was always arguing with him. I tended to do that. If they were hard, I always rebelled. Just as I was leaving, it came out. "Oh, you're Irish, I should have guessed." He knew all about Kevin Barry and people like that and he went, "*That's* why you're so rebellious".'

And so, Kevin Rowland recognised a kindred spirit in John Lydon, who was fronting the Sex Pistols as Johnny Rotten. He asked his mother if Lydon was Irish and she said, yes, there were lots of them back in Mayo.

'I was very pleased to hear he was Irish. And not a bit surprised, because he was rebellious. This guy was expressing how I felt and it was great, you know. And they were the cutting edge; they were the thing.'

Dexys Midnight Runners were the thing in 1979. They dressed like dock workers in homage to Elia Kazan's *On the Waterfront*. There was a brass section and energy and focus. Their first single was called 'Dance Stance' and it named the some of the greats of Irish literature – a roaring litany.

'I think it was the 70s when the thick paddy jokes really were at their most intense. You'd just hear them all the time. What made me laugh, in a sickening sort of way – there was a lot of, what I considered, not very intelligent people telling these jokes. I tell you what, these kind of jokes, they go into your psyche, and a part of me did feel second class for being Irish. It reached boiling point for me in '78, when I wrote that song. I just thought, "How can Irish people be stupid when they produce people like this?" It was great to write it, actually. It was cathartic.

'To be honest, I'd read Brendan Behan's *Borstal Boy* but hardly any of the others. I thought Brendan Behan was fantastic. I got a biography of his and on the jacket of it or early on, it said, the Irish have produced some great writers. Some people say he's got the brilliance of – and then it gave me this long list – Oscar Wilde, Sean O' Casey...'

There was meaning with the debut album cover that pictured Anthony O'Shaunnessey, leaving his burning home at Cranbrook Gardens, Belfast in 1971.

'Even the cover of the first album – it was green, white and red. I didn't think I could be blatant enough to have it green white and gold. But I was pleased and my mum and dad said to me, "Oh, that's the Mayo colours". I was putting in the references subtly. How I sold it to the band was, "This is like a troubled scene, it just happens to be Ireland". What happened was something turned, late '81, early '82. I remember thinking to myself, "Okay, now I can come out with Celtic". I think Van was singing about something 'Celtic', and I can come out now and be more Irish.'

This was realised on the *Too Rye Aye* album in 1982. It began with the Victorian parlour song 'Believe Me, If All Those Endearing Young Charms', a song that his mother would sing. The song 'Come on Eileen', Kevin supposes, was 'about growing up in a very strict Irish background and struggling with sexual feelings'. The record's pleading chorus dominated the summer and the UK singles chart was won.

With the *Don't Stand Me Down* album, he furthered this interest. On 'Just One of Those Things' he encounters some English socialists who have their defined opinions about conflict in the Middle East, Latin America and Africa. Kevin wants them to look nearby:

'How do you feel about Ireland?'
Ireland? Yeah, Ireland

That place, it's just across the sea.'

He repeats the question, this time asking them about Belfast, but their answers are still underwhelming and similar. Also on the album was a personal exploration called 'Knowledge of Beauty':

'I became very interested in Ireland, about where I came from. I went back over there. I had a look around and stuff. I wanted to find something that had some kind of meaning. The other things that I'd been experiencing with my work had become trivialised. So, knowledge of beauty: even though my mum was from what would be considered now as a poor background, she had this understanding of beauty and music and stuff. I wanted to call the song 'My National Pride' and my brother said, "Ah, it's a bit strong, that".

'I've gone through really negative periods of my life where I've blamed England for everything. You know, only Irish people are good and English and bad – and that's stupidity when I look back on it now. It's easy to do that and it's wrong. Now, I hope I've got some kind of balance with it.'

Shane MacGowan from the Pogues was also a Behan admirer. In the first of the band's songs, 'Streams of Whiskey', Brendan is the spirit walker who comes into Shane's dreams and shows him the secret of transcendental drinking. The writer becomes MacGowan's talisman. He keeps him safe during treacherous times, he provides eloquence, philosophy and the art of looking steady in a white shirt and the Clery's Sunday suit.

MacGowan was previously active around London's punk scene, inspired by John Lydon and reborn as Shane O'Hooligan. He sang with the Nipple Erectors and their second incarnation, the Nips. He was born in Kent but his people were from Tipperary and he lived there in the feral, summer months. After the Nips, there was a very brief interlude in a band called the New Republicans. Shane was joined by members of the Millwall Chainsaws and the New Bastards. Their only show was in April 1981 at the Cabaret Futura club in Soho, London, managed by Richard Strange. The set included 'The Patriot Game' and 'The Bold Fenian Men'. Shane had plundered his parents' record collection, finding favour with Luke Kelly and the Dubliners as well as the Clancy Brothers. Not all the clientele at the club were pleased with this, as Shane recounted to Ann Scanlon: 'There was a group of about 20 drunken squaddies who took exception to the songs and started pelting us with chips.'

The rebellious life had its limitations, then, and a fusillade of French fries from soldiers returning from a tour of duty in Northern Ireland was a setback. They regrouped in 1982 as Pogue Mahone (Póg mo thóin is Irish for 'kiss my ass') but when a presenter at BBC Radio Scotland put in a complaint they settled for the Pogues. Shane's Republicanism was implied at this point although their version of Behan's 'The Auld Triangle' left little doubt about the reason for the singer's incarceration. Shane explained the overall method: 'What we were saying is fuck everything.'

As a bonus, the Pogues accented the generosity of the group spirit. The first album sounded like the jukebox in Biddy Mulligan's, Kilburn. Shane's own songs sat respectfully beside the time-tested ballads and sundry Paddywhackery. By the second album, his writing was magnificent and the reach was all-inclusive. It was music for the stumblebums, bar flies and the lost, deracinated souls. Everybody was invited onto that rudderless, leaking raft.

Album three was *If I Should Fall from Grace with God* in 1988 and there was a Shane lyric called 'Birmingham Six'. He was directing attention to a miscarriage of justice, insisting that the wrong men were jailed in 1975 for the Birmingham pub bombs. Public interest in the cause had been growing, led by the journalist Chris Mullin who had written a book and authored a series of *World In Action* TV investigations. Shane's song also mentioned the Guildford Four, another disputed case from 1975. Supporters claimed that witness statements had been extracted by force.

'It's about people getting framed up by the British system of justice, or whatever you want to call it,' Shane explained. 'It specifically mentions the Birmingham Six and the Guildford Four but there's also a verse about the eight guys who were recently done by the SAS (in Loughgall, 1987). Basically, it's about anybody who's been locked up without any real evidence against them.'

'Birmingham Six' was subject to a ban by the Independent Broadcasting Authority (IBA). The ban was rescinded in 1991 when the convictions of the six were quashed.

The Pogues were self-regulating in that the band members had various left-leaning outlooks and a stake in the story. After his departure from the group, Shane became more outspoken with his politics. On *The Crock of Gold* in 1997 he unleashed a series of 'Paddy' variations, each of them outside the law. 'Paddy Rolling Stone' was an unquenchable bad boy. 'Rock'n'Roll Paddy' was fuelled on Elvis and Big Tom and his methods were appalling. 'Paddy Public Enemy No. 1' was based on the life of Dominic 'Mad Dog' McGlinchey who had served with the IRA and then the INLA before being killed in 1994. He was linked to a series of killings and admitted his involvement in the Droppin Well bombing of 1987 in which 17 died, including 11 soldiers. When asked about McGlinchey, Shane remarked, 'He was a great man'.

'Skipping Rhymes' was also on the album:

> *'We put the hood around his head*
> *Then we shot the bastard dead*
> *With a nick nack paddy wack*
> *Give a dog a bone*
> *Send the stupid bastards home'*

The first three words in the Andy White catalogue were '*Protestant or Catholic?*'. The song was 'Religious Persuasion', released in 1985 and it re-enacted a street showdown in Belfast during the conflict. In Andy's case, it had happened around Annadale, near the River Lagan. He was unharmed by the brief interrogation but for others it was the prelude to violence.

'I had that youthful self-belief and probably arrogance,' says Andy. 'I just thought nobody had said anything about what we were, in the medium that we were listening to. I'd always written poems since a very early age. Suddenly, they became songs at the start of the 80s. With that punk attitude and seeing John Cooper Clarke, I knew that if you had something to say, you just had to say it.

'I knew this was a perversion of religion. It had nothing to do with actual religion and that's why the song has got so many biblical references in it. If you tried to write a song about the religious conflict in Northern Ireland it would be impossible. I didn't think of it in those terms. I was just telling the ironic, hyperbolic version of what happened to me. I was a middle-class boy, but the Troubles affected everybody. It didn't matter if you were a middle-class boy.'

Andy had an earlier project called the Ghost of Electricity – noise and Dylan-inspired bravura. He had recently watched the Bob documentary *Don't Look Back* when it toured the art cinemas. At the same time, artists like Lloyd Cole and Roddy Frame from Aztec Camera were hipping young audiences to the troubadour strain and making the wearing of suede jackets permissible again. 'I remember thinking, "This is it." Every generation had to have these people. They looked like French poets from the 19th century.'

Rod McVey played the Hammond Organ – the Al Kooper in his Dylan equation. They recorded the *Rave On Andy White* album in Homestead Studios with the encouragement of producer Mudd Wallace and late-night whiskey fever. On 'The Soldiers' Sash', they took opposing anthems, spliced them up and desecrated the lot.

'It was like a punk reaction to the stuff they were throwing at us. It was absurd. I didn't do it as a conscious thing but humour is the way you have the most force. 'The Soldiers' Sash' was outrageous and funny to us. To make a complete farce out of it in the middle with 'I Am The Walrus' and stuff.'

Later songs were about love and whimsy, travel and surprise, but Northern Ireland returned to his work at intervals. In 1987, he read a story in *The Observer* about the Guildford Four. He read the Robert Kee book on the subject and made his call. 'It was obvious they didn't do it. I had hung around in enough London bars with stoned Irishmen to know, after reading detailed accounts of those who had been arrested, that they didn't do it. Whatever the circumstantial evidence may have been and whatever their political persuasion.'

Andy had delighted in the Dylan song 'Hurricane', his rolling defence of the imprisoned boxer Rubin Carter. Released as a single, the song was such a long, churning spell that the listener had to flip it over for the second instalment.

'It's a masterpiece and it's got all those details, and the lines are so good and the story comes from putting all those details together. If he'd just written the narrative, it wouldn't have worked. It really works like a song.'

So, this was a model for 'The Guildford Four' with its shifting perspectives and unfolding pain. There was mention of the Balcolmbe Street bombers, convicted IRA members who had admitted to the crime. There were dates and set pieces and an outro that lacked a conclusion because there was not one. Soon after writing it, Andy sang it on *The Late Show* on BBC 2. In his recollection, he did it without permission and was largely prepared for any criticism.

'When you've grown up in Belfast and you've said lots of things like I've said, you just get used to shutting lots and lots of it out. People don't want to discuss it with you and they definitely don't want to discuss your use of language or music or stuff, which I really treasure and which I'm really careful about. They just want to criticise you. Or punch you in the face. So, I got used not taking very much notice of it.'

But Gerard Conlon, one of the four who were imprisoned, did hear it, and after he was freed in 1989, he met Andy at the Finsbury Park Fleadh:

'I was also very wary of what they would think of it. I didn't know. There are so many walls up. It's not like everybody goes, "Andy, well done, it's great you wrote a song about it". People would be completely quick to jump on you – "Why are doing this, what gives you the right to do this?" So, you get critics talking like that but when I met Gerry Conlon, he said they listened to it in prison and they loved it. That meant such a lot to me. I had played it on the Dave Fanning show that's what they heard in prison.'

Another song that became part of Andy's repertoire was 'There Were Roses' by Tommy Sands. It was about two friends from the Mayobridge area, part of a community that was defined by music, art and open-mindedness. Both were killed, one as a reprisal for the other. The chorus has a crushing inevitability and Tommy sang it with a regretful softness.

'I played it when the Berlin Wall came down,' says Andy. 'There was a very long-running political festival in East Berlin called the Festival of Political Song. And it ran during the time of the Communist DDR. The only people booked were from Communist bloc countries, like Cuba, South America, Russia, but in 1989 the wall came down and the Committee could book whoever they wanted. And Tommy Sands was legendary in the festival. He had played it in the DDR. I had heard the song through Rod McVey and when I got there, Tommy Sands was God. They all knew that song. The narrative of that song is perfect. It just said everything. I think it's one of the greatest songs ever written. He found a particular and just widens it out to the universal in a way that folk music is used to doing.'

In 2017 Andy released an album, *The Guilty and the Innocent*, a return to political writing. He found that his new songs were fitting into good and bad camps. He was using a flat tone, holding on to some objectivity. The title track was the last piece of work. It had 12 verses and it returned the listener to Desolation Row, perhaps wiser, but also less judgemental. Andy had been home to Belfast during the marching season and the news reports interviewed children who were defiantly building bonfires close to a residential area. There was a stand-off and many inflammatory words.

'You can say what's happening and you can point it out in a poetic way, but you don't get to judge anybody, really. You can say, "These are guilty and these are innocent", but actually they're the same as us. All we went through is in us still.

'Bits of the world now have more serious experiences than we went through when we were growing up. Which is bizarre. Suddenly, the whole world talks constantly about terrorism, all the time. After the fall of the Iron Curtain, they replaced the enemy with the terrorist.

'Most people feel like artists feel, which is that kind of heartbroken, blank feeling of desolation. That's what art has to represent because nobody else is uttering it.'

John T. Davis, the film-maker who had made the punk documentary *Shellshock Rock* was working on a project around the Maze Prison in the later part of the 80s. He had been corresponding with Wilfie Cummings who was serving a life sentence. Wilfie had taught himself to paint and play guitar and had amassed a store of his own music. The prisoner was also writing to Vernon Oxford, a former honky-tonk singer whose Nashville career had been supplanted by gospel singing and old-time religion. John T. Davis saw a story emerging:

'It was about a fallen country and western singer who becomes a healer and preacher. He's sent as a missionary from this little church in Tennessee, to these little gospel halls here. He's bringing Jesus back to the Irish. It was a bizarre way of telling a story about the Protestant side of fundamentalism here. It allowed me to put Vernon on at the Liverpool Supporters Club at the top of the Shankill Road. And to go to Darkley.

'Finally, I wanted Vernon to play, like Johnny Cash, for the prisoners. The Northern Ireland Office said no but I filmed in the Prison Officers' Country Music Club. They were all dressed up in the satin and the fringes and the hats and toy guns. The only way I could get Vernon to perform in the Maze was to perform for prison officers. That's the way it happened. They had own quick-on-the-draw competitions, with toy guns. And during the day, they carried the live ammo. There's a sequence where one of the prison officers is singing 'Long Black Veil', a very profound murder ballad. I got a picture of an ashtray and burger and a gun on the table.'

'Wilfie wrote reams and reams of writing and songs that he'd put together. There was a particular day – I'd been up at the morning and he'd asked me to try and get some of his songs to Johnny Cash (who was playing in town). They were very much in the country and Irish tradition. if you like. I thought, "Maybe there's half a chance", because of Cash and his background. I smuggled the songs out, tucked them in my back in a jiffy bag and got through the security and went back to town and did my day's work and went to the back of the Ulster Hall and rapped on the door. The manager eventually came down. I said, "I've got these songs from a lifer in the Maze and I'd like very much to give them to Johnny Cash".

'That was that and I went round to the show, got in and was part of the audience. The prison officers where there with their flags and their gear. The second half of the show starts and Johnny Cash comes out carrying the jiffy bag and I fucking nearly died when I saw this. And he started to talk to the audience, he said, "These songs have been delivered to me, from the Maze Prison today" – and then the prison officers roared, waving the flags and everything – "and I'd like to do one of them". It turned out to be one of those Hank Williams-type monologue songs. It was called 'Halleluiah Joe'. It was about this guy in the back of the congregation who would shout Halleluiah at whatever the preacher had said. And so Cash did it and brought the house down. And I just teared up, I couldn't believe it.

'The prison officers loved it because they knew who it was – they knew it was Wilfie's stuff. It was a strange sort of thing that was going on there. They all knew him and there was a kind of camaraderie as well. They were country music fans as well, and Wilfie was trying his best to write country music. There was friendship there and they got very much off on the fact. I wasn't questioned afterwards for smuggling the stuff out.'

BIG DECISION

The Adventures turned a Bob Dylan lyric on its head when they sang, '*these times are not changing*. Instead of a flood tide of retribution, 'Broken Land' had rivers that ran too deep. History seemed stuck and while Pat Gribben had started writing the song with an image of riots in Soweto, he soon brought it home. The drum sound was vast and expensive but the uilleann pipes were calling.

The band's contract had been bought out by Elektra Records from Chrysalis, so they were now an American signing, a major label priority and they played 12 nights at Wembley Arena supporting Fleetwood Mac. 'Broken Land' was on many 'A' list radio schedules and it reached top 20 in the UK singles chart in 1988. Yet when singer Terry Sharpe went back to Belfast, the guy on the far side of the bar was still not impressed.

'Hey, Sharpie,' he said. 'Northern Ireland is not a publicity stunt.'

The same critic might have taken issue with Gary Moore in 1985. 'Out In The Fields' was recorded with his Thin Lizzy compadre Phil Lynott and seemed to imply a connection to the conflict. Parts of the video were filmed around Divis Flats but Belfast-born Gary was more circumspect when he talked about the song:

'The song was partially written about Northern Ireland. The video was all set against Belfast and the soldiers. It was just a general anti-war song but we thought because of where we came from and what it meant to us, we wanted to make it about that when it came to making the video.'

Other artists were unhappily involved. Tina Turner had charted in 1989 with 'The Best', a song that had previously been recorded by Bonnie Tyler. The song was then adopted by Johnny Adair and the Shankill UFF. 'Simply the Best' was the motto on their shirts when 50 paramilitary members joined the Orange Order protests at Drumcree in 2000. Johnny had a matching shirt for his Alsatian dog, Rebel. During the same summer, the UFF was involved in a summer 'culture festival' when the song was played out and masked men fired their shots in the air. Johnny Adair explained the scenario to *Hot Press*:

'What used to happen when UFF 'C' Company did a show of strength – that means hooded men coming out reading statements – before they'd come out, we'd have a function. And prior to them coming out, we'd blast Tina Turner's 'Simply the Best' for about a minute-and-a-half, and the next thing the hooded men would come out and the crowd would just be in uproar.

'So, the music industry must have heard about this, because somebody from Tina Turner's record company rang our offices – which at that time was the UDP (Ulster Democratic Party) offices on the Shankill – and asked would 'C' Company, and especially that man 'Mad Dog' Adair, kindly refrain from using Tina's song as their anthem for displaying guns and what have you. Ha, ha!'

Derry had an alternative soundtrack. One of the most striking acts from the city was Bam Bam and the Calling. They were wise to Echo and the Bunnymen, New Order and Orange Juice, taking notes from the Velvet Underground, Can, the Doors and old soul records. But the city had also made an imprint, as the band's vocalist Paul McCartney remembers:

'When we were kicking about at the extreme start of the 80s, the biggest thing in our head was not really the revolution in Ireland it was more to do with the cops, hassling us all the time. We felt it was getting a bit more Orwellian. Getting searched, houses getting raided. The technology was improving and cameras were looking in windows and stuff. That was our thing, a slightly paranoid dimension. A bit of unease there, like something sinister was happening.'

Raymond Gorman played guitar with them for a while in 1984. He had returned to Derry after graduating from University of Ulster and was also playing records at a club night called the Left Bank. The other DJs were Micky Rooney and John O'Neill, the former Undertone who'd barely played his guitar in the year since he'd left the band. John had lost his confidence but the club nights were joyous explorations of reggae, hip hop and musical outsiders like Pere Ubu and Captain Beefheart.

Raymond and John starting playing music, eventually borrowing the band name from a Bam Bam and the Calling song, 'That Petrol Emotion'. As with many alternative groups of that era, there was a plan, almost a manifesto.

'I remember me and John, we did sit down,' says Raymond. 'It was deliberate, we never really talked to the others about it we just kinda said to them, "This is how it's going to be"; there was no discussion. I remember we had quite a hardcore sorta song in the early days but we thought it was too much. The chorus was like, *'keep that finger on the trigger, let's just say that I'm a white nigger'*. And at first it was like "Yeah" and then it was like "naw, naw, naw, naw, this is no good, this is not right". So, we changed it then.'

Raymond had been on the Derry Civil Rights march with his father on October 5 1968:

'I got water-cannoned and chased off the bridge. I remember my dad saying to me, "You'll remember this for the rest of your life," you know? And I think it really has informed everything that I've done. I think I was very, very lucky growing up in Derry because I had access to both communities. I was obviously going to a Catholic school but all my friends on the street were all Protestant, and I was in the Protestant Cubs (Cub Scouts) and it was fantastic. We would go do stuff in the Church of Ireland church. They even took communion as well so it was really nice for me to be shown that at an early age so I could never, ever get into the entrenched views or whatever.'

John O'Neill had his own agenda at this point:

'The 1981 hunger strike had happened. I'd become more politicised. I was fully behind Sinn Féin. I could see that despite the maelstrom of violence and the recriminations that were happening that (there was) the intransigence of the Unionist Party and the British government. The Undertones had obviously stayed clear of all that sort of thing, so I just thought that we'd got a platform. We didn't wanna end like Stiff Little Fingers but even if we didn't necessarily feel able to write political-type songs we could at least mention something in interviews. It was great going all around Europe and trying to explain the Nationalist side of things 'cos obviously the British media at that time weren't allowing anybody to express an alternative view from the Unionist or their own point of view.'

The band moved to London in October 1984 and featured John's brother and fellow Undertone Damian and drummer Ciaran McLaughlin. They introduced singer Steve Mack, who was born in New York but more recently had been a resident of Seattle. The press release for the 1985 debut 'Keen' noted: 'That Petrol Emotion pledge to put a spanner in the works of ugly pop and to attempt to redress the balance on totally ill-informed coverage of Northern Ireland'. The Derry boys began printing their names *as Gaeilge* on the record sleeves.

'I'd got a bad impression of England,' says Raymond. 'A bit of a chip on my shoulder, most definitely. We were living hand-to-mouth. The first year was miserable so I think there was a lot of getting your armour on to protect yourself. To try and keep yourself at a distance. But what I also thought was that Irish names look really beautiful written down.'

The artwork drew attention to strip searches in Armagh Women's Prison, Diplock Courts, 'thick Paddy' jokes, the Prevention of Terrorism Act and the use of plastic bullets by security forces.

'All the Petrols' sleeves dealt with issues to do with the injustices against the Nationalist community,' says John. 'People had been blinded by the army or the RUC shooting plastic bullets at point blank range at people. They did it with impunity. There was never any outcry about it outside of the Nationalist community.'

The band moved from Polydor Records to Virgin in 1987. Their first release with the new label was 'Genius Move'. On the back of the sleeve there was a quote from Irish revolutionary Liam Mellows, who had taken part in the 1916 Rising in Galway and was executed by the pro-treaty forces during the War of Independence in 1922. The quote explained the need for an economic revolution as well as a political one. Perhaps confusingly, the quote was attributed to *The Politics of Irish Freedom* by Sinn Féin leader Gerry Adams.

'There was no need to put Gerry Adams' name to that whatsoever,' says Raymond, 'because it was from the Liam Fellows book. But John couldn't be arsed doing it himself, so he got our tour manager to sort it out. And, of course, he didn't know, so he put it in. And it was like, "Fucking hell!" And that's when we moved to Virgin and then when people must have saw Gerry Adams it was like, "Fuck this". I mean, 'Genius Move', when you think about it – that was when our momentum was at its most high. It should have been the one to push us through. And I think it was because of that sleeve. People just saw Gerry Adams; they're not looking at anything else, you know what I mean? It was a huge own goal. Huge.

'*The Sun* did a story about 10 bands that would shout off their mouths. It was basically a real hatchet job and we were one of the bands. It was basically saying we were the musical wing of the IRA. It really hurt me a lot, you know? I just thought, "No, you're talking about civil rights but you're perceived as the musical wing of the IRA". How could you win against that?'

The band had previously reached 42 in the singles charts with 'Big Decision' in 1987. It was a singular blend of groove, riff and message. Musically, John was saluting the Velvet Underground and setting Steve Mack up with the line '*plastic bullets chic headlines in store*'. The song title was a commentary on the British government and their tentative approach to Northern Ireland. 'Big Decision' was denied entry to the UK top 40 by Wet Wet Wet and 'Wishing I Was Lucky'.

That Petrol Emotion were touring America when the Enniskillen bombing took place. Damian recalls the scenario:

'We'd these guys in the dressing room, American Petrols' fans, and they were going, "Yeah, it's good, isn't it?" Arseholes. They thought it was a good thing for 'the cause'. We were all going, "Is this worth it? These fucking moron followers here – who turned out to be more right-wing than Reagan even?" Nah, that was a bad, bad time.'

The music was wiry, inventive, exciting and Steve Mack was a charismatic singer but this aspect was not always given its due. Raymond recalls a moment in 1988 when the profile was ready for a rethink:

'Me and Ciaran did the sleeve notes for *End of the Millennium Psychosis Blues* – that was all about Civil Rights. I thought, "I've nothing more to say anymore". Because there was some stuff I was a little bit uncomfortable with. I thought my whole thing was always "I'm not going to alienate my friends". My Protestant friends who I went to college with and stuff – I'm not going to alienate them. My whole thing was not to do that.'

The Belfast band Ruefrex came from the Shankill Road. Paul Burgess and Tom Coulter had attended the Boys' Model School, a few years younger than the Stiff Little Fingers intake. Their first single, 'One by One', was released by Good Vibrations and the lyric quoted from James Plunkett's *Strumpet City*. On stage, they delivered a formidable quake, but Paul Burgess was writing considered lyrics. He was looking to understand his locality but also aware of the violent context:

'Tyndale Community Centre was in the area where most of us lived. In keeping with our commitment to play for ordinary kids in their own communities we went up there to play. We used it a couple of times to rehearse, but, chillingly, we found out later that while all that was happening, the Shankill Butchers had been using that place as a staging post. While we knew there was a paramilitary element around and an affiliation to the centre, we had no idea about this and it was really, really shocking to us. Soon after, when that was exposed, the RUC came up and absolutely gutted the place, in a manner that it couldn't be used again, which was the best thing. They should have razed it to the ground.

'That particular group terrorised their own community as well. There would be stories of these guys going into petrol stations, filling up and driving off because no one was prepared to say anything. It was like the Wild West. Within their own community, they did what they wanted. So, you were aware that there was this renegade faction within the paramilitaries. Like, in the American Civil War there was the guy (William) Quantrill, who rode under the black flag, before the Confederacy, and nobody could say anything about him. So, definitely, you knew who they were and you knew what was happening.'

Paul had connections to the Workers' Party and accepted an invitation from the playwright Martin Lynch to perform in the Republican Turf Lodge.

'For four guys from the Shankill, aged 17 or 18, to be going in there at the time was fairly daunting. It sounds a bit of a cliché but it completely reinforced our analysis of the situation. We played on the Woodvale the night before we went into Turf Lodge. The kids were all dressed exactly the same, they enjoyed the songs that the Woodvale kids enjoyed. They weren't so keen on the songs that the Woodvale kids weren't so keen on. It reinforced to us that this was a pointless sectarian undertaking.

'We decided that we were going to try and do community centres. We maintained throughout a fairly uncompromising stance, in regards to where we were from and the fact that that did not necessarily follow that we would be Monarchists and knee-jerk, into all the usual stereotypical images that would attach themselves to our community. We put this out at every possible opportunity.'

They had a song called 'Cross the Line', a call for young people to break ranks. There was a 1980 BBC documentary of the same name, which focused on the desolation of the Shankill and the rough vigour of singer Allan Clarke, employed in timber yards and brush factories, quenched by Clan Dew in back alleys and determined to manage his anger. 'I still lose the head,' he says. 'It's just I learnt to control it more.'

They made an emphatic return in 1985 with 'The Wild Colonial Boy'. On the cover, an assault rifle is being packaged up, ready for delivery to Ireland. It was a remarkable song with a particular target: ex-pat fundraisers in the US, sending arms to the IRA.

'That was explicitly about NORAID,' says Paul. 'At the time of writing it was a big story, in regards to Irish-Americans going around funding arms shipments to Northern Ireland. So, it was written through the eyes of an Irish-American and it's obviously pretty scathing of that community. It was intended to be – in regard to an over-simplified analysis of the Northern Ireland situation.'

The lyric imagines an inhabitant of Wisconsin who thinks he is being true to his bloodline by donating money. The lyric wailed, '*eat up all your TV dinners, open up your wallet wide... and let your green be seen*'. A similar theme was also aired on the Stiff Little Fingers song 'Each Dollar a Bullet'. Burgess regarded this single as a final throw.

'The band had virtually ground to a halt when I decided I'd have a crack at England. I'd written 'Wild Colonial Boy' back in 1980, and always wanted to put it out as a single, so I talked the others into having one last shot at it before quitting. We recorded it off our own bat, with our own money, so we weren't going to compromise at all. We stuck the Armalite on the cover, put the lyrics on the back and didn't expect any BBC play because it was too hot to handle. It was going to be our last shot. This was the song we felt had to be done. For every reason. The totally unexpected interest aroused by 'Wild Colonial Boy' resulted in Ruefrex being touted as one of the UK's brightest young hopes.'

Ruefrex later released 'Political Wings', a discourse on the paramilitaries' dual policy of 'Armalite and ballot box'. It became a Republican strategy after the hunger strikes but neither did the song spare the Loyalist equivalents.

'It was pretty much a didactic thing, basically saying that the political wing from my community – and, I suspect, the political wing from the Republican community – really do not represent the people that they propose. '*What are you, street people or military staff?*' is one of the lines. One the cover, there's a Gerry Adams type figure as both the playing card terrorist and the politician – which was prescient now, looking back.'

The *Political Wings* EP also featured 'On Kingsmill Road', remembering the killing of 10 workers by the IRA in South Armagh. 'Playing Cards with Dead Men' looked at how the Loyalist community had been abused by the State, encouraged to be patriotic in wartime and then disregarded afterwards.

> '*And you're playing cards with dead men,*
> *but you're losing every hand.*
> *You cheat my people past and present,*
> *We'll live and die upon this land.*'

'We didn't try to walk the middle ground, in terms of Stiff Little Fingers, trying to be all things to all people. I think we advocated at an early stage that we never can be that. People will always see us for who we are and where we're from, anyway.'

Ruefrex did share with Stiff Little Fingers the will to support integrated education, particularly Lagan College in Belfast

'The fledgling Lagan College was two pre-fab huts. At the time, it wasn't about fundraising, it was about just bringing attention to the school. It fitted completely at the time into how we viewed the situation. It was something I was always interested in and I subsequently wrote a book called *Crisis of Conscience*, specifically about the education system in Northern Ireland and the necessity for integrated education. It was always a theme that ran through us.'

In 1988, Nanci Griffith was in the back seat of a Ford Cortina that was stopped by an Army unit in Ardoyne. The driver was Seamus O'Neill, production manager for a local radio station in Belfast and former drummer with the Bankrobbers. It was a disconcerting moment for the Texan folksinger but one of the soldiers was familiar with her music and was particularly fond of 'From A Distance', a Julie Gold song that Nanci had recorded in 1987. He asked for her autograph. She agreed, but on one condition. 'I said that I would give him anything if he just took his gun out of my face.'

She wrote a song about the encounter called 'It's A Hard Life Wherever You Go' and released it in 1989. True enough, she was in the back seat of the car in West Belfast, driving on the left side of the road and talking to Seamus the driver, who recognised a local child on the Falls Road and wondered what kind of a future the kid might expect. Nanci heard the commentary about the barbed wire and how difficult it was to find a way out, but she did not pass judgement. She was a visitor from America, a student of non-violence and aware of the shortcomings closer to home.

In the second verse she was in Chicago, watching an adult in a café queue abusing black people in front of his children. She imagined that he joined a Ku Klux Klan rally at night and that his kids watched him slip away in his robes, accepting this behaviour as normal. In the final verse, she recalled her liberal upbringing in the 60s, inspired by Martin Luther King and taking her news reports from Walter Cronkite, 'the most trusted man in America', on *CBS News*. The song expressed disappointment but also admitted some kind of complicity, that even Nanci was not absolved.

'When I wrote 'Hard Life',' she explained, 'what I wanted to express is that the hatred damages children and causes the cycle to continue. And we do a terrible disservice to the next generation, and to the future of the world when we pass on our hatreds to our children. And I hope the song expresses that not just in relation to Northern Ireland, but universally.'

On August 31 1994, the Provisional IRA announced 'a complete cessation of military operations'. Its statement continued, 'we urge everyone to approach this new situation with energy, determination and patience'. On October 13, the Combined Loyalist Military Command made their announcement. 'The CLMC will universally cease all operational hostilities as from 12 midnight on Thursday 13th October 1994. In all sincerity, we offer to the loved ones of all innocent victims over the past 20 years, abject and true remorse. No words of ours will compensate for the intolerable suffering they have undergone during the conflict.'

Between the two ceasefire declarations there was 'Zombie' by the Cranberries, words on the armed struggle and the blood lineage since the Easter Rising. In Dolores O'Riordan's view it was *the same old thing since 1916*. Dolores didn't want to commemorate the battles. The video made this more explicit as the British Army patrolled peace walls in West Belfast, children played in the wasteland and the names of the fallen were flaking off the walls. Interestingly, the band scenes were shot in Los Angeles. Dolores was daubed in gold paint and stood by a memorial cross, lilting her message that people were dying for a cause she could not follow. She sang of the men with their tanks, bombs and guns, a seeming echo to the old ballad 'Johnny I Hardly Knew Ye', or perhaps 'The Men Behind the Wire'. Finally, she turned to the paramilitaries and tried to understand their motives. '*What's in your head?*' she repeated, angry and disbelieving.

Dolores had written the song while touring the UK in 1993 – shortly after the Warrington bomb attack on March 20, when the IRA had targeted a shopping centre, killing two children, Johnathan Ball and Tim Parry. 'A lot of people need to grow up,' she told *NME* a week before the record's release. 'If these adults have a problem with these other adults, well, go and fight them. But don't stick a bomb somewhere where you'll hurt kids and ordinary women who never did anything to you. Some people might think they're getting their point across, but to me, it's pathetic, really.'

The Derry band Schtum weren't impressed. 'She's from Limerick, what the fuck would she know?' they told *Melody Maker*. 'You're talking about the last 25 years of a much bigger and wider problem that has gone on for hundreds of years.'

But Dolores felt that she had her own imperative. 'You should just let it go. That's my thing in life; I get over experiences and write about them. Life's too short. The last four years of my life have gone so fast. People shouldn't fall out over countries and territory so much. It doesn't matter. You should look to your grave, and that's your country.'

'Sunrise' by the Divine Comedy begins in the murk and ambiguity of Northern Ireland in the 80s. In the lyric, Neil Hannon puts out the idea that his birthplace, Londonderry is also known as Derry city. His home is Enniskillen but historically it's about the mythology of *Inis Ceithleann*, water and land and ancient footfalls. The singer gives his dues to the different narratives and steers a self-conscious path between them. Then, on November 8 1987, the bomb goes off at the Cenotaph on Remembrance Sunday and there is no easy way to walk that line:

> *'Oh, what a clever boy*
> *To Watch Your hometown be destroyed*
> *I knew that I would not stay long*
> *So, I kept my head down and carried on.'*

Eleven people were killed and 63 were injured by the IRA bomb. It was followed by claims and revisions, numbness and distress. Christy Moore began to re-evaluate his politics. Chris de Burgh wrote 'Remembrance Day' and dedicated it to Marie Wilson, who had died holding her father's hand in the rubble. '*I am ashamed to be Irish on Remembrance Day*', he sang. Bono was on tour in Denver and his onstage revulsion was captured in the *Rattle And Hum* film:

'And let me tell you something. I've had enough of Irish-Americans who haven't been back to their country in 20 or 30 years come up to me and talk about the resistance, the revolution back home, and the glory of the revolution, and the glory of dying for the revolution. Fuck the revolution! Where is the glory in bombing a Remembrance Day parade of old-age pensioners, their medals taken out and polished up for the day? Where's the glory in that? To leave them dying or crippled for life or dead under the rubble of the revolution that the majority of the people in my country don't want.'

Neil Hannon released 'Sunrise' on the 1998 album *Fin de Siècle*. The song had the benefit of distance, a chance for the writer to be more considered.

"Sunrise' was the most difficult song I have ever written,' he said, 'and it is still the most difficult to actually perform and I don't want to sort of make it into some sort of 'Sunday, Bloody Sunday' where I will never do it again. Because I will, because it is cool. But it was just so hard, it was like walking on eggshells trying to write the lyrics for that song.'

Yet he definitely wanted to dismiss the patriot game. In mid-song, he grows weary of the different semantics and name-calling:

'In many ways you want to put people's backs up – to not kowtow to the kind of general political correctness of the North. You are meant to talk in hushed tones about various situations, and I just wanted to lay on the line and say that, "You know, pretty much nothing is worth being buried for".'

But 'Sunrise' was also born into a peace process and so there was a cautious release in the final verse, the idea that transformation was possible. That's what makes the song resound as a mature work. However, it wasn't his first try. Interestingly, there was a previous Neil Hannon song on the subject. Back in 1988 he had released a collection of songs called *Exposition*. The band was October, named after a U2 album and featuring a musical accomplice, Lawrence Hoy. The music was very much of its time, with spatial guitars, a drum machine and too much flange pedal. 'Remembrance Day' summons the bottomless dolour of Joy Division as Neil tries to relate to the atrocity:

> *'I saw the wall, row upon row*
> *Of those who fell so long ago*
> *I watched them fall again today*
> *No uniform, no rifles, they*
> *Have lit a flame for all to see*
> *Not just for you, not just for me...'*

'Remembrance Day' may be Hannon juvenilia, but it comes directly out of the experience. There is no artistic cover. Neil looked by ruefully to this early creation:

'When I was teaching myself to write songs in the 80s I was definitely under the tutelage of Sting and Bono and I came up with some truly awful political statements, you know, very simplistic. When the Enniskillen Bomb went off and I wrote a song it was truly terrible. I called it 'Remembrance Day'. It's on some demo somewhere and I hope you never find it and, you know, I listened to it once about five years ago and I have since decided to never, ever think about it again because it is too awful. You know, it is very difficult to write things about the situation. It's very difficult to write pop songs about serious issues. So I generally don't.'

Therapy? did not go glibly into the new dawn either. Their method was contrary, the music was often cacophonous while Andy Cairns peopled his songs with crackpots and deviants. During their rise in the early 90s, one of the popular Celtic forms was the folksy, 'raggle taggle' sound of the Waterboys, the Hothouse Flowers and the Black Velvet Band. It was a time of fiddles and waistcoats and crushed velvet. In contrast, Therapy? delivered searing noise, a quizzical name and influences from American hardcore punk. They listened to Big Black, Hüsker Dü and Snuff and went touring with Henry Rollins and Hole. Their horror was often internalised. Some of the macabre characters in the music came from the gothic reaches of County Antrim.

'We used to be into kind of weird stuff when the band started,' says Andy. 'Watching weird documentaries, reading books about how rednecks in America would live. Then we sort of came to realise, the more we started practising out in Larne, that a lot of these people where living on our own doorstep. The kind of people that the Butthole Surfers would sing about – there were plenty of those characters in County Antrim.

'There was one guy in Ballyclare called Constable Cornflakes that wasn't in the cops, but he used to walk round dressed as one and pretend to be talking on a walkie talkie radio. There was another guy who use to cut the head off rabbits – it would be a Saturday night and the people would wake up on Sunday morning and all the cars in the Main Street had rabbit heads on their aerials.

'I used to have a summer job at Crazy Prices and a guy that I worked with, he went and sniffed glue. He got up and went home and in the next couple of weeks his mum and dad died within a couple of months of each other, he met his girlfriend, he got his dad's house handed down to him and he got a job with the Big Pink Truck company, independent trucks, and went around. He woke up a year later in bed and he was back in the field. He had been tripping for 15 minutes and he swears to this day that he lived a year of his life and woke up one morning back in this field.'

At the time of the 1994 ceasefires, Therapy? had sold 650,000 copies of their album *Troublegum*. They had found a rock audience without losing their indie heartland. But the work rate had been punishing and substances had been consumed. The sessions for *Infernal Love* involved the cellist Martin McCarrick and the sonic freedom challenged their new fanbase. The song 'Loose' was based on an LSD misadventure in Botanic Gardens, Belfast. And in their peculiar way, they acknowledged the changing political climate in Northern Ireland. The song '30 Seconds' considers the work of paedophile priests and addresses the vanities of stardom. There's a moment of reflection when Cairns looks back to his youth in Ballyclare and the Blue Lamp Discos that were organised by the Royal Ulster Constabulary. He charts a feverish journey that has caused the band members to crack in San Francisco but, most astonishingly, Northern Ireland may be hauling itself out a violent past:

> 'There's one thing that I should remember
> There is a light at the end of the tunnel.'

For Billy Bragg, this era was a chance to stress the smallness, the normality of a city that had earned the right to be unremarkable. His 1996 song 'Northern Industrial Town' saves the punchline for the end. Listeners may be thinking that he's fondly describing a mill town in Yorkshire or a revived Victorian sea port on England's west coast. It's a place that has a couple of football teams, some terraced houses, tolerable rain, decent bar bands and a fair economy.

> 'But it's not Leeds or Manchester
> Liverpool, Sheffield, nor Glasgow

It's not Newcastle-on-Tyne. It's Belfast
It's just a northern industrial town.'

Music was brought in to copper-fasten the peace. The Northern Ireland Office asked Van Morrison for the use of his closing line from the song 'Coney Island'. He agreed and so this uncharted era was signposted by a lyric: *'wouldn't it be great if it was like this all of the time?'* Van Morrison had previously imagined Linden Arden, a Celtic warrior archetype with his whiskey, his hatchet and his gun. Now he was singing in front of Belfast's City Hall, before President Bill Clinton and the First Lady, Hillary. It was November 30 1995 and the Christmas lights were switched on by the American leader. Van marked the occasion with music and was joined on stage by Brian Kennedy, a vocalist from the Falls Road who sensed the layers of significance:

'It wasn't lost on me how important it was that you had somebody who grew up where I grew up – a Catholic upbringing – and you had Van Morrison who grew up in East Belfast with a Protestant upbringing and we sang a song called 'No Religion'. I remember thinking, "I love the way that this is saying it without saying it. We are united just by being together." At that moment, what was very sharp and focused was co-existence. Literally, singing in harmony.'

Paul and Phil Hartnoll from Sevenoaks, Kent began recording as Orbital in 1989. They were named after the M25 road system, encircling Greater London, a passage to illegal acid house parties in fields, factories and warehouses. They were part of a loose federation of DJs, promoters and ravers, sourcing the music and a feverish tone from Chicago clubs. The UK scene was also inspired by the sense of open emotionality that some clubbers had experienced in Balearic locations like Ibiza. Use of the psychoactive drug ecstasy was coded in the music, the clothes and the empathetic gatherings. Altogether, it was a massive behavioural shift.

'Early house music had a very positive spin on it', says Paul Hartnoll. 'Punk was aggressive and angry and was sort of kicking against authority whereas dance music was positive, it was almost saying, "We're done with fighting, we're just gonna go over here and do our alternative thing". And that was potentially a more powerful thing than having to fight what you don't like. Just move away and say, "We're off, we're doing it". In and around London, it really scared the authorities, they really cracked down on dance parties when nothing bad was happening. You'd get 2,000 people at an illegal rave and nobody would get hurt. You wouldn't get the level of alcohol-induced violence that used to happen. That scared the authorities; there was a change.'

David Holmes was an early adopter in Belfast. He had come out of the mod scene that had been revived in the late 70s, playing Northern Soul at the Abercorn Bar as a teenage DJ and then realising that house music was absolutely of the moment.

'When the whole acid house movement happened, it was like a gift from the gods,' he says. 'Suddenly you were having the best night of your life, every weekend. It was just this constant source of energy, inspiration, new music coming from Europe, America, London, Manchester, wherever. We used to say that it was our 1960s, our Summer of Love, even though it was grey and miserable.'

House music had been played at the Plaza on Donegal Street, a members-only gay club that also tolerated the goths, rockabillies, hip-hop aficionados and other fringe dwellers. Around the same time, DJ Peter Spence set up in the sweaty confines of Tokyo Joe's while Richardson's Social Club and the Playpen were hosts for an occasional night called Joy. The club flyers reflected the rushing colours, the cosmic intentions, peace signs and great blue planets.

David Holmes and his friend Iain McCready worked at Zakk's hairdressers. Their first major house promotion took place at the Members Room (aka the Thruppeny Bit), an annex of the King's Hall on September 25 1989. They called the event Base. David's mother was just back from a family visit to Chicago. At the request of her son, she visited a specialist record shop and came home with an impressive collection of white label releases. The club nights continued and each one raised the standard for sound and production. A few months later and Iain McCready got hold of 'Chime', the first recording by Orbital on the Oh Zone label.

'When I heard it the first time it just completely blew me away,' says

David. 'Like so many records back then it was life-changing. We used to play it at the Art College and people would be breaking down. Incredible moments when you put on the right records at the right time, which was pretty much all the time.'

David rang Orbital. They agreed to come over and do a live show at the Conor Hall, part of the Art College. This was Space Base 4, May 12 1990.

'I'd got this call from David,' Paul Hartnoll recalls. 'He said, "Would you come and play in Belfast?" I was 22, naive, my only experience of Belfast was what I got fed by the British media so I said, "Is that gonna be alright? Are people not gonna kill us if we come over there?" He said, "Ah no, that's fine, we'll look after you" and laughed at me, the way that he does. And he sorted us out.

'He gave us a tour of all the scary parts. He took us down the Falls Road. We saw British Paratrooper kinda guys, standing around pointing guns at people and lowering their rifles. I'd never seen anything like that before. It was horrifying, really.

'David took us to a pub for the first night. Everyone was so friendly. 'We asked people, "What are you? Are you Catholics or Protestants, what's the story?" And they went round the room, "Oh, I'm brought up a Catholic… Oh I'm brought up a Protestant… We're going out with each other, our parents can't know, but we don't care." There was this real unification within the whole dance music community that was building up there, through David's clubs and other clubs, that was breaking through boundaries that I thought in my naivety were solid boundaries.

'Then we played at the Art College. And, honestly, we hadn't done anything so electrifying. The audience went absolutely mental. We were so inundated, trying to get off the stage, people grabbing us. David Holmes just stood at the side of the stage laughing at us. He said, "You can't go, you're gonna have to do that song again", and made us come back on again and play 'Chime', again. That was probably our first ever encore.'

David had also talked Orbital into staying at his mother's house on 475 Ormeau Road. She made them an Ulster fry the next morning. Part of the payback was a cassette tape of unfinished Orbital demos. One of David's friends, Glenn Leyburn, had just passed his driving test, so they listened to the cassette obsessively for weeks as they rolled. They were overwhelmed by the second track on the tape. Holmes gave the writers his feedback. 'I contacted the Paul and Phil and I said, "This track is completely blowing our minds".'

Encouraged by this, Paul returned one afternoon from his shift in a pizza restaurant and worked on the four-track demo of the unnamed track. Phil's partner was about to have their second child, so he was putting together a birthing tape. He decided to include a piece of music called 'O Euchari in Leta Via' by an America soprano, Emily Van Evera. The recording dated to 1985 but the music was early medieval plainchant by Hildegard of Bingen, a German Abbess, mystic and philosopher. Paul remembers that there was an epiphany of sorts:

'Phil was wearing headphones I couldn't hear what he was doing. He just lifted his headphone off and went, "Hey, hang on, listen to this". He pulled out the headphones and it was beautifully sailing over the top of the track. And that was how the vocal line ended up getting onto the track. Total fluke and chance but what a great ending to that track. It just seemed to hit a moment.

'We decided to name it 'Belfast' because we'd had such a positive experience. It had been so beautiful coming here and we'd met so many nice people, that we just thought, "Wouldn't it be good to actually name something that's beautiful and soft and lovely about Belfast and put it out in England where everybody had this completely different view of the place?"'

For David Holmes and his friends, this was the greatest endorsement:

'The next minute I know it surfaces and it's called 'Belfast'. We knew why it was called 'Belfast', so it was really beautiful because we'd never experienced anything like that before. We were definitely wet behind the ears, young and hungry and excited and full of enthusiasm. It was just a magical time and what's really incredible is, some of the music that they were making back then have remained actual total classics – in the world of music, not just electronic music.

'I've seen Orbital play many times. At Glastonbury, in front of how many thousands of people, this road of emotion and knowing the story that led back to that track becoming 'Belfast' always puts a real smile on my face. It brings me back to that time. Innocence and complete and utter joy.'

WE'VE GOT TO CARRY
EACH OTHER

John came on from stage left and David made his appearance from the other side. They walked cautiously, past the microphone stands, the amplifiers and the effects pedals. The pair met in front of the drum riser and with some ceremony, they shook hands. David crunched down firmly, but John was also a practiced gripper. There were a few more reassuring pats, taps and exchanges and 2,000 school children roared over the awkwardness.

It was momentous enough but then Bono stepped in from behind, took their nearest arms and raised them over his head, like prize-fighters. Encouraged by the cheers, John Hume and David Trimble raised their spare arms so that the three of them traced out these emphatic V shapes. The international news cameras were reeling while the stills photographers grabbed the next day's cover shot. The world was presented with the vision of two guys in their relaxed-fit shirts, dad ties and pleated suit trousers, winging it with the singer of the biggest band in the world. Bono was more recognisable with his spark-plug physique, the patrol cap and his Fidel Castro chic. It was the strangest confederation of characters. For weeks now, people had been recklessly hurling the word 'history' into their conversations. But here it was, May 19 1998 at the Waterfront Hall in Belfast, one of those actual moments.

It was remarkable because David Trimble and John Hume were leaders of the largest political parties of Northern Ireland: Ulster Unionist and SDLP. They represented the less extreme ends of the debate and yet they had never shaken hands in public before. Not during two years of talks with US Senator George Mitchell. Not even on the delivery of the Good Friday Agreement, April 10 or on those few weeks of fierce and dirty campaigning afterwards. Now here they were, with three days to go until the agreement referendum vote and the Yes deal finally got a shake.

The context was a rock'n'roll show. U2 from Dublin, the band Ash from Downpatrick, plus Trimble and Hume. It was a self-conscious exchange of north and south and perceived religious persuasion and politics. If it didn't balance, it would fall. The Corrs rang up at the last moment and offered to play but, sadly, it would have shifted the scales adversely. Meantime, there was an ongoing worry about the import of popular music, about loose minds and attitudes. This was new territory for the political parties and the risk was considerable. A flippant phrase or an incriminating press cutting could do damage.

The Yes team was already practicing a series of rebuttals. They worried that rogue stories of Ash and some youthful drug misadventures might surface. There was the issue of the U2 song 'Sunday Bloody Sunday' and how that might be played out as a Republican anthem. Would Bono be perceived as a wooden horse? Earlier that day, the Ulster Unionists' senior campaign officers had also met at their Glengall Street headquarters and they had aired extreme misgivings. But Trimble held his resolve and the show was still on.

Opponents of the Yes vote had ridiculed the gig and the involvement of the Ulster Unionists and the Social Democratic and Labour Party. Robert McCartney of the UK Unionist Party called it 'silly and superficial'. Ian Paisley from the Democratic Unionist Party put it thus: 'it is quite evident that Mister Trimble has joined the pan Nationalist front. And he's now going to rock and *roll*. He's rocking anyway. And he'll be rolling after the 22nd.'

But there was malevolence in the stories also. Paisley's sources told him that Bono had once burnt a Union flag at a gig in Boston. The fact was never substantiated, but still Paisley put out the story on Radio Ulster's *Evening Extra*. More informed U2 listeners were pointing out that the band had made an issue out of the white flag in their concerts, railing against violent Republicanism. Hence the proclamation 'this is not a rebel song' when Bono introduced 'Sunday Bloody Sunday' at Phoenix Park in 1983, at Red Rocks Colorado and also Maysfield Leisure Centre in Belfast, when he said that he would never sing it again if the audience so wished. Most emphatically, U2 had played the song in Denver just after they had received news of the Cenotaph Bombing in Enniskillen in November 1987, an IRA bomb that left 11 dead. The moment was captured in the film *Rattle And Hum* when Bono was moved to proclaim, 'fuck the revolution'.

The singer had actually been in Belfast on the night that the Good Friday agreement had been thrashed out. The *Hot Press* Awards took place at the BBC's Blackstaff Studios on the evening of Thursday April 9. The big names of Irish Music had gathered for this annual event and there were masses of pop fans at the rear entrance of the Europa Hotel, screaming out for Ronan Keating. Twenty yards away and a rump of protesters had settled outside the Ulster Unionist headquarters. There were members of the UK Unionists, the Spirit of Drumcree group and the Protestant Civil Rights Group. They sang 'The Sash' while David Trimble discussed the peace package with his team inside. Glengall Street had been in the music event schedules as the appointed spot for the musicians' limos, so an alternative plan was taken.

Bono marked the occasion during the Awards, making reference to another pop singer's recent arrest in Los Angeles for a 'lewd act' in a public toilet in a Beverly Hills park:

'What's the difference between Ian Paisley and George Michael? At least George Michael will talk to anyone.'

After the Awards, he spoke about his earliest impressions of Belfast:

'When I was a little kid, I used to come to Belfast all the time. It was just part of growing up. And then all of a sudden, we just stopped going. I asked my old man, "Why aren't we going?" And he just said, "Well, it's not the same".

'Well, every time I've been here, I've found it to be joyful. It's easy to be a party town, like New Orleans or one of these places that just knows how to get drunk. It's not like that in Belfast. There's something going on. I met Lou Reed a few days ago and he played with us in Belfast in the 80s some time [1987]. It took him a year to recover from it – he said he'd never experienced anything like it. You meet that around the world. People in Belfast probably think, "Yeah, we're a great town", but when it's coming from people like Lou Reed – forget U2, forget the locals – when it's coming from people who have no stake in it, it must count.'

Regardless, Sammy Wilson of the DUP had made capital of the U2 connection at an anti-agreement rally in Banbridge. In his imagined Bono setlist, he was dedicating 'Acrobat' to David Trimble and his 'political gymnastics', while 'Helter Skelter' would be a critique on his crashing popularity. 'Running to Stand Still' would be thematic of the Yes campaign while 'Hold Me Thrill Me, Kiss Me Kill Me' was an indicator of the Unionists, getting cosy with the Republicans, Gerry Adams and Sinn Féin.

But Bono saw a parallel to another headline-grabbing night at the National Stadium in Kingston, Jamaica. Back then it was Bob Marley who had headlined the One Love Peace Concert in front of 32,000 people. The country was riven by killings and political extremism. So, on 22 April 1978, Marley was asked to officiate. It was a masterclass in charisma and timing. He massed up the euphoria in his music, and when the rapture was at its fullest, he had called out to Michael Manley from the People's National Party and Edward Seaga from the Jamaican Labour Party. It was an unscripted move from the singer, so the opponents were compelled, reluctantly to make their way to the stage. Bob held up their arms and thus music was able to suspend the ill feeling, to make a connection.

The Belfast moment at the Waterfront was absolutely going to be stage managed, and Bono had some input. David and John were not going to speak from the stage. It was all about the visuals and the symbolism. Their suit jackets would be too formal, so they would be set aside. They were to approach this evening like a music event. They needed to steel themselves for the blinding spotlights and the disconcerting noise and to look upwards, reaching for the people in the back row. Simple as. And then Bono would prep the audience for their appearance:

'Two men who are making history, two men who have taken a leap of faith out of the past and into the future...'

Two months before on St Patrick's Day, influential figures from the voluntary sector, the unions and business interests had met to discuss the likely referendum and how they might give it a positive steer. They were provided with a space at the Europa Hotel on Great Victoria Street and they searched for a different dynamic. The daily meetings started at 7.30am and they often locked up around midnight. They wanted to build relationships and to create space for ideas.

They recognised that the high-level talks with American Senator George Mitchell were the first line of discussion and progress. Also, there had been other methods and back stories. The South African peace process had provided a series of milestones, from the release of Nelson Mandela in 1990 through to CODESA (Convention for Democratic South Africa) to elections in 1994. Study visits had allowed the Irish-British contingent to see this model while providing a context for arch-enemies on the visits to be nudged and encouraged. Thus, alongside the headline stories, there was covert preparatory work.

There wasn't a name for this Belfast-based network at the start – just friends and associates with an active persuasion. They looked at the importance of words and nuances and decided that the term 'Voluntary' wasn't emphatic enough. And besides, the paramilitaries had used that word already. So they talked about themselves as the Third Sector. Elsewhere, the pressure lines were around the State and the combatants. The bombings and assassinations continued while the Europa network looked for other shades and opinions. Chiefly, they needed to get ready. George Mitchell focused everyone's minds when he announced that his wife was expecting a child and that he would wrap up on April 10, Good Friday. This hastened a 20,000-word agreement and a vote on the Referendum, May 22.

Quintin Oliver left his job at NICVA (Northern Ireland Council for Voluntary Action) to head up the Yes campaign team. The party leaders were exhausted at this point and so the remit was to take a load off, to sustain momentum, clarity and the life-changing value of Yes.

'It was coming to an endgame, says Quintin. 'And that was where we got together to say, "Well, the politicians will be tired, they will have done a deal hopefully, we don't know the shape of it but that doesn't matter, because if the two governments and the eight parties do a deal, it's gonna be pretty good and it will represent something". Therefore, we should prepare to explain it to the people and to persuade the sceptical people who might think it's a sell-out that, actually, it may represent a step forward.'

They took advice from Nigel Smith, who had led the cross-party Yes campaign for the Scottish Devolution Referendum of 1994. Positivity, they heard, was a crucial note. And it should be bold and attractive. The campaign should never look like it was put together on a kitchen table.

'Therefore, all our materials were brilliantly and professionally designed. So, invest in design, invest in creativity and that's where the arts and culture came in as a huge benefit to it. And invest in the message. So, clarify your message. Hone it down to two or three simple points. You're gonna have a complicated, constitutional document that is gonna be very hard to explain, even if it is sent to every household. So we knew we had to create a wonderful image of positivity from the 20,000 legal, constitutional words. And that's where the creativity was so key. That's why we had poets and artist and musicians working alongside us to achieve that.'

Ian Paisley's Democratic Unionist Party was outside the deal, and so was the UK Unionist Party. The key supporters were John Hume's SDLP and the Ulster Unionists – led by David Trimble but with many internal disagreements within the party. Other participants included Sinn Féin, Alliance, PUP, UDP, the Northern Ireland Women's Coalition and Labour. Some of them were hostile to each other. It would not have been practical to get them around a table – there had only been two plenary meetings during the talks, on Day One in 1996 and then another, some 700 days later, when Senator Mitchell asked them for their consent. So, the Yes campaigners were obliged to work as brokers, patching together ideas, one-on-one.

Legally, Quintin's team needed a name, so they chose the Referendum Company. They regretted it later when various sources confused them with James Goldsmith's Referendum Party. Even British Telecom got it wrong, and directed Goldsmith enquiries to Belfast. But there were more testing issues ahead, chiefly about the decommissioning of arms, police reform and the early release of paramilitary prisoners.

The so-called Balcombe Street Gang had been arrested after a six-day siege in a flat near Marylebone train station in London in December 1975. Members of a Provisional IRA active service unit, they were given 47 life sentences at an Old Bailey trial in 1977 – found guilty of seven murders and conspiracy to cause explosions and false imprisonment. They were Martin

O'Connell, Harry Duggan, Edward Butler and Hugh Doherty. In 1998, they were transferred to the high security wing of Portlaoise Prison, near Dublin. On May 10, they were given temporary release to attend the Sinn Féin *Ard Fheis* at the RDS Hall in Dublin. They were given an ovation of almost ten minutes and were received by party president Gerry Adams as 'our Nelson Mandelas'.

Michael Stone was a loyalist paramilitary who had attacked an IRA funeral at Milltown Cemetery in 1988 with grenades and a semi-automatic pistol. He killed three people and injured 60. He later admitted to three other murders. In 1998, he met with the Secretary of State for Northern Ireland, Mo Mowlam, at the Maze prison, part of a delegation that represented the Ulster Defence Association and the Ulster Freedom Fighters. He was on temporary parole when he attended a political rally for the UDP, the political wing of the UDA. When he entered the Ulster Hall on May 15, 1998 he was also given an ovation. British PM Tony Blair said he could sympathise with feelings of 'revulsion' from the public. 'The timing was unfortunate, to say the least.'

Ian Paisley felt vindicated in opposition: 'The bubble burst, the Yes campaign was built on froth and it is dissolving into nothing.'

Quintin Oliver recalls the feeling of alarm. 'The polls plummeted when Adams welcomed the Balcombe Street Bombers as 'our Mandelas'. The polls plummeted then, but not across the pitch. Then Mo Mowlam released Michael Stone as, in her view, an equal and opposite effect – that somehow this would boost Unionism and they would be proud that their representatives would be released from prison. This was, however, a shallow and incorrect understanding of the standing of Loyalist paramilitaries within Unionism and Protestantism – which was totally different than Nationalism or Republicanism. The polls plummeted further the day after Michael Stone paraded into the Ulster Hall. I can remember that vividly.'

In October 1997, U2 had released 'Please', a song that alluded to the peace process in Northern Ireland. Or rather, the lack of any sure progress. In the lyric there was shrapnel and false prophets, flags and bloodlines. Larry Mullen played a martial snare drum, just like he did in the days of *War*. Months were torn off the calendar but the anxiety was unceasing. Religion was used to divide and subjugate. Bono called it 'a mad prayer'. The lyrics asked an unknown figure to go beyond masochism and victimhood ('*so you never felt alive until you almost wasted away*') and to open up to redemptive love. Elvis Costello said it was one of his favourite songs and when Bono heard his stripped-down rendition, he declared that Elvis was showing U2 how to play it all over again.

'Please' was a feature of the *Pop* album, a record about being lost in the supermarket, about glowing surfaces and screaming vacancy. The concept had prompted them to take a giant lemon and a neon arch on their stadium tour. The visuals often borrowed from 60s pop art and so it was not unusual to see the cover of the 'Please' single paying homage to Andy Warhol's vivid screenprints. But instead of Marilyn Monroe, Elvis, Jackie Onassis and Liz Taylor, U2 provided a less alluring montage: Trimble, Hume, Adams and Paisley.

Various people had sounded out Bono about a likely referendum and the Yes campaign. The SDLP had mutual connections such as the film director Jim Sheridan and the barrister Hugh Mohan. Then again, John Hume and his wife Pat were personal friends. There was a growing expectation that Bono might do a press conference, at least. Jim Sheridan was in Belfast to support the agreement on Thursday May 14. He met Tim Attwood from the SDLP at the Wellington Park Hotel and when he learnt of the difficulties, he passed on Bono's number and urged Tim to make an urgent call. There was no signal inside the hotel, so Tim stepped outside and rang. The response was positive.

'I know John a little bit,' Bono recalled a few days later. 'We were asked to help out with the Yes campaign and I felt that I didn't want to be part of any one community. I just feel that's not what U2 are about really. So I said, if you can bring together John and David, we'll do something. I was very surprised when they both came back and said that they wanted to do it, to be honest with you. We could do a gig. So Ash stepped in, they're a boss rock band, they're just on it. And I think that most importantly, the people need to see these two men together. Forget us, we're up from the south and we wouldn't dare patronise people up here, but it was still nice to throw in our tuppence worth.'

Tim Attwood then called David Kerr, Director of Communications for the Ulster Unionist Party. He was at the party's headquarters on Glengall Street. David remembers feeling incredulous.

'My first reaction was, "Are you serious?" We had nothing left in the tank. I just said, "Look, I think it's a brilliant idea". I literally went from one office to the boardroom. David Trimble was there with Ray Hayden [his media relations advisor] and a few others. I said, "This is a brilliant opportunity to reset the public focus in the final week of the referendum campaign. It's the best opportunity we have to bring people out who are at present disconnected from politics and who may not vote, or actually worse than that, can be persuaded to vote against it on purely moral grounds". David accepted the logic and Ray agreed.'

Tim Attwood contacted one of Belfast's biggest music promoters, Eamonn McCann, at Wonderland. He was in the men's department of the London department store Fortnam & Mason's. He had a meeting in the city and had forgotten his tie, but the call took precedence. 'Give me five minutes,' he told Attwood. He arranged himself at a window seat, apologised to the staff and made the necessary arrangements. Very fortunately, the Waterfront Hall was free on the following Tuesday. Ash were in Rockfield Studios near Monmouth in Wales, finishing their second proper album, *Nu Clear Sounds*. But absolutely, they would play the gig and sure thing, U2 could borrow their gear for the night. So, they put in a swift rehearsal, packed up the van and drove north to Stranraer for the ferry over to Larne.

The two bands held a series of phone discussions about likely material. 'Give Peace A Chance' was an early call but Ash didn't care for it. Thankfully, 'Two Little Boys' by Rolf Harris was also rejected. Bob Marley's 'One Love' was considered a bit obvious and 'People Get Ready' by Curtis Mayfield was maybe not obvious enough. Bono thought of 'Strangers in the Night' by Frank Sinatra but it didn't carry. However, the Beatles' songbook was worth another try. Perhaps not 'We Can Work It Out', but certainly, 'Don't Let Me Down'. That was when John Lennon was singing out of his skin in 1969, still grieving for his mother Julia, but looking to Yoko and a love that has no past. Perfect.

'That was my idea,' says Edge. 'A bit cheeky, but appropriate for the moment.'

The Yes campaign had three important events on the schedule for the final week. On the Monday, a 75-foot banner was unfurled outside the Europa, the most bombed hotel in the world. It was simply one word: Yes. On Wednesday there was a planned photo opportunity with Tony Blair, Trimble and Hume in the grounds of the Dunadry Hotel, County Antrim. That was a conscious echo of the Clinton-Arafat-Rabin image on the lawn of the White House in 1993. It was all about recognising statesmanship, giving authority to Trimble and assuring those undecided voters in his camp. Thirdly, they had the Waterfront gig on the Tuesday. It was potentially valuable for the campaign, but always an unknown quality.

'There was discussion,' says Quintin. 'There was some apprehension because Bono was Bono. From the south. Bono was a rock musician. Not exactly the target audience we were after. We were after Unionism. We knew that Nationalism was on board for the Agreement because it was progress, regardless. So, it wasn't exactly our target. It [the Waterfront gig] was young people but they were actually pretty good. We were actually going for an older demographic, a Unionist safe conservative demographic. We did actually debate, would this actually be helpful, or would it be a hindrance?'

The first business of Tuesday was the meeting of the bands and the political parties on Lanyon Place by the River Lagan. U2 had flown in from London in a five-seater jet. The sun was up, a rare appearance in an otherwise dreary spring. The new arrivals walked up to the hosts. It was like *High Noon*. Edge wore the cowboy hat with the vented crown while his colleagues sauntered over in their Miami-Cubano casuals. And then many handshakes. The suits were hospitable and so were Ash in their skater boy attire. A journalist asked Bono how this assembly might persuade the doubters.

'I dunno,' he said. 'We can *deafen* them. That's probably the job of rock and roll. We just wanted to be part of an event that represented both sides on the community. And we're just big fans of Ash and they're a pretty cool band. So I hope we can highlight the good things when there's a lot of folk out there highlighting the bad.'

John Hume had played an exhausting part in the agreement process and the years of spadework that had prepared this chance. He had been a feature in the political rough-house since the early days of the Civil Rights movement, making a case for non-violent methods while also presenting the Nationalist case. His face was a map of strain and perpetual difficulty. Now, he wanted to talk about the how Tim Wheeler and Ash were voicing a fresh aspiration.

'It was all summed up by Tim in words I heard him speak earlier today when he said, this his generation is the generation that fully understand this problem and they want to be the last generation who has it. And the future generations will put this quarrel behind them.'

Ash had been schoolboy wonderkids in the mid-90s, taking time off from Downpatrick High for rowdy tours, delivering five top 40 hits and a number one album. Tim wrote with panache about the teenage dream and space adventures, but he was self-aware also. His father George was a District Court Judge and therefore a 'legitimate' target for the paramilitaries. He knew exactly what a threat amounted to. Later, he would write this up in an extraordinary song called 'Sheltered Youth', about a friend's house in mourning, a body bag outside the toy store, the doctor leaving his daughter's wedding to save lives after the Loughinisland massacre.

'My dad worked for the court service,' Tim says. 'We had to check under our car for bombs every day. We had bulletproof windows in our house, which I actually decided to test one day with my friend. I was bragging to him about it and we got a catapult he said, "If I got this catapult and fired a stone at your window would it bounce off?" I was like, "Yeah, it's bulletproof". So, we did it and of course bulletproof glass takes the impact and it cracked. My dad had to pay to get it replaced.

'It's strange how when you're a child, though, you don't take these things so seriously. You don't realise. The Army is around and there are all these terrible things on the news every night, but as a kid, you just get on with things and you think that's normal.'

As he faced up to the Yes gig, he was 21. Along with Mark and Rick, Tim wrote out a press statement that concluded, 'The 'No' vote offers no hope. If we don't say Yes, what's the alternative? We want our country to move into the future. Let's get it together.'

Upstairs at the Waterfront, Ash joined Trimble for a press conference. Charlotte, their new guitarist, was also present and they had assumed some extra stature. Tim, normally bashful, spoke well. 'We really, genuinely believe in this. People get involved in politics because they want to improve their image or to get publicity. But this is something we believe in.'

David Trimble emerged differently also. He revealed a fondness for Elvis, alongside Strauss and Vaughan Williams. When the newspaper guys asked him about the last gig he attended, his comeback was delayed. And then he remembered. It was Ben E. King, some time ago. Yet he also spoke eloquently about his eldest daughter Victoria, how she was very much looking forward to the Waterfront gig later. That's what everyone should have been able to do during the previous 30 years, he supposed.

'David was a difficult man to try and prep for press conferences,' says David Kerr, 'He usually had an MO that went something like, "Look, I know what to say myself". I was genuinely really worried that he was going to make an idiot out of himself or say something really daft. When he said actually, I'm a big Elvis fan, I almost fell over. I did not see it coming, because I knew he was an opera fanatic. Obsessive about Wagner and all types of classical music but at no stage, in the time I'd worked with him, had I ever realised he had any interest in any type of popular music, never mind Elvis. I could see Tim and the others starting to look at him and go, "Well, maybe you're more interesting than we thought you were". And then of course, the mood lifted.

'You very rarely ever saw a softer, human side to him in any type of context. Maybe he was slightly socially awkward about doing it, but when he did, it was very powerful for him.'

Just as they were wrapping up, John and Tim started talking about a mutual acquaintance, the Reverend Knox, recently moved from Downpatrick to Harmony Hill in Lisburn. Later, Bono and Trimble conversed about the gospel power of the hymn, 'Amazing Grace'. These were unusual but helpful connections.

The Yes gig needed a compere. Mike Edgar from Radio Ulster had been approached but the BBC had insisted on his impartiality. So, the job was offered to this freelance writer who was firstly startled by the spin-doctors and dust-busters who demanded to see the speech in advance. Truthfully, there was none. Instead, it was fitting to read the Ash statement out in full. The 2,000 school children, mainly Sixth Formers and higher education students, understood. This was an audience that appreciated the urgency and surprise on the night.

Ash played some new songs, but also batted out the reliables such as 'Oh Yeah', 'Goldfinger' and 'Kung Fu'. There was a gap before they resumed with Edge, Bono and 'Don't Let Me Down'. The roughness was less important than the sense of occasion. And then there was the handshake.

Bono asked for a few moments of silence afterwards, to remember those that had suffered since 1968. He didn't get absolute quiet. There was a bit of singing and random shouts. And then the politicians stepped away. John Hume was overwhelmed, in tears.

The U2 song 'One' had been partly inspired by Edge's marital problems in 1990 but the lyric had become highly adaptable over the years. This plasticity had served as a requiem for AIDS sufferers and an anthem for a reunified Berlin. 'One' was about the dynamics of the band itself, it would come to reflect on Bono's relationship with his father. At the Waterfront, it morphed into something else. It was about the various responses to living in the north of Ireland: one, but not the same. As always, the song urged the listener to feel the tensions and to roll with the paradoxes. Souls were moved. And Bono slipped in a coda of 'Give Peace A Chance' – his second Lennon reference of the night.

John Lennon's spirit was definitely in the house. 'Stand By Me' was most famously performed by Ben E. King but Bono was singing it like John on his *Rock And Roll* album. To Tim Wheeler's alarm, he was almost handed the first verse, but his mind went blank, Bono resumed and the moment passed.

Backstage, the musicians and Yes campaigners watched TV as the story was already high up the agenda on the evening news. Trimble had just gone off to another interview. Hume was spent and weary, but he knew that the night had been won. Bono went off to a private room where he met some families that had been damaged by conflict, including Sarah Conlon. Her husband Giuseppe and her son Gerard had been falsely imprisoned for the Guildford Pub Bombings. Bono had worked on the soundtrack to the Jim Sheridan film, *In The Name Of The Father*, which told that account. He asked Sarah what she thought about the gig. 'It was very loud,' she said.

Bono asked the management to fetch in some beer for the guests, not just the mineral water that was set in front of them. The company included Paddy Lavery, whose father Martin had been shot at home in December 1993 while he wrapped Christmas presents. There was Paddy Cameron, whose father James had been killed in 1993 in retaliation for the Shankill bombing. The painful inter-connection of the conflict was furthered by Alan McBride, who had lost his wife Sharon and her father John Frizzell in the Shankill bomb that had killed ten, including one of the bombers. He had been on a TV news feature the night before and Bono had asked for a chance to meet. And so it transpired, as Alan remembers:

'He came over to me and said, "You're Alan McBride – I was very impressed about what you had to say last night about forgiveness". I had to stop him, because I hadn't forgiven anybody at that stage, and I still haven't. I don't know what he thought he heard me say, or maybe he misunderstood what I was saying.

'So I had to correct him. Basically, I said you have to let go of the hurt of the past. But to actually forgive someone is a step too far because for my mother-in-law who'd lost her daughter – if I was ever to say publicly that I forgave anybody, she would never forgive me. And I care about her. So I know I wouldn't have said I forgave them, but I probably said something like, "We need to go beyond this and let go. And not let the hurt hold you back."'

This meeting impacted on Bono as he stated later in the evening. 'I couldn't say anything at the time, but now I think, if someone like that can vote Yes, there is hope. That's what this is about for me. Maybe we can help swing it.'

Edge was happily impressed. 'We'd just finished the tour, our road crew had gone off and we had to use Ash's instruments. And they were very generous. They covered all our screw-ups. But the night wasn't about us really. It was about John and David. It was just amazing. All the hairs on the back of the neck time. We were as ropy as fuck. We used Ash's gear, we didn't bring anything. I'd never played that guitar before we started, so it was interesting, but the vibe was what it was all about and the crowd just got it. They got the idea of the moment and they were so into it. That's what was so exciting.'

The arms-aloft image made the covers of most of the papers the following day. On the Thursday, the Ulster Unionists took out a full-page advertisement in the *Belfast Telegraph*, with a shot of the Waterfront audience taken from the balcony. The faces of the school children were beaming and enthralled. 'Don't Let Them Down', the strapline read. The Waterfront gig had put youth onto the agenda in a very tangible way.

The turnout for the referendum vote was 81.1%. The Yes vote was an emphatic 71.1%. Music's importance was the subject of some debate.

'It was a very significant moment,' Tim Attwood stresses. 'It symbolised everything the Good Friday Agreement was: orange and green, Unionism and Nationalism, coming together. It changed the dynamic. The polling company suggested that between the Tony Blair pledges and the U2-Ash gig, it added six to seven per cent to the turnout. And that made the difference between Unionism saying Yes and No.'

Quintin Oliver is mildly sceptical. 'I don't buy that, actually, but fair play to them. I don't think individual events have huge significance in critical yes-no debates like this. I think they're part of the narrative, part of the framing, and we were certainly conscious that we needed the last week to be positive. I don't think you can say, "Well, I changed my mind as Bono sang", or "because he got Trimble and Hume to shake hands". I don't think voters behave like that. I think it's part of a context.'

David Kerr is sure that the event was pivotal. 'I'm not someone who's prone to revisionism. We had been sitting at about 67%. Had we ended up with that type of vote, we would have had a problem, straight away, with what I would call the legitimacy of the Yes vote. It would have been hard to say it was genuinely cross-community, that it had the confidence of both communities. That concert pulled 80 to 100,000 votes into the ballot boxes. It got people to vote who normally never voted. In the final analysis of that concert, it was a truly historic moment, certainly in the history of Northern Ireland. I have no doubt in my own mind that rock and roll drove the referendum vote over the magic 70% mark.'

CHAPTER NINETEEN

HOW LONG MUST WE
SING THIS SONG?

In February 2018, Bono responded in writing to the following questions.

On the 2014 song 'Raised by Wolves' you return to the story of the Dublin bombing of 1974. Its impact was re-enacted when you played it live. Had there been a longstanding wish to write about this, or did the memory reassert itself in recent years?

I was mulling over my long-term obsession with how ideas are in some quarters more valuable than people, i.e. wondering why someone would take somebody else's life... is there such a thing as a just war and all that? And I realised this was an obsession that started early on in my life when the Troubles made themselves known to me personally. I had experience of sectarian violence as a pre-teen in Butlins holiday camp, during the week of the 12th of July where rival gangs clashed but it was in 1974 when there was a coordinated bomb attack in Dublin. On any normal Friday at that time I would be at the bus stop a few yards from where the first blast hit... there was a bus strike that day so I cycled to school. My best friend's brother Andrew Rowan, or Guckpants Delany as we called him, did not escape... his father helping to carry the dead and the wounded after he had locked Guckpants in his van screaming and roaring. Guckpants never really recovered from it...

I called him when we were recording 'Raised by Wolves'. I hadn't spoken to him in years. He told me that he carried a piece of shrapnel from that day with him wherever he had lived over the years. Then, putting down the phone, he went to find it. I asked him why. He told me he was interested in this little piece of the thing that tried to kill him. But I think it was more that he lost a little piece of himself that day… that the piece of metal symbolised.

There may be a connection between the Dublin-Monaghan bombings and the Miami Showband killings in 1975. Did the latter event register when you were growing up?

The Miami Showband killings also shocked and appalled us… it's a story that needs to be told more than it is. As was rightly pointed out to me when I talked about the attack on the Bataclan club in Paris. The Miami Showband massacre was actually the first terror attack on music in our time.

How important was it to hear Stiff Little Fingers singing about the conflict in 1978?

Even more than the Clash, SLF showed us how we could dramatise local issues and make them global. 'Suspect Device' was just genius and of course 'Alternative Ulster' more than contributed to Edge's drone-like guitar sound… it was a clarion call for another land… one yet to be discovered… the land of the imagination.

Around the time of the *War* album you were waving a white flag. Were you were trying to remove the orange and green from the U2 experience?

Yeah, I thought of it as a kind of John Lennon move… a bit of performance art, a bit of stirring things up. And a bit of genuine disgust at flags in general. I would cut up the tricolour, which I'm sure was very upsetting for people who had put their lives on the line for that same flag… with hindsight, I apologise for that now. But sometimes we can put our nation ahead of our decency, and that's when you have to question the whole project of nationalism.

'Sunday Bloody Sunday' still polarises some listeners. The likes of Feargal Sharkey have been critical of the song. How do you regard the song now?

What a beautiful voice that man has, and he put his whole person behind his politics in every which way except with his music and it's totally understandable that the Undertones would have been annoyed to see U2 traipse across the globe singing about their town whilst we lived in the safety of the south... I get it... our teenage kicks were a little more earnest... in truth it's a lyric about how the original Bloody Sunday, Easter Sunday, was at the heart of both communities and how Christianity had been hijacked for people's political ends... one community dominates the other, etc. I'm not sure it's a very well-written lyric if I'm still having to explain it. A better idea than a lyric, indeed a better tune.

The Enniskillen Bombing of 1987 provoked a very emotional response during a U2 gig in Denver on the night of the news broke. It stayed in the edit of *Rattle And Hum*. How important was it to document this reaction?
I found it excruciating and to this day try to avoid ever having to witness myself in such a self-conscious rage. Some things have to be said though. You can't become a monster to defeat a monster. I only recently heard a replay... it must have been an anniversary... of [Enniskillen bombing survivor] Gordon Wilson's interview, when he describes being under the rubble with his daughter and her last words... so full of forgiveness, so inspiring, so humbling. His faith gives you faith.

You co-wrote 'North and South of the River' with Christy Moore. There was a lot of give-and-take with Christy's original lyrics. How significant was the line, '*I've been doing it wrong all of my life*'?
Christy is a very extraordinary fella... there's a lot to be learnt from his humility. I think at the time of writing he was nauseous at the more extreme Unionist and Republican response to the Troubles. He wanted to be humble about how the character in the song got to hold such heart-felt revolutionary convictions. He is a naturally empathetic person.

Elvis Costello says that 'Please' is one of your best songs. How did you come to write about the halting rhythm of the peace process?
'Please' is a song about fundamentalism wherever you find it... political or religious. It's particularly noxious when combined... it's roughly directed at a well-educated upper-middle class revolutionary I knew at the time...

There was a lot of them about… still a few… the kind who would never pull the trigger but they would raise a lot of money for the guns. Some, believe it or not, claimed to be believers in the Church.

At the 1998 Waterfront Hall gig in Belfast you encouraged John Hume and David Trimble to shake hands. How do you measure that moment, on reflection?

Shaking hands was an obvious symbol… the best idea I had on that day was asking both men not to speak. An unusual restriction for a politician. But we knew the photo was everything and we were scared of booing from one side or the other… what's less well-known is that after a meeting back stage I left the two men on their own and told everyone outside that they didn't want to be disturbed. I think they lasted about seven minutes. This was of course before the Nobel and all that. Ash were key to the success of that whole event and moment… what a songwriter Tim Wheeler is.

You mentioned some of the names of the Omagh Bombing victims in the song 'Peace on Earth'. As a songwriter, is there a delicacy required when you put real lives in a lyric?

This is a great question and the answer is of course, yes. It's very easy to trivialise unknowable lives when you sing about them. I remember when we used to, during Zoo TV, have live satellite connections with Sarajevo under siege. On one night in Wembley stadium we were told 'We know you'll go back to your concert and leave us to die, just tell those who are trying to kill us to hurry up'… hard to recover from that.

There's a cache of songs about the conflict. There are sentiments from Paul Brady, the Cranberries, Van Morrison, Sting, the Undertones, Bananarama, Simple Minds, Stiff Little Fingers, Paul McCartney, John Lennon and more. Is it a valuable legacy?

Yes. And especially Bananarama. Pop music is a more radical purveyor of political messages than rock.

BROKEN THINGS

Twenty-nine people were killed in the Omagh bombing, August 15 1998. The red Vauxhall Cavalier had been parked on a yellow line on Lower Market Street. There was 500 pounds of explosive made from fertiliser in the boot. It was the last day of carnival week and there were tourists over from Donegal and visitors from Spain. Others were doing the weekly shop, looking for school uniforms for the start of the new academic year or sorting out new boots and jeans in the market town.

Northern Ireland people had been toughened to some degree by 30 years of conflict but this was the worst loss of life in a single event during that time frame. It happened 13 weeks after the Good Friday Agreement, at a time when the political parties and the main paramilitary groups had given their assent to the Mitchell Principles: peaceful, democratic means, disarmament and the absence of force and coercion. There was a deal of lightness and trust, even vulnerability coming back to civic life and so the grieving over Omagh was acutely felt.

It was the work of the Real IRA, former members of the Provisional IRA who did not accept an Agreement that was short of a United Ireland. They had been planting bombs that year in Banbridge, Moira and Portadown and the public was getting accustomed to hearing the term 'dissident' on the news. After they had parked the Vauxhall and taken a ride back towards the border in a scout car, they had phoned in several warnings to the

Ulster Television newsroom and the Samaritans office in Coleraine using their agreed code, 'Martha Pope'. But the warnings had talked up a bomb on Main Street when no such place existed, and had also mentioned the Courthouse, further up the hill. So, the police were moving people down in the direction of the Cavalier when it had exploded.

Afterwards, 232 people were treated in hospital. Most of these were women. Five teenagers were among the dead. There was a generational loss when Avril Monaghan, pregnant with twins, died with her mother Mary and her 18-month-old daughter Maura. The church leaders called a day of mourning on the Sunday and it was determined that there would be a Memorial Day on Saturday 22 at the Courthouse.

All of the main political parties and dignitaries from the Irish Republic were represented at the service plus an estimated 60,000 people, backing down Market Street and across the Strule River. Red drapes were fixed at the top of the steps and this is where the solemn speeches were made. All week, people had been talking about revulsion, evil and futility, using phrases that had lost their impact after decades of condemnation. There would be a minute's silence at the time of the explosion, 3.10pm plus a speech in Spanish to recognise the loss of Fernando Blasco Baselga, a 12-year-old boy from Madrid who had come over with a student exchange programme. Music was also part of the schedule and Juliet Turner had accepted the invitation to sing.

She had been raised on the family dairy farm at Tummery in the Parish of Dromore and attended school in Omagh, 12 miles away. Music was an important part of the church life of Togherdoo Methodist Church and Juliet later saw this as a confidence builder. She studied English and History at Trinity College Dublin where she played parties and pubs and wrote folksy, quizzical songs. She worked in a Christian aid and development agency and recorded her debut album, *Let's Hear It For Pizza* in Glasgow in 1996. Her voice had a searching quality and she sang in her an unashamed Tyrone accent.

Reverend Robert Heron was Minister of Trinity Presbyterian Church in Omagh. He was helping to organise the Memorial Service and he called a colleague in Belfast, Steve Stockman, Presbyterian Chaplain at Queen's University who presented a Sunday evening music show on BBC Radio

Ulster called *Rhythm and Soul*. Robert was asking to contact Juliet Turner, who had appeared on Steve's programme.

'Juliet was reluctant,' Steve later wrote. 'I can remember her on the phone with me saying that she was on her way home to Omagh and was going to meet Robert but didn't feel she had any songs that were appropriate. Robert then phoned back. Juliet had given him the same story... no songs.'

Steve suggested a song called 'Broken Things' that Juliet had performed on his show. This was the work of Julie Miller, a Texan artist who had suffered an abusive childhood, leading to self-harm and a visit to Bergen Pines Mental Hospital, New Jersey. She had embraced Christianity and settled with her husband Buddy in in Nashville. 'Broken Things' was on her second album *He Walks Through Walls* in 1991. It was about severe pain and disrepair, the voice of an abased soul and the decision to get it mended.

'Well I heard that you make old things new
So I give these pieces all to you.'

Juliet sang this without ceremony on the steps of the Courthouse. She was relatively unknown, she did not have a record deal and there was no expectation from anyone at the service. Yet she gave voice to the distress of the occasion. She knew some of the injured, as all the locals did, and she provided empathy. Just like Julie Miller, she allowed herself to surrender to the song. For many, this was the essence of the service.

Evidently it translated into the live TV broadcast. BBC Online was logged by requests. International viewers wanted to know more about this singer and to purchase 'Broken Things'. But there was no studio recording and she did not intend to meet that demand. On August 26 she issued a statement from Dublin, via her manager Derek Nally:

'Juliet Turner has been surprised and touched by the response to the song 'Broken Things', which she sang as part of the Memorial Service in Omagh for those killed and injured in the bomb blast there ... one of the reasons the song 'Broken Things' touched people so deeply at the service was because it sidestepped all the politics surrounding the blast, and expressed the feelings of the ordinary people who had been hurt...

'Juliet realises that there might be many people who do not understand some of her reasons for not releasing 'Broken Things' as a tribute single. Juliet will try to make her own contribution to any kind of healing process that takes place in Omagh, but she does not want to be the focus of any more attention.'

Eventually she recorded the track for a benefit album, *Across the Bridge of Hope*. Released in 1999, the album was co-ordinated by Tim Hegarty and Ross Graham. There were tracks from the Corrs, U2, Van Morrison, Paul Brady and others. The impact of Omagh was channelled on a special edition of *The Late Late Show* in Dublin and a song by Def Leppard called 'Paper Sun'. This came directly after the news coverage from the town. 'We had the telly on with the sound off and basically wrote our own soundtrack,' Joe Elliott explained.

U2 set a few of the names into 'Peace on Earth'.

'Sean and Julia, Gareth, Ann and Breda
Their lives are bigger, than any big idea.'

And Juliet Turner continued with a music career, managing the habitual questions. Mostly she was gracious, but there were times when she wearied of being the artist that had carried a song at a grievous moment. There was an instance in 2004 when she was vexed at being this point of focus.

'They ask these stupid things like, how did you feel at the Memorial Service? What kind of stupid question is that? They never ask how are things up there now or how are the people of Omagh recovering and taking a step forward. They're only interested in the music thing and my perspective, which isn't really relevant. All I did that day was get up and sing a song. And I didn't even write the song. I wish people had more interest in what's going on there.'

CHAPTER TWENTY-ONE

WASHED IN THE BLOOD
OF THE LAMB

September 26 1998.

It's Saturday night at the Waterfront Hall in Belfast, and the Reverend William McCrea is fronting a sell-out gospel show. People have paid as much as £12 to witness the Free Presbyterian singer from Stewartstown giving praise and reviving some of that old-time religion. There are many white-haired grandmothers in the auditorium, but occasionally you see a few young men with tidy haircuts and earnest eyes. There are 40 other singers on stage, waiting their chance to come forward and testify. This includes a harmonising act called the Kingdomaires, as well as Crimson River, who raise up the notes like barber shop singers, a popular attraction at the gospel quartet conventions.

Amy Roberts, a middle-aged performer, is prompted to tell the audience about her former life in showbusiness, before she was led to the Lord in 1990. She's shuddering as she remembers this existence when she sang 'in the world', and not in God's presence. She was 'heavily steeped in alcohol' and was desperately unhappy. Now, she has a new song to sing. 'I just want to please the Lord', she says, and the audience claps in approval.

William McCrea has cut well over 20 albums, recording in Nashville, but only using born-again personnel. He has a light, personable tone, not unlike vintage American singers such as Pat Boone or Hank Locklin. But the well that he drinks from – and which his flock seem to love most of all – is the music that's imbued with the sound of the Appalachian Mountains and the holy rollers who took the form onwards.

There's a kinship there, since many of the Scottish-Irish emigrants made their way through Ulster and on to the Blue Ridge Mountains and beyond. And so that winsome, simple form of expression has been exported back to Ulster. Hearing McCrea and his peers is like opening a window back to the Louvin Brothers or the Carter Family, when it was acceptable to be sentimental and home-loving and to wed the Bible with a guitar and the voices of true believers.

But there are concessions to technology too. McCrea performs many tunes, such as 'He Is My Everything' and a new number, 'The Preacher on the Fence', over a pre-recorded backing tape. At one stage, the technology fails and he is piqued for a moment. But he ultimately puts it down to Divine Will.

William's light mood conceals a momentous life. In 1969, he underwent a religious rebirth after hearing Isabella Paisley preach about Hell in a tin hall in Magherafelt. He was inspired to follow Isabella's son Ian into politics, but he lost his Mid Ulster seat in the last UK election to Sinn Féin's Martin Mc Guinness, when the Nationalist vote united against him. Three of his cousins have been killed by the IRA and his own home has been strafed with bullets. He believes that capital punishment is 'a scriptural principle', and does not regret his decision to share a platform in 1996 with the late Loyalist Volunteer Force leader Billy Wright, nicknamed King Rat. 'I support the right of a person to make a political statement without threat', he told the *Belfast Telegraph*. In 1975, William led a prayer service at the funerals of Harris Boyle and Wesley Somerville, UVF members who died while planting a bomb in the van of the Miami Showband.

None of this is mentioned at the Waterfront. William is singing praise and selling tapes, CDs and a new video. He is also joining the audience in prayer. 'Are you washed in the blood of the lamb?' he asks, appreciating that much of this flock is safely gathered in.

September 27 1998.

The Reverend Ian Paisley is in the house on Sunday morning, offering up praise at Martyrs' Memorial on the Ravenhill Road, Belfast. It's a large, plain building that has witnessed many events since 1969 when 6,000 people celebrated its opening.

Several hundred have gathered this morning. Many of them are of pensionable age. Almost all the women wear long dresses and hats to cover their modesty. This is an adherence to the advice of Saint Paul in 1 Corinthians 12:6, which says, 'If it be a shame for a woman to be shorn or shaven, let her be covered'. The congregation shout 'Amen' and 'Halleluiah' during the service. At one stage, the Reverend isn't pleased with the volume of the 'Amen' and asks to hear it again, louder.

The area beneath the pulpit is made of unadorned breeze blocks. To the left is a Union flag and a banner that says Jesus Christ Is Lord. To the right is the flag of Ulster and the unfurled message, Salvation To The Uttermost. There is no choir. Women rarely serve in senior positions.

Paisley is less combative in church than his familiar television persona suggests. He leads into the first hymn, relishing the words, '*almighty love inspires my hearts, and pleasure tunes my tongue*'. This is 'Now Shall My Inward Joys Arise', from Isaac Watts, born in 1674, sometimes referred to as 'the Godfather of English Hymnody'.

Music is important to Ian, just as long as there is a spiritual dimension. During his election victories, he celebrates by singing from the Doxology – 'Praise God, From Whom All Blessings Flow', a 1674 piece by Thomas Ken. There are many election victories and, mindful of Paisley's honorary doctorate from Bob Jones University of South Carolina, this piece of music is sometimes known as the 'Doc's-ology'. In terms of secular music, the man is not approving and has pronounced that 'line dancing is sinful, as any other form of dancing, with its sexual gestures and touching'.

He welcomes visitors from Canada and England and makes some mildly amusing remarks about people missing the light refreshments in the mid-week meeting and having to go to the chippy down the road. But the preacher also embraces a wary dimension in his prayers, praising God for throwing his opponents into confusion and railing once more about the ecumenical trend and the World Council of Churches. This is poison to the fundamentalist mind, and Ian refers to this development as 'the days of apostasy'.

Paisley resists this movement almost as much as he opposes modernism or the Roman Catholic church. He calls the latter "baptised paganism" or "the mother of harlots". He takes the Bible reading from Isaiah 41. Shortly before this section in the Scripture, the Prophet had been predicting the Babylonian invasion of Israel and the breaking of the Jewish Nation. But now he wants to stress the supremacy of God. 'I will uphold thee with the right hand of righteousness,' is the word from above. Ian urges his congregation to conquer fear and dismay. 'There's enough dynamite in this text to blow away all your hopes and fears', he roars.

His son, Ian junior, nods in agreement from his seat in the balcony. Like his father, he too is a member of the recently elected Northern Ireland Assembly, but he doesn't seem to have the preacher vocation. Ian junior's twin brother Kyle is a man of the cloth, but is less inclined politically. Meanwhile, the DUP is taking on a more secular character under the likes of Peter Robinson and a number of University-educated "Duppies".

Many people feel that when Ian senior retires, the church will be diminished. But the Big Man has already rejected this in a famous speech. 'When I die, The Lord will send some young Joshua to lead us into the promised land', he said. He reminds us, smiling, that he is 60 years on the road to Heaven, and calls for an evangelical revival to ease his work. After this service, he will be headed for Newtownards, Randalstown and Kells, visiting other flocks, on an indefatigable trail that aims to keep the Free Presbyterian people holding out for deliverance, clinging steadfastly to that old rugged cross.

SING OUT LOUDER

Ursula Burns also bills herself as The Dangerous Harpist. Her performances are dramatic, lurching and strange. On the song 'Being Born' she transforms into a baby that's in the amniotic sac, blissful and unaware. Then she realises she's going to make her arrival on the Falls Road, Belfast, 1970 and the panic rises. '*They're killing each other out there!*' squeals the newcomer while the mother's contractions begin. '*Put me back. There's been a mistake. I need to speak to the Boss!*'

As the dreaded event happens, the baby imagines how it should have been. A happy birth in Honolulu, a diet of organic baby food, vistas of trees and lovely flowers. Instead, the Belfast home is being prepared for curfews, riots and CS gas canisters. '*My mother's just put the towels and vinegar around the windows to stop the tear gas from getting in,*' she hoots. '*I'll be 27 before I realise that I don't have to be plastered, drunk.*'

The audience laughs at the enactment but also understands that this might have been Ursula's own birthright. She wasn't quite born in a crossfire hurricane but neither did she know the most peaceful surrounds or social advantages. Some of her listeners may feel lucky that they have escaped this accident of birth.

Ursula also has a recent song called 'Heartbreak Was Heartbreak'. She plays it on the piano and again she looks back at an eventful youth. The words were triggered by an old photograph of the security gates around

Belfast, with the bag searches, body checks and turnstiles. She came to realise that there were layers of her memories that seemed to exist in black and white. The newsreels and the freeze-frames were all monochrome.

But as she reviewed these life moments there was a splash of red. It was remembrance of a pool of blood on the Falls Road in 1988. This triggered a memory-rush of attacks and reprisals that had started with the killing of three IRA members in Gibraltar on March 6 1988. At the funerals, ten days later, Loyalist gunman Michael Stone attacked the mourners in Milltown Cemetery with a gun and grenades, killing three people. This resulted in more funerals and at one of these, on March 19, army Corporals David Howes and Derek Wood drove their car into the cortege, perhaps by accident. They were removed by the crowd, beaten and shot.

'When I looked at the photographs, so many years later,' Ursula says, 'I got a flash of the red in the black and white photograph. Like, I remembered seeing blood on the pavement, then I realised that there's a traumatic element. Even though no one in my family died and there was no direct trauma that was impacting on me, people around me were being impacted and you were dealing with their emotions.

'And the energy, when the black flags went up on the Falls Road – the atmosphere was so thick and heavy. Those black flags used to really upset me. So, in the song 'Heartbreak Was Heartbreak', I get flooded in my mind with all the three-word sayings. Normal sayings that we were hearing, and some that weren't that normal:

'Bring in the bins
He's so thin
Do his knees
Let's go play
Riots are on
It's a grey day'

'It's the realisation that what we grew up in wasn't normal.'

Ursula was in school at St Louise's during the Michael Stone attack. From the barred-up window of her typing class she could see into the graveyard, but the students were instructed to keep looking straight ahead and to concentrate on getting their letters in line. 'Repressed memory,' she says. 'And then it comes back.'

The whiplash effect of trauma and conflict has been a regular songbook feature since the ceasefires. Bono examined his memories of the 1974 Dublin and Monaghan Bombings in 'Raised by Wolves'. Van Morrison sang 'Ancient Highway' and followed the East Belfast waterways, remembering '*all the people living in the nightmare hurt that won't go away no matter how hard they try*'. Tim Wheeler put his anxieties into 'Sheltered Youth'. In Anthony Toner's 'Exit Wounds' there's a messy incident with a drunk policeman, a Walther PPK handgun and a boy who's astonished when the weapon is fetched from a sock drawer and placed in his hand. Anthony tells it like Kris Kristofferson and the action is dangerous in a Raymond Carver, haphazard way:

> '*My friend had seen this all before and he sat at the foot of the bed,*
> *He knew when his dad was on the rum and coke, it would*
> *sometimes turn his head.*'

Iain Archer described an upsetting recall with the song 'When It Kicks In'. Back when it happened, he was in a band called the Mighty Fall with Brian Houston and Johnny Quinn. They had set up outside Dr Robert's record shop on Church Lane when somebody stepped from the crowd at the corner and put a limpet bomb on a police car:

'It was like a cartoon. You know when you see these shreds of metal tearing out of things, just monstrous. There was a lot of carnage. I started to explore my memories and my reflections about where we are and what's going on. The original title was 'Truth Drug'. I was thinking, "What does it take to have a change of mind or a change of heart, if you're this hell-bent on destruction and damage?" I couldn't imagine anything other than something mind-altering – to change people's dogma or people's will to kill. That's where the song erupted from.'

There was a chance for post-conflict revisionism when the film *Good Vibrations* was released in 2013. It fixed Terri Hooley, his record shop and punk rock into the foreground of late 70s Belfast. Back then, it was perceived as frivolous, even a freak show, but here was a re-telling of the obstinacy, effrontery and important safe places in that subculture. Music was upheld as a life-affirming force in the film, part of the resistance movement. The screenplay, by Glenn Patterson and Colin Carberry, was caustic and also sentimental. Stories were compressed but faithful to the essence. There were indeed a dozen locations for the Good Vibrations shop after he left Great Victoria Street. His business places were damaged, burnt out and bombed in various campaigns. Terri was also beaten up by paramilitary gangsters over non-payment of protection money. Some of the names were changed. The film was praised in many international film festivals and Hooley was rightly gifted his victory lap.

'I cried the first time I saw it,' says Terri. 'I still cry every time I see it. Then I realise what a dick I was and that I drank too much. But I think the film is about freedom. It could be any trouble spot in the world – anywhere that people have had enough and want to do something different.'

The film also provided fresh interest in the original punk bands that were reforming and touring abroad. Now they were regarded as authentic and in demand.

'The film might not have done massive box office,' says Greg Cowan from the Outcasts, 'but it changed my life. I'm now 57, Martin is 62 and we're basically a touring band. I haven't gone two weeks within the last month without being away – in France, Germany, Switzerland. It might be seven hours in the back of a van but I fucking love it.'

Likewise, the Defects, who have played the Rebellion punk festival in Blackpool most years, have released new albums and issued a formidable statement on the peace process with the song 'Riot Free Zone'. The band's singer Buck is surprised at the direction of travel. 'The maddest gig we've ever done was in Union in Los Angeles. The crowd was all Mexican. From the minute we went on I thought, "How do these people know all about us?" They were so enthusiastic, so much energy. We went off and it was just nuts, the way they were shouting for us.'

The Harp Bar, long demolished, was remembered with a plaque on Hill Street in 2012. Hooley walked his people to the site, he called the punk parade 'our traditional route' and rubbished the Lord Mayor in an

entertaining, scattershot ramble. One of the organisers of the plaque was
Maureen Lawrence, who was also commemorating her own teenage passage
through alternative Ulster:

'We all ended up getting married and having children. We call them the
'lost years' before everybody re-grouped later on. When I first watched *Good
Vibrations* at the Ulster Hall it was emotional, and we were having a great
laugh about it and just delighted that somebody had done this film and
the soundtrack was great. But when I went to see it the second time and
took my kids and sat in the middle of them, I cried all the way through it.
Because when we watched the premiere it was Terri's film and his life story.
But when it watched it the second time it was as much my story as anyone
else's. Every time the bombs went off, my kids kept looking at me to see my
reaction. It absolutely hit that feeling of what it was back then.'

One outcome of the ceasefire was a rise in property values. Bap Kennedy
watched this with some concern and in 2007 he produced 'Boomtown', a
meditation on the so-called 'peace dividend'. Talk of violence and revolution
was being replaced by the chatter of the bourgeoisie, pleased with their
soaring equity. Meantime there were kids standing outside the City Hall in
Belfast, dressed in the designer threads of quasi-cool culture. *'Don't know
how lucky they are, they never heard a bomb,'* he sang, grumpily. Bap had the
voice of a disenfranchised veteran:

> *'I can't afford to live on a dead-end street,*
> *Things are getting so bad I might join the police.'*

From 'SS RUC' to career opportunities in the rebranded Police Service
of Northern Ireland, that was one way to measure progress. But Bap did
not sound convinced. There was a related note in 'Sailortown' by Anthony
Toner, a fleeting love song in a different era, where the paramilitary graffiti
is fading but the urban renewal and apartment blocks are causing other
varieties of stress.

Music was co-opted into cultural tourism – the belief that the cities could
be re-branded and that the reputation and finances of Northern Ireland
would benefit from landmark events and exhibitions. Belfast was host to

the MTV Europe Music Awards in 2011 and a potential world audience of 1.2 billion. In the north-west there was some soul-searching before the Maiden City made a bid for the UK City of Culture. Their delivery of the 2013 programme aimed to make a marketing positive out of the Derry-Londonderry schism, to roll with the contradictions. The additional tag of 'Legenderry' looked for a lightness, a third way into a city with identity issues.

Both bids sought the endorsement of Snow Patrol, Northern Ireland's biggest musical export at the time and top five in America with 'Chasing Cars' in 2006. The band assented in both cases, allowing the Derry-Londonderry submission to use the song 'Just Say Yes' in a promotional video.

'It's very hard to have anyone agree with anything in Northern Ireland,' Gary Lightbody from Snow Patrol explained. 'You don't hear 'yes' an awful lot, which is why using 'Just Say Yes' for the City of Culture was a great triumph. The word 'yes' is a really important word in the new Northern Ireland.'

Gary was also co-founder of the Oh Yeah Music Centre in Belfast (this writer was also a co-founder), a social enterprise aimed at raising the community value and industry potential of music in Belfast. Himself and David Holmes had also been co-producers of *Good Vibrations*. There was a recorded gesture from Snow Patrol, 'Take Back the City' which he called 'a love song to Belfast'. Gary regarded the place as 'a flawed work of art' and the song was a call for generational and creative change: '*now it's time to make your own demands*'.

Van Morrison returned to Cyprus Avenue on August 31 2015. It was the occasion of his 70th birthday and a touchdown on a famous setting from the *Astral Weeks* album. Organised by Eastside Arts, the two performances on the site saw international visitors from 19 countries – the 'Vanatics', who were now regular attendees at the singer's home shows and who had become a warm-hearted fraternity on social media. This was cultural tourism in a beautiful, intimate form, among the trees and the Victorian landscaping, paradise revisited. It was hoped, but not expected, that the singer would play the song that honoured the setting. Van did not sing 'Cyprus Avenue', but he did sign off with 'On Hyndford Street', a sublime call to his early years on the terraced streets nearby. He summoned a trance-like state and positioned his audience in the swooning present. '*It's always being now*,' he sighed, with magisterial effect.

There has been post-ceasefire agitation from the LGBT+ community, notably Susie-Blue from Derry, who has railed against homophobes and inequality on 'People Like Us' and 'Be A Lady'. Pride marches in Belfast and Derry have combined colour with dissent and reform proposals that have already succeeded in the UK and Ireland and so the attainment of marriage equality in this remaining outpost is a mission drive and a likelihood. In the same spirit, music initiatives like Women's Work have campaigned for fair opportunities and they make their case with positive-minded festivals and events. In many cases, the obstacles are religious and political fundamentalists with fixed minds and a tendency to work out prejudices and favouritism through arts and funding bodies and State mechanisms.

A young Derry band called Blue Jeans changed their name to Touts, local parlance for paramilitary informers. Many gable walls have carried the message that 'Touts will be shot' and so the band channelled this anxiety and outsider stigma. Their music drew on the Undertones and Stiff Little Fingers, the oil and water of Ulster punk. They wrote it into songs like 'Bomb Scare', 'Sold Out' and particularly 'Political People', a howling denouncement of green and orange slapstick.

'I didn't really plan to write a political song,' says vocalist Matthew. 'I just thought, "I have to write another song". And then a People Before Profit leaflet came in the door. That's how that happened. It's not political. It's political commentary, more.'

People Before Profit, a manifestly leftist political party, was represented in Derry by Eamonn McCann, who was elected to the Stormont Assembly and scored many anti-austerity points in his tenure, 2016-17. His contrary tendencies have imprinted on musicians like Paddy Nash and the Wood Burning Savages. The latter are led by Paul Connolly, a lightning-catcher for rage and disgust. In the tradition of Woody Guthrie and Pete Seeger, his guitar bears a written message: 'Ulster Says Know'.

The Rubberbandits were wilfully contentious when they released 'Up Da 'RA', a stream of garbled history and knee-jerk Republican sentiment. They name-checked Sean South, the Potato Famine and Éamon de Valera. They sang about hardships in prison and imagined an afterlife for the martyrs.

'And to all the patriots who have died before in the Irish wars?
I know you're up in heaven smoking a joint with Tupac and Bob
*   Marley.'*

'When I was growing up in Limerick,' says Blindboy Boatclub from the Rubberbandits, 'the cool thing to do was to support the IRA. But the kids that were doing it, they didn't know what the IRA was. They would draw a picture of Bob Marley and then a speech bubble that says, 'Up The RA'. And it became utterly meaningless. And that's what the song is about, the sheer meaninglessness of the IRA to a Southern, Limerick audience.'

Satire swung the other direction in *Trainspotting II* when the characters Renton and Simon entered a Loyalist club in West Scotland. Their motives were criminal and to fit in with the locals they created fake 1690 tattoos, commemorating the Battle of the Boyne. Later, they guessed this would be the PIN number on many of the stolen bank cards. Their plan was waylaid when they were asked to sing and Renton improvised with a bloodthirsty ballad that pleased the regulars.

'It was on the field of battle
Of hope we were bereft
And by the time that it was over
There were no more Catholics left.'

Joshua Burnside from Lisbane, County Down was less inclined to humour. He put out 'Red and White Blues' in 2017, questioning the summer practice of painting kerbstones in patriotic colours and flying flags in Loyalist areas. In the lyric he says that he was raised in this community, with a grandfather in the Democratic Unionist Party, but now he does not agree with the ritual. He is tired of the territorial displays and repeats that he is not afraid. Rather, he is repulsed.

'Putting flags where no-one wants them
Marching where they know it taunts them...'

Organisations such as Beyond Skin have recognised that many cultures now feature in Northern Ireland as immigration brings a potential richness. So, the Shankill Road Defenders may perform in concert alongside players from Kurdistan, India and Ghana. In the same spirit, L'Orchestre des Refugies et Amis is a rolling collective of voices, persuasions and incoming joy, sometimes anchored around the generous personality of homeboy Joby Fox.

Before he became a recognised musician, Joby was a problem child and recreational rioter in West Belfast. When he was 14, he staged an attack on a Bedford lorry full of soldiers. He had sourced some petrol and established a position on Kennedy Way, ready for the target. There were more than a dozen juveniles involved, already skilled at launching petrol bombs, as Joby recalls:

'Fuckin' direct hit, like. We didn't hurt anybody but because there was so many of us they thought it was much more sinister. It was well organised. And I fuckin' organised it! It was like military precision – we'd a couple of dicks (look-outs) out and factored in the windspeed and all that shit. And then they brought us up to Castlereagh (interrogation centre). Two days in Castlereagh and then brought us down to Townhall Street police station and the guy says, "You're going to the Home". And when they brought us up into court the judge seen how dirty we were and he says, "Get these children home and get them washed!" The Great Unwashed! So, we were lucky, like.'

He came from a family of ten and was raised in the Riverdale area of Andersonstown, a relatively pleasant space. They had pictures of the Sacred Heart, Martin Luther King and Che Guevara on the wall. His mother sang in bars and clubs and encouraged an older brother to perform in a duo called the High Spots. When the conflict started, Joby was able to look down from his house and watch the Army setting up at Musgrave Park below. As a nine-year-old, he witnessed the aftermath of a shooting on Finaghy Road when three workers were targeted in a car and one was killed. 'No child should ever have to deal with that.' Later, his own family was drawn into the worsening situation:

'My older brother was 17. He got involved in hijacking a bus and he was arrested. And when he was arrested he had to declare – or it was put on him – that he was a member of the IRA. There was still political status at the time so that's sorta how that went. And he was in the camp with the

IRA guys and that changed his life. It definitely changed our life – the whole exterior thing that was going on, the whole conflict itself was beginning to rage. Five years in jail. It just rebounded through the whole family. The British Army started coming on to the streets and started to do more of the security war and we were considered a Republican family and we were raided all the time. They were kicking in our doors.'

He trained himself to use a catapult, firing one-inch staples with accuracy. He was aiming to get his projectile into the open hatch of a Saracen personnel carrier. He had rehearsed the act in the local scrapyard, using a biscuit tin to test his reach. Then he picked a spot at the end of a convenient alley and bided his time for a six-wheeler.

'I whacked this fuckin' soldier, the poor bastard, and I took an 'L' shape out of his forehead, I'm sure I did. I didn't take his eye out or anything, thank God. I took a bit of flesh off. He crashed, apparently. I didn't hang around to find out. Off I went…'

Another Fox brother was at Queen's University, preparing for a career as a civil engineer. He took Joby into town, to a session at a student house where the young hooligan heard Van Morrison's *Astral Weeks* for the first time. This was another kind of recreation and he came to relish his encounters with the album. A special ritual was enacted. 'I smoked a bit of dope, lay with the speakers on the ground and listened to *Astral Weeks* and it sent me to another place. That's when the Pandora's Box opened, you know?'

He heard some neighbours rehearsing in a band called Uncle Waldo and so he started helping them shift their gear. By the end of the 70s he was playing bass with the Bankrobbers and they finally signed a singles deal with EMI. They had a song called 'Harry's Blocked', which was a coded comment on the H-Block protests. They made a TV appearance on *Whistle Test*. Ahead of their band footage, the BBC show put Belfast into context by unspooling old news archive of a street riot. Sure enough, there was a young Joby in the film, clodding bricks at the army near the bottom of Fruithill Park.

'And that intensity – I brought that intensity into music. For me, I needed to find a place for that too, I really did. So, when I got into music I fuckin' went at it. Full on. Bang! And it helped.'

A few years after the Bankrobbers folded, Joby moved in London, earning a wage as a courier and playing with old friend Bap Kennedy and some other exiled Westies. The late 80s were an era of mass emigration, and so Energy Orchard had a ready-made audience of lonesome Irish drinkers and a clutch of songs that fitted the mood. They had a residency at the New Pegasus in North London where they perfected their wayward tone. Many of the songs were written by Bap, including 'Somebody's Brother', which remembered the bad days at home:

'I've counted the coffins, felt the wind of despair
I've grown numb to murder, and I'm too drunk, too drunk to care.'

Joby had been carrying a song around since his previous band and Bap was very fond of it. It was called 'Belfast' and since he had only known a few guitar chords at the time, it had a simple, sad form, almost a drone. The Bankrobbers had tried a faster version but now it was finding its true pace. He used to play it at house parties and everyone thought it was special. The lyric had been written after Joby left his girlfriend home one evening and was walking back through Ladybrook Park.

'What fed into it? A riot. I remember I came back down to the bottom of this road and the British Army had dispersed everybody but they'd been firing a few rubbers and that sulphur used to hang in the air, just under your chin – and the smell of it. I remember walking through it and there was no one around, just me sauntering through this. Nobody else experiences this, not in the UK anyway. This is very different. And you got this kinda eerie, kinda sparky feeling about it.'

The band signed to MCA Records and 'Belfast' was their first single in 1989. Produced by a Van Morrison associate, Mick Glossop, the tune was now expansively sad and it reached 52 in the UK chart. It was their most successful release but Joby took some criticism about the line, *'you're like heaven, you're like hell'*. They said it was a cliché but the author did not apologise. 'Who gives a fuck? 'Cos that's what people experienced here. It was a great place but it was also a fuckin' hell of a place too.'

After Joby returned to Belfast, the song became a personal keepsake and a Troubles memento. Even if the song had remained as a historic piece, he was still going to have local respect, and the potential to use the lyric in workshops and international gatherings around the theme of conflict resolution. This was the case in December 2012, when he visited Israel and met with Palestinian musicians. He had a new EP called *End of the War* and many stories to tell.

'I was with a bunch of musicians from the Golan Heights. I was in Tel Aviv and I was looking at the TV, chatting to these people and I ventured to say that maybe people in Israel could learn something about the Irish-Northern Irish peace process. I was strategic in the sense that I didn't say it at the start of the week because I encountered a few hard-line reactions – conversations I didn't want to be in – that I started.'

However, the TV news was showing a different aspect to life in Belfast. There had been a ruckus in the City Council over the flying of the Union flag at the City Hall. The Unionists wanted to retain the flag, 365 days a year. Nationalists and Republicans wanted it removed and the Alliance Party brokered a compromise, to fly the flag on designated days. The outcome was met by Loyalist riots in the city, especially in the East, plus a reversal of political goodwill and a frustrating development for Joby to explain to his new friends:

'I'd just been lauding the fuckin' Irish Peace Process and then that happened. Culturally scundered! And then I was home, just looking at the youth of East Belfast. And who did I see? Me. And the way I grew up. I'm coming 50 years of age now; it's gonna happen to these guys now. These Protestant youth, they don't know what's really going on and they're gonna be the ones who've got the (criminal) charges - because I've a couple of charges, for rioting and all that there. And now there's these guys, they're gonna get fucked over and they won't get a job or they'll feel second-class citizens or whatever the case may be.

'And I felt very strongly about it and I thought to myself, "No, I'll write this third verse and I'll play the song the way I always wanted to play it anyway". So, I re-recorded it and put the third verse in there. I made my point as an artist and said, "That's what I think and there you go" – I don't give a fuck what happens after that. I felt gratified, I felt good about it.'

The third verse of 'Belfast' is looking for direction out of a bad place. A hand reaches for a hand and recognises that extra distance can still be achieved. Such were the sentiments that put the Civil Rights people on the road in 1968. It was the shaky connection that Christy Moore was stretching for with 'North and South of the River'. Joby had his variation on the riff and the intention to do more.

'I've got strong social and political views, what I learned from being in the conflict. It was never straightforward. They weren't black and white issues, they're very complex, they're trans-generational, they're historic, they're about identity. Then it goes into philosophy. Who are we? Who are we as human beings? What is our relationship to this fucking planet here? What's the right thing to do?'

In October 2015, Joby travelled to the Greek island of Lesbos to help with refugee relief. Dinghies were arriving from the Turkish coast, overloaded with people. He was pulling babies out of the water, making tearful reports home, empathising because he had lost one of his own children in infancy. He made a series of return visits and determined to succeed with a funding drive to purchase a rigid, inflatable boat with an Irish name, *Mo Chara* (My Friend). The boat was purchased.

Joby's humanitarian work has been self-willed, emotionally driven. Not everyone has approved but he will not be checked by caution or narrative. His actions have an unorthodox line that took him out of wild youth in a riven city during a brutal era. According to the received script, he might have achieved less and been conditioned by habitual actions and reactions. He has refused the expectations. Neither will he talk in post-conflict platitudes.

'I've always wanted to talk about this, I've always felt guarded because I was in the music business and I didn't want to put myself out there so that it would be perceived to be on one side or the other. I didn't want to do that for a variety of reasons. I felt, as the years have gone by, I'm entitled as an individual to talk about my experience. There doesn't have to be an equivalence to everything that I say about my own experience.'

Joby looks bemused. It's been a valuable life. Something to learn from.

'I'm out of the trenches, man. I'm well out of the trenches.'

ACKNOWLEDGEMENTS

Thank you to the following people who have given generously with their interviews over a period of time:

Peter H. Aiken, Harvey Andrews, Iain Archer, Tim Attwood, Blindboy Boatclub, Bono, Adrian Boot, Paul Brady, Michael Bradley, Paul Burgess, Jake Burns, Petesy Burns, Ursula Burns, Ruth Carr, Henry Cluney, Greg Cowan, Matthew Crossan, John T. Davis, Anne Devlin, Barry Devlin, Keith Donald, The Edge, Brian Faloon, Joby Fox, Raymond Gorman, Wes Graham, Paul Hartnoll, Michael 'Hendi' Henderson, David Holmes, Terri Hooley, John Hume, Dave Hyndman, George Jones, Brian Kennedy, David Kerr, Glenn Kingsmore, Maureen Lawrence, Des Lee, Kyle Leitch, John Lennon (Belfast), Jona Lewie, Alan McBride, Colin McClelland, Eamonn McCann, Paul 'PJ' McCartney, John McElhatton, Ali McMordie, Joe Moody, Christy Moore, Gary Moore, Joe Mulheron, Ian 'Buck' Murdoch, Fionnbarra Ó Dochartaigh, Máirtín Ó Muilleoir, Damian O'Neill, John O'Neill, Dolores O'Riordan, Gordon Ogilvie, Quintin Oliver, Jim Reilly, Chris Roddy, Kevin Rowland, Feargal Sharkey, Cathal Smyth, Nick Stewart, Stephen Travers, Tim Wheeler, Andy White, Brian Young. Regards also to Ralph McTell for his quotes and Victor McCullough for the correspondence.

British Council Northern Ireland has been most helpful in bringing this book to completion. Arts Manager Colette Norwood has been particularly supportive and respected the ambitions of the story when others were more cautious.

Maurice Kinkead at Eastside Partnership made a creative and very welcome intervention at a key stage of the work.

John Thompson was kind enough to involve me as an Industry Fellow at the Institute for Collaborative Research in the Humanities at Queen's University Belfast, 2014-16. This was a significant help and the Institute is greatly missed.

I received some funding assistance in the early days from the Arts Council of Northern Ireland, under their Support for the Individual Artist Programme. This allowed me to pull together decades of impressions and storylines into a basic draft. Damian Smyth helped to get things started.

Colin Harper has been a fundamental supplier of proofreading and production smarts, music knowledge, contacts, singular humour and sounding-board services.

Thank you, Brídín Murphy Mitchell and Régine Moylett at RMP.

Typesetting expertise by Tom Seabrook. Appreciation to Alistair Graham for the great, evocative photos, to Stuart Bell for the cover artwork and Donna Morrow for transcription assistance.

Gráinne Mooney in Paris made it possible to source the Gilles Caron cover image. Salutations to Louis Bachelot and Francisco Aynard for the necessary permission.

Cheers to old colleagues at *NME* who let me write up with the first sketches of this story and to Charlotte Dryden and the Oh Yeah Music Centre team who helped it to grow into an actual exhibition.

Shout-outs to those who I've worked with at the BBC, including Mike Edgar, Paul McClean, Rigsy, Davy Sims, Susan Lovell, Jimmy Devlin, Cathy Moorehead, Tony Curry, Ruairi Cunningham, Maggie Doyle, Owen McFadden, Peter McCaughan and Peter Stewart.

I'm happily in receipt of considerate deeds and encouragement from Debbie Patterson, Kate Elliott, Máire Brennan, Tim Jarvis, Sarah Hughes, Sean O'Neill, Lyndon Stephens, Vinny Cunningham, Claire Archibald, Malu Halasa, Malachi O'Doherty, Steve Stockman, Steve Mack, Colin Coulter, Sean Kelly, Maeve Quigley, Anthony Toner and Tim Newell.

With continued gratitude to the libraries of Belfast and also the Public Record Office of Northern Ireland and CAIN (Conflict Archive on the Net).

This book is for Lily, Rosalie, Betsy, Collette, Margaret and Jim Bailie.

1. Take A Look Where You're Living

About the Stiff Little Fingers gig at the Bataclan, Jake says: 'We tried to make it as normal a gig as possible. Although there was a much smaller audience than we would have normally had, and a larger media presence, I guess that was to be expected. Once we'd played it, we tried not to talk about it again as we didn't want to be seen to be making any capital out of it at all.'

Jake on the gig at Custom House Square, Belfast, 2017: 'It was a nerve-wracking evening, not least because the monitor system stopped working just as we were about to take the stage. Belfast gigs are always emotionally charged affairs simply because we still consider them 'hometown' shows, but as they go, Custom House Square was a particularly good one.'

2. We Are Not Afraid

Fionnbarra Ó Dochartaigh's book, *Ulster's White Negroes: From Civil Rights to Insurrection* (AK Press, 1994) has details of other DHAC activity.

The PBS American Masters documentary *Pete Seeger: The Power of Song* (2007) is a useful insight into the development of 'We Shall Overcome'.

Bernadette Devlin quotes taken from her autobiography, *The Price of My Soul* (MacMillan, 1969)

'He laid great emphasis upon the brotherhood of man rather than the Kinship of Christ.' *Protestant Telegraph*, April 13 1968. Quoted in *Persecution Zeal: A Portrait of Ian Paisley* by Dennis Cook (Brandon, 1996)

'McCann planned on flaunting an unwritten law...' as stated at Eamonn in *War and an Irish Town* (Pluto, 1993)

'Our conscious, if unspoken strategy was to provoke the police...' Eamonn McCann quoted by Simon Price and Geoffrey Warner, *Belfast and Derry In Revolt* (Irish Academic Press, 2012)

'Over and again, along Rossville Street...' Eamonn McCann writing in *Spirit of '68: Beyond the Barricades* (Guildhall, 2009)

'The gable wall of St Columb's Street' from Eamonn McCann's historical recollection. These days, the city geography puts it at the intersection of the Lecky Road, Rossville Street and Fahan Street.

3. The Viaducts of Your Dream

Eamon McCann quotes on *Astral Weeks* from *Hot Press*, October 28 1998

'We want to show that most young people are not interested in hatred...' *City Week*, July 17 1969

The Free Derry Fleadh and related stories are documented in *No Go: The Free Derry Story* (Open Reel Productions, 2006). Producer-Director: Vinny Cunningham; Writer-Producer: John Peto. This followed on from Open Reel's 2004 documentary *Battle of the Bogside*.

4. Behind the Wire

'Sessions musicians are an ecumenical breed...' Cel Fay quoted in the *Belfast Telegraph*, May 17 1985

'A greater market than many of the major labels imagine...' *Music Week*, September 20 1975

Bobbie Hanvey and Martin McBurney quotes from a Billy McBurney obituary, BBC Online, February 11 2016

The culture of the tartan gangs and the identification of Robert Bates on the cover of the Dexys Midnight Runners sleeve are discussed in Gareth Mulvenna's *Tartan Gangs and Paramilitaries: The Loyalist Backlash* (Liverpool University Press, 2016)

'That day was probably the biggest evacuation since World War Two...' *North Belfast News*, March 2006

5. They Shot the People Down

There's a good overview of Lennon's political connections in Peter Doggett's *There's A Riot Going On* (Canongate, 2007)

Johnny Rogan examines the Irish Republican encounters in *Lennon: The Albums* (Calidore, 2006)

'Bloody Sunday had unleashed a wave of fury...' quoted in David McKittrick and David McVea's *Making Sense of the Troubles* (Viking, 2012)

'He thought it was too inflammatory...' quoted in *The People's Songs: The Story of Modern Britain in 50 Records* by Stuart Maconie (Ebury, 2014)

'My family comes from Ireland...' *Uncut*, June 2007

'That was his little cotton wool protest...' Henry McCullough talking to the author, 2004

'It seems likely that they were gleaned from some boozy New Yorker...' *Irish Times*, August 7 1972

'People on the extremes of Unionism would have dismissed it as a rebel song...' *Galway Advertiser*, February 7 2013

6. The Pound's So Old

'Yes, oh yes, I think it was...' Rory quoted in *Melody Maker*, January 8 1972

'The emergency services had just removed the dead...' Gloria Hunniford talking on *The Troubles I've Seen*, ITV, October 27 2008

'It broke my dad, crippled him...' Chris Roddy quoted in *The Vacuum*, Issue 3 2003

'There were 500 deaths, 2,000 explosions and 10,000 shooting incidents...' David McKittrick and David McVea's *Making Sense of the Troubles* (Viking, 2012)

'It was the first time I'd ever given up on my country...' George Jones returned to Northern Ireland after an unhappy period of time working in South Africa. He played with the reformed Clubsound. They had a popular residency at the Railway Bar in Antrim. 'Then we brought out 'Peace: The Time Is Here'. That was taken from an album by the Freshmen. We started putting this in at the end, instead of a national anthem. And in the Railway and every big club we played at, Catholic or Protestant, everybody stood up and held hands. That's how strong the feeling was from Joe Public. They were tired, they wanted peace.'

7. A Million Miles

'They were almost ruthless in pursuing their objective...' Gerry Anderson, quoted in TV documentary, *The Day the Music Died*, BBC, 2005

'Suddenly, we became a place *not* to go

to...' Jim Aitken on *Arts Extra*, Radio Ulster, July 29 2005

'It was a time of your life when you saw headlights behind you...' Barry Devlin talking to the author in 2006 for the BBC TV documentary *So Hard To Beat*

'I couldn't have refused Jim Aiken...' *Belfast Telegraph*, February 3 2015

8. I Wanna Riot

'Bombs... bombs... bombs...', from *The Clash* by the Clash (Readhowyouwant, 2014)

'This was a case of people saying, look, I've had enough...' from *The Clash* (Readhowyouwant, 2014)

'The Social Security made me open the letters...' Quoted by Marcus Gray in *Last Gang in Town: The Story and Myth of the Clash* (Fourth Estate, 1995)

'I feel we might be rubbing their faces in it...' Ian Birch story in *Melody Maker*, October 29 1977

'They'll think we're here to entertain the troops...' Caroline Coon story in *Sounds*, October 29 1977

Quotes from Adrian Boot, Caroline Coon, Gavin Martin, Chris Salewicz, Paul Burgess and Maureen Lawrence taken at *A Riot of Our Own: A Symposium on the Clash*, University of Ulster, Belfast, June 20-21 2014.

'I just felt like a dick...' Ian Birch story in *Melody Maker*, October 29 1977

Brian Young and Joe Strummer quotes from Sean O'Neill and Guy Trelford, *It Makes You Want to Spit: The Definitive Guide to Punk in Northern Ireland, 1977-1982* (Reekus, 2003)

9. You Ain't No Friend of Mine

Gerard McWilliams and Ivan Clayton both feature in *Lost Lives* (Mainstream, 1999)

'I decided that I'll just have to go out and party...' from the BBC Radio 4 documentary *The Godfather of Punk* (2012)

'The great thing about Terri...' from the BBC Radio 4 documentary *The Godfather of Punk* (2012)

'Hell-soaked liquor traffic...'. Quoted by Bob Purdie, *Politics in the Streets* (Blackstaff, 1990)

10. Alter Your Native Land

Jake Burns interviewed by the author for a BBC Radio 2 documentary, *Breaking the Barricades* (2003). Produced by Paul McClean. Supplemented by a Jake interview with the author in 2018.

'The great thing for people who weren't able to make music about punk...' from the BBC Radio Ulster documentary *Year Zero* (2007). Produced by Owen McFadden.

'The roadblocks, the riots, the constant hassle, in fact the sheer paranoia of everyday life...' from Roland Link's *Kicking Up A Racket: The Story of Stiff Little Fingers* (Appletree, 2009)

'They employed a black and white photo of an incendiary, device...' a copy of the inlay card is reprinted in Roland Link's *What You See Is What You Get: Stiff Little Fingers 1977-1983* (Colourpoint, 2014)

'Catholic kids took us on a guided tour of the Falls...' from Daniel Rachel's *Walls Come Tumbling Down* (Picador, 2017)

'People would Sieg Heil at a few shows...' from Daniel Rachel's *Walls Come Tumbling Down* (Picador, 2017)

11. Casbah Rock

'Feargal helped out in the weeks before, delivering the competitor tickets...' Adapted from a Feargal article about his youth in *City of Music: Derry's Musical Heritage* (Guildhall, 2008)

'It wasn't until people remarked on it...' Michael Bradley interviewed by the author for a BBC Radio 2 documentary, *Breaking the Barricades* (2003). Produced by Paul McClean.

'He was like Neal Cassady, without the amphetamines...' from *Teenage Kicks: The Undertones* (2001). Directed by Vinny Cunningham.

'I remember a record company ad...' Michael Bradley interviewed by the author for a BBC Radio Ulster series, *So Hard To Beat* (2007)

'We were only 20 minutes away from beautiful beaches...' John O'Neill interviewed by Hannah Gibson for a City University of London Dissertation, 2014.

'Johnny Green, Road Manager and trusted fixer...' He recounts his part of the story in *A Riot of our Own* (Orion, 2003)

'I suppose we were conscious of getting reviewed...' John O'Neill interviewed by the author for a BBC Radio 2 documentary, *Breaking the Barricades* (2003). Produced by Paul McClean.

'Joe Strummer interrupted a Clash gig in Madrid...'. Story from Chris Salewicz, and *Redemption Song: The Definitive Biography of Joe Strummer* (HarperCollins, 2006)

'Possibly, the pressure to write about the Troubles may have got to Damian and John...' Michael Bradley interviewed by the author for a BBC Radio Ulster series, *So Hard To Beat* (2007)

'During one of our many tedious meetings...' Michael Bradley interviewed by the author for a BBC Radio 2 documentary, *Breaking the Barricades* (2003). Produced by Paul McClean.

'The typical English view is that both sides...' *NME*, July 20 1985

12. It's a Professional Career

'They looked like little kids...' Elvis Costello, *Unfaithful Music and Disappearing Ink* (Viking 2015)

'The Irish accent was important because the treatment of the song is very traditional...' interview with Kris Needs, *Zig Zag*, November 1985

'Don't Fraternise' noted in Malachi O'Doherty's *Gerry Adams: An Unauthorised Life* (Faber, 2017)

13. A Rebel I Came

'If I have a hero, it's him...' *NME*, October 29 1988

'I find I've reached a point in my life...' *Hot Press*, September 5 1991

14. They Take You Down to Castlereagh

'Their own songs included 'Gestapo RUC'...' According to an interview with Olaf Tyransen in *Hot Press*, May 11 2007, the Offensive Weapon repertoire also included 'We Killed Your Kid with a Plastic Bullet'. Johnny remembered, 'hundreds of skinheads used to come to hear us play. We were totally crap but it was always a buzz playing gigs. It made us feel important and popular. We loved it, while it lasted.'

Johnny Adair was on weekend parole on April 31 1999 when he attended a UB40 gig in Botanic Gardens, Belfast. He was shot in the head at point blank range by an unknown attacker. While a bullet fragment lodged in his head, he was relatively unharmed. This was either due to moisture in the gun cap, excessive gun oil or perhaps the weapon had been tampered with by security forces.

'A 'P' Check was a police search...' Also referenced in the Ex Producers song 'P-Check' (1979)

15. Rough Justice

'They were in a Holborn flat...' as mentioned by Roland Link in *Kicking Up A Racket: The Story of Stiff Little Fingers* (Appletree, 2009)

'He was shot from behind and died by the gates of St. Aidan's.' *Lost Lives* (Mainstream, 1999)

Gary Kemp quotes from his autobiography, *I Know This Much* (Fourth Estate, 2009)

'Harry's Game' by Donegal family group

Clannad was also perceived as a lament for the conflict. Released in 1982, it was the theme to a Yorkshire TV drama about the search for an IRA gunman. The music was produced by Richard Todd, who had engineered 10cc's 'I'm Not In Love'. The haunting, multi-layered vocal took the record in the UK top five. The Irish language lyrics were based on the grandfather's book of proverbs, one of which spoke of man's vanity when framed against the divine scheme of things.

16. Wreckage Down on Main Street

'There's a perception that all Irish people can sing about...' *The Guardian*, May 15 1987

'I was very isolated at the time...' *Hot Press*, September 15 1999

'Just because you were born in a stable...' *Melody Maker*, November 2 1985

The act Denim released a strangely evocative single in 1992 called 'Osmonds'. Lawrence Hayward, formerly of Felt, sang about 70s pop culture and working-class style but paused in the middle to remember his home town of Birmingham:

'In the 70s there were lots of bombs
they blew my home town up
and lots of people were killed
on the news the relatives cried.'

'There was a group of about 20 drunken squaddies...' quoted by Anne Scanlon, *The Pogues: The Lost Decade* (Omnibus, 1988)

'What we were saying, is fuck everything...' Anne Scanlon, *The Pogues: The Lost Decade* (Omnibus, 1988)

'It's about people getting framed up...' Anne Scanlon, *The Pogues: The Lost Decade* (Omnibus, 1988)

'He was a great man...' Shane MacGowan talking to the author, 1998

The John T. Davis film with Vernon Oxford, *Power In The Blood*, was released in 1989.

17. Big Decisions

'The song was partially written about Northern Ireland...' Gary Moore interviewed by the author in 2006 for the BBC TV documentary *So Hard To Beat*.

'When UFF 'C' Company did a show of strength...' *Hot Press*, May 11 2007

John O'Neill interviewed by the author for *Across The Line*, BBC Radio Ulster, 2015

'If he just took his gun out of my face...' Nanci Griffith speaking to Ivan Little, *Belfast Telegraph*, February 22 2013

'The hatred damages children and causes the cycle to continue...' Nanci Griffith in conversation with Joe Jackson, *Hot Press*, October 31 1999

Colin Parry, father of Tim Parry who died in the Warrington Bomb, only learnt about the meaning of 'Zombie' on the death of Dolores O'Riordan on January 15 2008. He told RTE's *Morning Ireland*: 'I'm sorry to say I didn't know about the song until yesterday when my wife told me. When I heard the song was about Warrington, I listened to it as carefully as I could to the words. I was very moved, certainly by the singing voice of Dolores and the song itself but it was the sentiment behind it that was particularly captivating. For an Irish band to sing about the tragedy of my son and Johnathan dying is obviously very poignant.'

Dave Mustaine from Megadeth created a deal of controversy at the Antrim Forum on May 11 1988. Introducing the band's version of 'Anarchy in the UK' he was apparently upset at a missile thrown from the crowd. 'Give Ireland back to the Irish!' he shouted. 'This one's for 'the cause' – Anarchy in Ireland!' The audience was conflicted, Megadeth were escorted out of the venue and Mustaine wrote the self-depreciating 'Holy Wars... The Punishment Due' by way of an apology.

Andy Cairns interviewed by the author for a BBC Radio 2 documentary, *Breaking the Barricades* (2003). Produced by Paul McClean.

Therapy? were planning to use an Ian Paisley sample at the start of their 1998 single 'Church of Noise'. The audio was from a Paisley interview with the author in 1994 during an *NME* tour around Northern Ireland with Andy Cairns. When asked about his favourite music, Paisley responded, 'Good Christian music. Music with the gospel in it.' On the advice of their record company the sample was not used.

Brian Kennedy interviewed by the author in 2006 for the BBC TV documentary *So Hard To Beat*.

Paul Hartnoll and David Holmes interviewed by the author in 2016. Featured on *Across the Line*, Radio Ulster.

David Holmes was inspired by the Guildford Four film, *In The Name Of The Father* to write the instrumental 'No Man's Land' in 1995. His soundtrack work has sometimes referenced the conflict, including *Resurrection Man* (1998), *Hunger* (2008), *Good Vibrations* (2013) and *1971* (2014).

18. We've Got to Carry Each Other

"Two Little Boys' by Rolf Harris was also rejected...' Sean O'Hagan was party to the song discussions amongst U2. He related this in his *Observer* feature on the day's events, May 24 1998.

'Sheltered Youth' by Tim Wheeler appeared on the deluxe version of his 1994 solo album, *Lost Domain*.

19. How Long Must I Sing This Song?

Andrew Rowan is also the subject of the U2 song 'Bad'.

'There may be a connection between the Dublin-Monaghan bombings and the Miami Showband killings in 1975.' It has been purported that UVF members, associated with the Glennane Gang, carried out both acts. Thirty-four people died in the Dublin-Monaghan bombings on May 17 1974.

20. Broken Things

Steve Stockman recounts his involvement with the choice of 'Broken Things' in his blog *Soul Surmise*, March 12 2017

'They ask these stupid things...' quoted in *Hot Press*, February 25 2004

21. Washed in The Blood of The Lamb

Parts of this chapter were written by the author in 1998 and previously published in *Hot Press*, October 28 1998

22. Sing Out Louder

'It's very hard to have anyone agree with anything in Northern Ireland...' quoted by Mark Carruthers in *Alternative Ulsters: Conversations on Identity* (Liberties, 2014)

'The two performances on the site saw international visitors...' According to Eastside Arts, Vanatics were representing USA, Canada, Australia, New Zealand, South Africa, Ireland, France, Belgium, Denmark, Germany, Spain, Italy, Holland, Norway, Switzerland, India, Sweden, Austria and Cyprus.

BIBLIOGRAPHY

Anthony, Gene, *The Summer of Love* (Celestial Arts, 1980)

Bailie, Stuart, *Popular Music: Troubles Archive* (ACNI, 2009)

Bailie, Stuart, *The Ballad of the Thin Man: The Authorised Biography of Phil Lynott and Thin Lizzy* (Boxtree, 1997)

Bailie, Stuart, *The Cranberries: In Your Head* (UFO, 1995)

Beresford, David, *Ten Men Dead* (Grafton, 1987)

Berger, George, *The Story of Crass* (Omnibus, 2008)

Bradley, Michael, *Teenage Kicks: My Life as an Undertone* (Omnibus, 2016)

Campbell, Sean, *Irish Blood, English Heart: Second Generation Musicians in England* (Cork University Press, 2011)

Carruthers, Mark, *Alternative Ulsters: Conversations on Identity* (Liberties, 2014)

Carruthers, Mark and Douds, Stephen (eds.), *Stepping Stones: The Arts in Ulster, 1971-2001* (Blackstaff, 2001)

Clerk, Carol, *Kiss My Arse: The Story of the Pogues* (Omnibus, 2006)

Connolly, Frank (ed.), *The Christy Moore Songbook* (Brandon, 1989)

Cooke, Dennis, *Persecution Zeal: A Portrait of Ian Paisley* (Brandon, 1997)

Costello, Elvis, *Unfaithful Music and Disappearing Ink* (Viking 2015)

Dawe, Gerald, *The Rest Is History* (Abbey, 1998)

Denselow, Robin, *When the Music's Over* (Faber, 1990)

Devlin, Bernadette, *The Price of My Soul* (Pan,1970)

Devlin, Paddy, *Straight Left* (Blackstaff, 2000)

Dillon, Martin, *The Shankill Butchers* (Arrow, 1990)

Doggett, Peter, *There's A Riot Going On* (Canongate, 2007)

Gilbert, Pat, *Passion Is A Fashion: The Real Story of the Clash* (Aurum, 2005)

Goldman, Albert, *The Lives of John Lennon* (Bantam, 1988)

Gray, Marcus, *Last Gang in Town: The Story and Myth of the Clash* (Fourth Estate, 1995)

Green, Johnny and Barker, Gerry, *A Riot of our Own* (Orion, 2003)

Griffiths, Stuart, *Pigs' Disco* (Ditto, 2013)

Harper, Colin and Hodgett, Trevor, *Irish Folk, Trad & Blues* (Collins Press, 2004)

Hayes, Dermott, *Sinéad O'Connor: So Different* (Omnibus, 1991)

Heylin, Clinton, *Can You Feel the Silence? Van Morrison: A New Biography* (Penguin, 2002)

Hippsley, Paul (ed.), *City of Music: Derry's Musical Heritage* (Guildhall, 2008)

Hooley, Terri and Sullivan, Richard, *Hooleygan* (Blackstaff, 2010)

Kemp, Gary, *I Know This Much* (Fourth Estate, 2009)

Link, Roland, *Kicking Up A Racket: The Story of Stiff Little Fingers* (Appletree, 2009)

Link, Roland, *What You See Is What You Get: Stiff Little Fingers 1977-1983* (Colourpoint, 2014)

Lister, David and Jordan, Hugh, *Mad Dog* (Mainstream, 2003)

MacDonald, Ian, *Revolution in the Head: The Beatles' Records and the Sixties* (Pimlico, 1998)

McCafferty, Nell, *Vintage Nell: The McCafferty Reader* (Lilliput, 2005)

McCann, Eamonn, *War and an Irish Town* (Pluto, 1993)

McClenaghan, Pauline (ed.), *Spirit of '68: Beyond the Barricades* (Guildhall, 2009)

McKittrick, David, Kelters, Seamus, Feeney, Brian and Thornton, Chris, *Lost Lives* (Mainstream, 1999)

McKittrick, David and McVea, David, *Making Sense of the Troubles* (Viking, 2012)

Moloney, Ed and Pollack, Andy, *Paisley* (Poolbeg, 1986)

Morrison, Bill, *Big Hand for the Band* (Motelands, 2015)

Moore, Christy, *One Voice: My Life in Song* (Hodder and Stoughton, 2000)

Mulvenna, Gareth, *Tartan Gangs and Paramilitaries: The Loyalist Backlash* (Liverpool University Press, 2016)

Murray, Charles Shaar, *Crosstown Traffic: Jimi Hendrix and Post-War Pop* (Faber, 1990)

Norman, Philip, *John Lennon: The Life* (HarperCollins 2008)

O'Doherty, Malachi, *Gerry Adams: An Unauthorised Life* (Faber, 2017)

O'Neill, Sean and Trelford, Guy, *It Makes You Want to Spit: The Definitive Guide to Punk in Northern Ireland, 1977-1982* (Reekus, 2003)

Parker, Stewart, *High Pop* (Lagan, 2008)

Prendergast, Mark J., *Irish Rock* (O'Brien, 1987)

Pietzonka, Karin, *And the Healing Has Begun* (Author House, 2013)

Prince, Simon and Warner, Geoffrey, *Belfast and Derry In Revolt* (Irish Academic Press, 2012)

Purdie, Bob, *Politics in the Streets* (Blackstaff, 1990)

Rachel, Daniel, *Walls Come Tumbling Down: The Music and Politics of Rock Against Racism, 2 Tone and Red Wedge, 1976-1992* (Picador, 2017)

Rogan, Johnny, *Lennon: The Albums* (Calidore, 2006)

Rogan, Johnny, *Van Morrison: No Surrender* (Vintage, 2006)

Salewicz, Chris, *Redemption Song: The Definitive Biography of Joe Strummer* (HarperCollins, 2006)

Santelli, Robert, *The Big Book of Blues* (Pavilion, 1994)

Savage, Jon, *England's Dreaming: Sex Pistols and Punk Rock* (Faber, 1992)

Scallon, Dana Rosemary and Murray, Ken, *All Kinds of Everything* (Gill & Macmillan, 2007)

Scanlon, Anne, *The Pogues: The Lost Decade* (Omnibus, 1988)

Smith, William, *Inside Man: Loyalists of Long Kesh* (Colourpoint, 2014)

Travers, Stephen and Fetherstonhaugh, Neil, *The Miami Showband Massacre* (Hodder Headline, 2007)

SELECT INDEX

Lutton, Davy, 108
Lydon, John, 192, 199, 201
Lynch, Martin, 214
Lynott, Phil, 83, 188, 209

MI5, 67-8
MacColl, Ewan, 48, 164
MacConnell, Mickey, 165
MacGowan, Shane, 121, 201
Mack, Steve, 212-3
MacLiammoir, Michael, 17
Mad Lads, the, 80
Madness, 192-3
Mandela, Nelson, 172, 179, 231, 233
Manfred Mann (group), 68
Manilow, Barry, 140
Manley, Michael, 230
Mao, Chairman, 60, 169
Marcelles, Fr Tony, 35-6
March on Washington (1963), 16
Maritime (Hotel), 33, 42, 73, 80
Marley, Bob, 10, 137, 230, 235, 261
Marmalade, 37
Marquee (venue, London), 148, 188
Marshall, Graham 'Grimmy', 108, 111
Martin, Bill, 68
Martin, Dennis 'Dino', 51
Martin, Gavin, 103, 105, 137
Marvelettes, the, 145
Marvin, Lee, 53
Marx, Karl, 59
Mason, Alison, 123
Mason, Roy, 166
Maudling, Reginald, 64, 79
MC5, the, 63, 145
McBride, Alan, 240

McBurney, Billy, 44-7, 135
McCann, Eamonn (Belfast promoter), 105, 235
McCann, Eamonn (Derry activist), 13, 16, 18-9, 22, 25, 27, 31-2, 38, 63, 168, 260
McCarrick, Martin, 222
McCartney, Linda, 68
McCartney, Paul (Beatle), 65-6, 68, 245
McCartney, Paul (Derry musician), 210
McCartney, Robert, 228
McCausland, Eileen, 109
McClelland, Colin, 36-7, 39, 130, 132-3, 136, 138, 141-2
McCoy, Brian, 84-5
McCracken, Henry Joy, 118
McCrea, Reverend William, 250-1
McCready, Iain, 224
McCrory, Sam 'Skelly', 179-81
McCrudden, Eddie, 76, 78
McCullough, Henry, 66
McDermott, Tommy, 25
McDonagh, Owen, and the Bogside Men, 46
McDonald, Country Joe, 19
McDowell, Kenny, 80
McDowell, Mississippi Fred, 40
McElhatton, John, 118
McFarlane, Brendan 'Bik', 166
McGlinchey, Dominic 'Mad Dog', 203
McGonagle's (bar), 122
McGowan, Shane, 121, 201-3

McGuigan, Chuck, and the Bogsiders, 45
McGuigan, Paddy, 47-8
McGuinness Flint, 68
McGuinness, Martin, 175
McGuinness, Tom, 68
McGuire, Séan, 45, 72
McGurk's Bar, 76
McHale, Tom, 45
McIlwaine, Kerry, 123
McKeague, John, 53, 148
McKee, Silver, 71, 79
McLaren, Malcolm, 100, 110
McLaughlin, Ciaran, 212
McMillan, Art, 49
McMordie Hall, 106, 145
McMordie, Ali, 127, 129, 135, 172
McTell, Ralph, 75
McVey, Rod, 204, 206
McWilliams, Gerard, 113
Mekons, the, 121
Mellows, Liam, 212
Memphis Slim, 40
Men of No Property, the, 48, 126, 169
Merville Inn, 140
Miami Showband Massacre (1975), 73, 96, 243
Miami Showband, the, 72, 83-91, 243, 251
Middle of the Road, 47
Midgely, Hilary, 123
Mighty Fall, the, 256
Miller, Buddy, 248
Miller, Julie, 248
Milligan, Terry, 77
Milltown Cemetery, 190, 233, 255
Millwall Chainsaws, the, 201
Mingus, Charles, 29
Mitchell, Senator George, 228, 231-2
Modern Jazz Quartet, the, 29
Mohan, Hugh, 234

Molloy, Matt, 167
Monochrome Set, the, 121
Monroe, Marilyn, 234
Moody, Joe, 120
Moondogs, the, 126, 148
Mooney, Frankie, 20
Mooney's (bar), 129
Moonlighters, the, 26
Moore, Christy, 5, 17, 161, 163-77, 197, 219, 244, 266
Moore, Gary, 209
Morelli, Tony, 76
Morrison, Van, 29-32, 69-70, 223, 245, 249, 256, 259, 263-4
Mortimer, John, 59
Motown (record label), 151
Moving Hearts, 168-72
Mowlam, Mo, 233
Mulheron, Joe, 48-9
Mullen, Larry, 233
Mulvenna, Gareth, 52
Murdock, Ian 'Buck', 177
Murphy, Lenny, 58
Murvin, Junior, 94

Nairac, Captain Robert, 88-9
Nally, Derek, 248
Nash, Paddy, 260
National Blues Federation, 40-1
National Front, 179-81, 93
Nazareth House Céilí Band, 44
New Bastards, the, 201
New Order, 200
New York Dolls, the, 108, 144
Newport Folk Festival, 16
Nicholson, Jack, 154
Nick Knack Paddy Whack, 184
Nipple Erectors, the, 201
Nips, the, 201
Nixon, Richard, 64

(TROUBLE) SONGS

Stuart Bailie is a music writer and broadcaster, based in Belfast. He has been a music industry professional for over 30 years, writing for *NME, Mojo, Uncut, Q, Vox, The Times, The Irish Times, Classic Rock* and *Hot Press.* He wrote the authorised story of Thin Lizzy, *The Ballad of the Thin Man,* in 1997. He has written TV and radio documentaries on U2, Elvis Costello, Glen Campbell and Thin Lizzy. He wrote and narrated a BBC TV history of music from Northern Ireland, *So Hard to Beat,* in 2007. He is a co-founder the Oh Yeah Music Centre in Belfast and was its CEO from 2008-16.

Stuart Bailie encounters the Reverend Ian Paisley, Belfast City Hall, November 11 1994. Photo by Steve Double.